Graeme Innes AM. ___ ___ , company director. In 1995 he was made a Member of the Order of Australia for his work on the development of the *Disability Discrimination Act 1992*, and in 2003 he was a finalist for Australian of the Year. Graeme's work as a human rights practitioner has spanned more than 30 years and includes his role as commissioner at the Australian Human Rights Commission where he led work on Australia's ratification of the UN Convention on the Rights of Persons with Disabilities and the Same-Sex: Same Entitlements Inquiry. Graeme also directed the merger of four blindness agencies to form Vision Australia, an agency that he then chaired. He is currently the chair of the Attitude Australia Foundation, a start-up aimed at using media to change attitudes towards Australians with disabilities, and he also serves on the PricewaterhouseCoopers Diversity Advisory Board and the Life Without Barriers Board. Visit Graeme's website graemeinnes.com

Graeme Innes

FINDING A WAY

UQP

First published in 2016 by University of Queensland Press
PO Box 6042, St Lucia, Queensland 4067 Australia

www.uqp.com.au
uqp@uqp.uq.edu.au

Cover design by Christabella Designs
Cover photograph by Kim Christopher Welinski
Cover Braille by Leona Holloway, on behalf of the Australian Braille Authority
Typeset in 12/15.5 pt Adobe Garamond Pro by Post Pre-press Group, Brisbane
Printed in Australia by McPherson's Printing Group, Melbourne

'One Strong Woman to Another' by Asmine first appeared in *Mascara Literary Review* Issue 16, October 2014 in the essay "Writing and Complexity at the Borders of Humanity" by Janet Galbraith. Reproduced with permission.
'Blind Tiger' by Rob Wallis and 'Treasure Island' by Brendan Doyle sourced from *Eureka Street* Volume 23:10, "Asylum Seeker Sonnet". Reproduced with permission.
'Mother' by M, 15 years, detained 13 months from *Our Beautiful Voices* by Writing Through Fences, Mark Time Books, 2014. Reproduced with permission.

Cataloguing-in-Publication entry is available from the National Library of Australia
http://catalogue.nla.gov.au

Innes, Graeme, author.
    Finding a way / Graeme Innes.
    ISBN 978 0 7022 5407 9 (pbk)
    ISBN 978 0 7022 5726 1 (epdf)
    ISBN 978 0 7022 5727 8 (epub)
    ISBN 978 0 7022 5728 5 (kindle)
    Subjects: Innes, Graeme.
    Blind – Australia – Biography.
    People with disabilities – Australia.
    Families – Australia.
362.41092

Inside front cover (*top to bottom*): Graeme aged three with Sir Robert Helpmann; Graeme riding a bike; Graeme graduating with a law degree.
Inside back cover (*top to bottom*): Graeme and Maureen on their wedding day with son Leon; Graeme with daughter Rachel; Graeme sailing.

University of Queensland Press uses papers that are natural, renewable and recyclable products made from wood grown in sustainable forests. The logging and manufacturing processes conform to the environmental regulations of the country of origin.

To my mum and dad, who gave me a great start in life and have been two of my best supporters all the way through.

Contents

Introduction

It had been raining steadily for four days, and the question of whether the fete would go ahead on Saturday was constantly up for discussion at the family dinner table. I was about 12, and very excited about the event taking place in the hospital grounds where we lived, as Dad was the CEO. I was the strongest proponent of going ahead, whatever the weather.

Saturday dawned, and the rain continued. 'They'll have to call it off,' said Mum. 'The ground is far too boggy.'

'No, they won't,' I said, eternally optimistic.

'I know what we'll do,' said Dad, who had always been an ideas man. 'We'll move the fete from outside on the lawn to inside in the hospital roof space.'

The volunteer set-up crew readily agreed, so at 6 am the full-scale operation of moving the contents of 20 stalls, soft drink machines, fairy floss makers, public address systems and all of the paraphernalia required for a successful fundraiser began.

My mum and sister were in charge of the cake stall, carrying what they already had stored at home to the hospital and up in the lift. My dad and brother were wheeling trolleys of soft drink boxes to and fro, and carrying the bags of ice necessary to keep them cool. The family tradition of 'all hands on deck' was deeply ingrained in me, and I was desperate to help. But that would be a challenge for a blind 12-year-old, where the environment was wet, muddy and constantly shifting. My face fell further and further as one after another of the set-up crew told me there wasn't anything I could do.

As it had done often in the past, and would do again and again during my life, my dad's warm hand on my shoulder saved the day. 'There's more than enough jobs for everyone today,' he said. 'The only puzzle is working out which one you can do. And I've solved the puzzle. Come and drive the lift.'

The lift was the pinch point for the whole operation. Everything and everyone going to the fete had to go up in the lift. And due to the high demand from the ground floor and the roof, it was constantly tripping out and causing delays.

'I'm going to override the automatic system and put this on manual, and I want you to drive it,' Dad said to me. 'If this lift doesn't keep going we won't have a fete.'

I couldn't have been prouder. I stood two centimetres taller, and spent the next 12 hours driving that lift – eating and drinking while going up and down, and strategically selecting quiet times for rushed toilet breaks. No-one else was touching those controls. There was no way I was letting down my dad, or risking the fete not going ahead.

This story encapsulates my book and my life. It shows me learning from my parents that I was not the kid who was blind, but an integral part of a functioning family unit; I understood that we, with our Christian values and ethics, and as well-off members of Australian society, had a social obligation to support those not so fortunate. As Grandma used to say, achieving success is 10 per cent inspiration and 90 per cent perspiration.

I learned from my family that most things could be achieved – the challenge was finding a way.

In this book I share my memories of 60 years on the planet – happy memories of love and support, tough memories of challenges and failures and positive memories of achievement. I share the unique experience of a life without one sense, but with heightened awareness of the information gained through others. I also share the advocacy for change for people with disabilities that has been a constant companion in my life.

I have woven stories throughout the book. I have learned that not only are stories the way we develop and pass down our culture, but they are also what remain in people's memories. This is constant, whether they are told by voices in the ear, words on a page, images on a screen or a combination of all of those. If you get a laugh from one of my stories, or find useful a piece of wisdom I have gained, then my book will have been a success. One of these pieces of wisdom, which came from seeing my daughter become the questioning and feisty teenager that I once was, is that no lesson told by an adult has anything like the effect of one you learn yourself.

Of course, there are regrets in my life. But overall I'm satisfied with the part I have been able to play in the lives of my family and friends, and in Australian society. I'd like to share it with you anyway.

So, you've paid your money, enjoy the story. And of course, let me have any feedback on Twitter or Facebook.

Graeme Innes AM
@graemeinnes
facebook.com/GraemeInnesAM

1
Early years

There's a photograph of me in the arms of Sir Robert Helpmann as he spun the chocolate wheel at the fete. I don't remember it, but the camera doesn't lie. And I would know, wouldn't I, as a person who has been blind since birth. I didn't look particularly pleased about being held by a famous dancer, with the whirring noise of a chocolate wheel close to my ear. Perhaps my face was a sign of things to come in that I would indicate clearly when I didn't like something.

We're not sure why my eyes did not form properly during gestation. Perhaps it was measles, or some other virus that Mum had. That was the original theory, although it was later supplanted by one of contact with the fumes of paint or some other similar chemical. It's an issue that has puzzled some minds for quite a time, but mine is not one of them. 'You play the hand you are dealt the best way you can' has always been my philosophy. You don't fret about why you were dealt that hand.

The doctors' bedside manner was sadly lacking when they told Mum and Dad of my blindness after I was born in 1955. 'Your son's eyes have not properly formed,' they said. 'He is totally blind, and that won't change.' Mum remembers it as a very harsh message, but perhaps in hindsight it was the right approach. Take the hit, and start planning for and dealing with the consequences was certainly the course Mum and Dad adopted.

Perhaps it was their country town upbringing – Mum in Parkes and Dad in Bathurst. Perhaps the fact that I was their second baby helped, with my sister Robyn having been born two years earlier. Or perhaps they didn't see many other alternatives. Whatever the case, that practical approach – treating me as one sibling and an equally important member of the family, rather than as the 'special' kid with the disability – has paid me back in spades during life.

They brought me home to Petersham in Sydney's west and did all the normal stuff you do with a new baby. Robyn was apparently pleased with my arrival. She loved me and bossed me around in equal measure, and was proud of my achievements. These characteristics of our relationship have continued throughout our lives.

*

Mum and Dad were children of the Great Depression. Mum's father – who died in 1958 – was a blacksmith in Parkes. They came to Sydney during the Second World War, where Mum then trained as a nurse. She met Dad at the Masonic Hospital where she worked and Dad's mother was a patient. Their relationship blossomed.

Mum's mother, Madeline, whom we knew as Grandma, lived in Strathfield when I was born. We moved to Ashfield when I was six, and Grandma moved into our old house in Petersham. Visits to Grandma's house are some of my fondest early memories.

Dad's father, Hilton, known as Mick, fought in the First World War, incurring a knee injury and being gassed in France. He returned home and worked on the New South Wales railway, and Dad followed him into that profession. Mick's first wife, Olive, died in 1949 and he married Claire some years later. We called them Pappa and Nanna, and I first remember them living in Marrickville. They had a frangipani tree in their yard, and I loved the strong smell and the soft touch of the petals as they fell. I have loved that smell ever since.

Dad came to Sydney as his career with the railways progressed. He told wonderful and exciting stories of pushing a hand-trolley along the tracks to check them, and how you had to quickly get it off the tracks if a train was coming. Perhaps I gained my love of trains from these stories. Or perhaps it was the many train trips I took as a child with Mum, who didn't drive. These train trips have continued into my adult life. My wife, Maureen, has a smile in her voice to this day as she tells people that I will only live in houses within walking distance of a railway station.

Dad followed the Protestant tradition for males of his generation, and joined the Masonic Lodge. As well as a community activity, the NSW Masonic Lodge soon became his employer, and he worked in Castlereagh Street in Sydney for a number of years.

When Mum and Dad acquired our Petersham house from a Mr Shoe, it came with a mantel clock that pealed Westminster chimes. This clock remained in the house while Grandma was living there, and only joined us in Ashfield after her death. I love those chimes. They evoke memories of visits to Grandma, and her tucking me into bed in what was then her spare room. And, later, of the warmth and sounds of the coal fire in the dining room in our Ashfield home. I missed that clock terribly when I moved out of home, and pre-emptively 'acquired' it when my parents moved to Gerringong on the NSW south coast. I have had it with me ever since.

*

My brother, Brian, was born four years after me, and Mum could not come home from hospital for several weeks because either Robyn or

I had some childhood illness, which could not be allowed to infect the new baby. We were looked after by a housekeeper while Dad continued working. She probably did an excellent job of looking after us, but my childhood rang with stories from Robyn and I of how the housekeeper checked our schoolbags every day to make sure we had eaten our lunch, and punished us if we didn't. She cooked dinners we did not like. We could not leave the table until we ate them. Worst of all, she wouldn't let us run down the street towards the station to meet Dad, like Mum did.

Being allowed to meet Dad on his way home was a special treat. I remember crashing into his suited legs, and the smell of the newspaper print from *The Sun*, which was always under his arm. If I told him I had been good he would let me carry the paper home, but I always had to wash the newsprint off my hands afterwards.

As well as the clock in Grandma's house, Mr Shoe had left us the contents of his back shed. Once I knew of its existence, I often spent time there, with or without permission. It was full of tools and equipment, a fascinating hidden treasure for the exploring hands of a young boy. There were wonderful shapes that I later learned were planes, chisels, awls, lasts for repairing and making shoes, and tins and boxes of various shapes and sizes containing screws, nails and hinges. There were also incredible smells – paint, vinyl, leather, grease (which was the cause of one ban from the shed after my white shorts and hands became smeared by it).

The best part was the grinder. This was bolted to the workbench, and consisted of a wheel that could be turned by a handle. If turned quickly, it made a very satisfying noise to a young boy, similar to that of a chugging engine. So the shed became my boat, in which I had many thrilling adventures. I towed big ships out of Sydney Harbour or cruised in search of pirates. I fought the Second World War alongside some of my heroes from the ABC radio serial *The Kraite*, the story of brave Aussies who fought the war, and went behind enemy lines, in an old fishing boat. I was the captain of my boat, of course, busily turning my grinder as the boat chugged along.

*

Grandma recognised my early love of boats and trains, and some of the best times we spent together were on what we called our transport days. We would catch two buses from Petersham all the way down to the Darling Street wharf. We would enjoy our picnic lunch in the park on the harbour, where I revelled in the tooting of tugs and ferries, and the sound of the wash on the sea wall. Grandma painted wonderful word pictures of the boats as they passed, describing their vivid colours, and we had lots of fun giving them names. As Grandma told me about each boat, I would develop a story of where it had been or where it was going, and what adventures it was having.

Then came the best part of the day, when we caught the ferry to Circular Quay. This involved a little boy bouncing up and down on the wharf as we waited for the ferry to pull in, listening to the exciting noises of the motor running, the propeller churning water, commands being yelled, gangplanks sliding out and hitting the wharf, and the inevitable tooting. I learned what the number of toots meant, and that memory has been a useful one as my time on boats has morphed from my imagination to reality.

Holding tightly to Grandma's hand, I then had the exciting walk along the gangplank, above what I imagined to be that dangerous strip of shark-infested water, and onto the ferry. We always sat outside, of course, rain, hail or shine. I remember the rocking motion, the feel of the sometimes wet wooden seats and the always wet mooring rope, and the smell of engine grease, painted wood and salt water. And after the return trip on the ferry, we took the train from Circular Quay.

Having a three-transport day – bus, train and ferry – was the norm. But if I was really lucky, and it was wet or Grandma was a little tired or unwell, we would also catch a taxi, which counted as a fourth type of transport. Those were the days of which I dreamed, when we could sit in the back seat of the taxi – or, if I was very lucky, I could sit in the front – and ply the unknown man at the wheel with questions, while I listened to the constant click and rumble of the meter, or the chatter on his radio. I would often tell him that he should call in on this or that job, or tentatively reach out and touch the controls and the microphone.

I would come home from these days absolutely worn out by my own curiosity and excitement. Grandma would prepare me my favourite dinner, pop me in a warm bath, then hustle me off to bed, where I went to sleep listening to serials on the radio, and the wonderful ticking and chiming of the clock.

2
Mountjoy

I'm sure Dad was very excited when he won the job as chief executive at the Masonic Hospital in Ashfield. With not much more than his Bathurst school education, he had worked his way up as a clerk, on the railway and in the Masonic Lodge. The job was a major promotion, giving him responsibility for all non-medical issues at the hospital, as well as for the infrastructure and grounds, and we would live in a beautiful old two-storey house on the premises called Mountjoy.

Most of our friends and acquaintances were, I am sure, pleased for Dad and us. But the concern I remember, as a six-year-old, was how I was going to cope with the stairs, which wound their way to the second floor. This concern has been a continuing theme in my life, but I have never shared it. One of my regular and somewhat terse responses is: 'It's my eyes that don't work, not my legs.'

For a young family growing up, Mountjoy was a dream come true. From a small cottage on a corner block, with an adequate backyard and a shed, and a busy road along one side, we moved to a large house with verandas and balconies on two sides, numerous out-buildings, an area of trees at the front that we called 'the bush', a long gravel driveway with a circle at the end, and two large areas of lawn for games. The grounds, gardens and buildings required constant upkeep and maintenance. Yet they provided Robyn, Brian and me with a very large and mixed environment where we could play and explore in relative safety.

*

It took me a while to understand that I was different from other kids. But as I grew up, I did start to wonder why I bumped into things more often, why I could not run around and follow people as other children did, and how it was that they appeared to know much more about the broader environment than I did. I worked a lot of it out from sounds, and information I had gained from conversations or previous experiences, but I did start to realise that other people could do something that I could not.

I don't remember thinking that this was unfair – just that it was a little strange. I do remember deciding that I would have to develop strategies to deal with this annoying lack of information, as I could see no reason to let it limit me. So I began to do that.

I worked hard at memory, and keeping maps of my environment in my head. To this day, even as my memory is more stretched, I still have a fairly good grasp of areas I am familiar with. I also learned to ask more questions about what was happening, or what was around me, and my family supported me by painting great word-pictures from which I could garner much information.

My wife, Maureen, has become one of the best impromptu audio-describers I have ever met. She has also developed the skill of weaving her word-pictures into general conversation, so that it does not feel like something special she is doing for me.

I also taught myself to retain this information. This was both so that I could make use of it later, but also so that I could refer to it in conversation in similar ways to others around me. I did not avoid words like 'look', 'sight' and 'see', because that would have made my conversation stilted and different.

My possessions were usually kept in the same place, so that I could put my hand on them easily when I needed them. This skill development has benefited me to this day, and it is unusual for me to lose something. My family support me very much in this regard. Maureen either has, or has developed, an amazing skill for putting things in the same place, and remembering that place even when I forget. And my daughter, Rachel, while not being the tidiest person herself, constantly chides her friends not to leave chairs or other items out in the paths of travel. She has developed the technique of making a noise between a squeal and a squeak when I am about to run into her or something else, and saved me (and her) much pain and embarrassment.

At a young age, I also learned to bluff when I did not know, to pretend I understood more than I did, so that I could acquire further information and fill in the gaps at a later time. This is a skill I have honed over the years. As a young boy I had a very good ear for sounds and voices. I could identify car makes by the sound of their engines, and amazed adults used to test me on it. But I often pretended I knew someone or something when I didn't, and usually worked out who or what it was before people realised my bluff.

I modified children's games and activities to 'level the playing field', and suggested or encouraged activities at which I knew I could perform well. I played rugby league on the big grass areas between the house and the hospital with my brother and his mates. They were all around four years younger than me, so my superior weight and strength compensated somewhat for my lack of sight. I didn't get the ball as much as they did, but once I got it I rarely let it go.

When we rode our bikes on the gravel drive I could follow the sound of the other bikes, and so crashed less frequently than I should have. My parents were not keen for me to have a two-wheeler bike because they felt I would find balancing at the slower speeds at which I needed to ride much harder than on my tricycle. But when my sister and brother started to ride two-wheel bikes and scooters I was determined to do the same, and just took theirs until my parents gave me my own.

Inevitably, as someone who could not see, I had some major misconceptions about what things looked like. I thought for a long time that birds were just like small cats or dogs with wings, because I had been able to touch a cat or a dog but not a bird. I could not understand why the Sydney Harbour Bridge was referred to as the 'coat-hanger' until much later in life when I felt a scale model. The shape of Sydney Harbour really confused me until I felt a map. And only recently, while attending an audio-described performance at the Sydney Vivid Festival, when light was projected onto the sails of the Sydney Opera House, did I really come to understand the shape of the sails. Even today, I can be caught out with an assumption about a thing or a place that is just fundamentally wrong because I have not seen it. It's a bit of a shock, but I normally get past it.

*

My parents were keen to ensure – right from the start – that I contributed equally to our lives. This was partly because they knew that the whole family would gain a greater benefit if everyone 'pulled their weight'. But they were also determined to ensure that I would not be treated differently because of my disability. The same expectations were placed on me as on my brother and sister; I received the same rewards of independence and opportunities. Mum or Dad, and increasingly I, just had to work out how I could best meet those expectations and take those opportunities.

I realise now just how much these family activities benefited my later life and career. They taught me many things: to work as a team, and plan to maximise the contribution that all team members could make; to enjoy the process of a shared challenge and a shared reward; to not limit someone by setting the expectations bar low; and when expectations are not met, to search out a different process by which they might be achieved. Life was about finding a way.

Life was also about giving thought to how a task might be done so that it included others. If Mum was cleaning or shopping we would often do it with her. If Dad had to rake the gravel drive or sweep leaves or rubbish into piles for composting or burning, we would do it as a family. This meant that sometimes one person was not doing things at peak efficiency – although you tried to achieve that whenever you could – but the overall result was more efficient, and everyone gained from the shared experience. Fantastic life lessons!

Many of these values arose in part from the religious commitment that was a central part of our family. Church at Holy Trinity in Dulwich Hill was a regular weekly event, and Mum and Dad both played significant roles in the congregation. As part of those values, we were always taught that we had a somewhat privileged place in society; we had an obligation to recognise and sometimes challenge disadvantage, and to demonstrate fairness and ethical behaviour. I remember Dad's outrage when he was offered a bribe while an alderman – as they were called at that time – on Ashfield Council, and his determination both to refuse the offer and to be very public about his refusal.

As a teenager I drifted away from the church and church activities, but never that far away from God. The moral compass I gained at that time has guided me through much of my life. In the past few years, Maureen and I have again come to appreciate the value of participation in a church community, and that closeness has reinforced the compass direction.

*

As well as fond memories of Mum's mother, Grandma, I have clear memories of Dad's father, who we called Pappa. After his second wife, Claire, died, and as he became older, he came to live with us at Mountjoy. The end of the veranda, which ran around two sides of the house, had been closed in and turned into a sunroom. This was his diurnal space. He would sit there reading the paper and smoking his pipe. I think I gained my love of the smell of pipe tobacco from him, and I took up pipe smoking when I went to university. This, mixed with the smell of the newspaper ink as he turned the pages of his *Herald*, was a heady mix for me.

Sometimes, Pappa would read out things from the paper that he thought may be of interest to me. They were usually of more interest to him, yet I loved having people read me information that I could not get in other ways. I was a voracious reader of Braille from quite a young age, but the material available in Braille was limited and dated.

On other days, Pappa was just not interested in reading to me. The only sounds we would hear from him were his grunts of annoyance as he read something about which he was unhappy, and his asthma-like cough. As well, of course, as the sounds of lighting, smoking and cleaning his pipe. He had been gassed in France in the First World War, and this cough may have been a result of that. He had also been wounded in the knee. The two options he was given at the time were to have his leg set so that he could never bend it, or to wear a caliper for the rest of his life. He chose the second, and the creak of the leather as he walked, and the smell of the leather straps, were – for me – his other constant companions.

*

As with any big old high-ceilinged house, Mountjoy was cold in winter. As a family we dealt with this by gathering around one of the few heat sources, and then at night running upstairs to bed and quickly getting under the covers on top of our electric blankets. The fact that I could read under the covers, and not get cold hands while holding the book, was always a benefit for me. It was a further benefit, both for me and my brother, Brian, who shared a room with me for a while, that I could read in the dark. However, it was a continual frustration for Mum, who always wanted me to be asleep before I was ready. Eventually she gave up on the going-to-sleep requirement, and many was the night where I stayed awake late finishing a volume of Braille.

Most books came in many volumes of Braille. The Bible, which I had in my room, was in 26 or 30 volumes. Sharing my passion for reading, Mum took me into the Royal Blind Society in William Street, where I met the librarian Louise Long, who also shared my reading passion. She became a firm friend for many years. I did not often see her, but I would ring her up to discuss my reading selections. On very special occasions, I would go into William Street and be allowed to browse the shelves, and pick books for myself. Louise was not keen on my choice of Zola's *The Drunkard*, but at my entreaties she put it on my list. However, to an eight- or nine-year-old boy, the title was far more fascinating than the content, and it was one of the few titles I sent back unread.

Books regularly arrived from the Royal Blind Society in wicker baskets. Hearing the clunk of the new basket on the wooden veranda was always a moment of intense excitement for me. What had Mrs Long sent me this time? I would devour the books, particularly during school holidays, often surprising her when I phoned in a few days' time to ask for a new basket.

Braille has played an incredible part in my life, providing me with a script with which to read and write. Most people who are blind, particularly those who lose their sight later in life, do not learn Braille. They rely on listening to speech, synthetic and real, and they input through a QWERTY keyboard, or through dictation. Sadly, some teachers discourage even young children from learning Braille, asserting that technology using voice is adequate. I believe they are wrong.

Just like any script, Braille takes time to learn. But once learned, even to be able to read notes or labels slowly pays you back for the rest of your life. As an active rather than a passive form of reading, memory retention from reading in Braille is higher than that from reading using voice.

I do not dismiss the value of recorded audio material. There is far more of it available, and it can often be a good way to quickly read through a large document. But for study or concentrated work, reading in Braille cannot be beaten.

*

The primeval human desire for fire and warmth has always been strong in me. Perhaps I gained it from my father's love of following fire engines and being a spectator at fires. The urban myth in our family was that he almost missed my arrival because he had raced out after a fire engine when Mum was about due to go to the hospital.

One of the heat sources in Mountjoy was a coal-burning cozy. The start of winter was always marked by Dad's decision to light the cozy – something I encouraged him to do earlier and earlier in the year. It had to be heated with paper and then wood before coal – or coke – could be put into it. Once this fire was lit we would keep it burning all winter.

I was often sent to fill the coal scuttle from the heap at the back of the house, and as I grew older I was allowed to pour the coal into the top of the cozy. I was forever sticking the poker in the round door at the top to see how far the coke had dropped, and whether I could pour in more coal. Mum was a very tolerant woman, but not always forgiving of the coke and ash I liberally distributed through the dining room where the fire sat.

When we went on holidays to a friend's cottage in Lawson, in the Blue Mountains, I always wanted to light the chip-heater, which heated the water for our baths. I was always keen to build up the campfires we had when Brian and I were in the Boys' Brigade. And on one occasion as an adult I was saved from burning our house down in Perth by the arrival of a friend. I had been there alone and let the open fire get too big – so much so that it had crept out of the fireplace and started to lick around the wooden supports of the mantelpiece.

Many people were concerned about me dealing with fire, and how dangerous it could be to both myself and the general environment. I did burn my fingers occasionally, and have had the odd minor catastrophe. But usually, as with many other things in my life, I worked out ways to minimise the risks so that I could fully participate. I very rarely accept limits on what I want to do.

*

At Mountjoy I would lie on the floor next to the cozy, after school and at night, listening to the radio. Radio introduced me to news and current affairs, and I am still a current affairs junkie. These days, though, current affairs come to me much more via Twitter and RSS feeds.

But I also gained a love for serials, and would listen regularly in the afternoons or evenings. I was a devoted member of *The Argonauts Club*, and 'Dracon 14' was my number. I just loved stories, and the radio gave me the words while my imagination created the pictures.

My love of cricket was reinforced by hearing Alan McGilvray and others commentating, both from grounds around Australia and in places as far away as South Africa and England. The first cricket series to which I listened was from South Africa in about 1962 or 1963. I vividly remember McGilvray's outrage at South African Jock Irvine neutralising the effect of Johnny Gleeson's finger-spin by padding away the ball with his pad. He had put excess of whitener on the pad, to make it harder for Gleeson to grip the ball.

As well as sharing my passion for reading, Mum shared my passion for cricket. We would take a picnic lunch and make a day of it in the Ladies Stand at the SCG for Sheffield Shield matches. We always sat in the front row just behind the picket fence, and the sounds of bat on ball, running feet and calls from all parts of the field by the players were explained for me by the ABC commentary. Cricket on the radio, as described by Greg Champion, has been a constant part of my life ever since. I now listen to it on the internet rather than the unreliable crystal set, which used to bring the tones of the BBC's John Arlott, Brian Johnston and Trevor 'Barnacle' Bailey to my ear late into the nights of an Ashes series.

Cricket remained my passion, but while growing up I also enjoyed tennis and football. The thwack thwack of ball on racquet as Laver, Newcombe, Roach and Rosewall 'owned' the Australian Open, with commentary from many ABC doyens, was a familiar January sound. Winter was marked by rugby league calls from Frank Hyde, Rex 'Moose' Mossop and Ray 'Rabbits' Warren on the commercial stations, as well as Alan Marks and others on the ABC.

The Western Suburbs Magpies were our team. Brian and I had cups with the then 12 league teams on them, and we would line them up according to the league table at the end of each weekend round. As we grew older, Brian and I would go to the football to support Wests. I still remember the sounds as the ball was kicked, bodies collided and players yelled. I particularly recall being one of those who banged on the tin fence at Lidcombe Oval when Wests scored a try.

One of my favourite early childhood memories was the New Year's Eve party that we regularly attended at Uncle Fred and Auntie Audrey Brown's house in Ashfield. Uncle Fred had acquired a huge fire station bell from a Blue Mountains fire brigade when they had modernised and installed an electric one. He used to ring it every New Year's Eve and, as I grew tall enough to reach it, he used to let me ring it with him.

After his untimely death – the event that I observed to most upset my dad – their house was sold and I acquired this bell. It was hung at Mountjoy, where I continued Uncle Fred's tradition. I also regularly rang it each time Wests scored a try in a semi-final or final game.

I stored that bell in Mum and Dad's house in Gerringong when Dad finally retired from the Masonic Hospital. Then it took up space in the garage in my own houses in Sydney, with me never quite getting around to hanging it up again so it could be used. A few years ago, when we moved into an apartment, the Museum of Fire in Penrith was pleased to receive it back for display. Given Dad's close friendship with Uncle Fred and Dad's love of following fire engines, it was a fitting way to close that circle.

*

Dad used the car when we travelled on weekends or holidays, or when he'd to go meetings. I travelled with him whenever I could, often accompanying him to Parents and Citizens meetings at North Rocks school and reading a book or listening to the radio in the car while I waited for him. It was wonderful to spend this time with my dad and have him all to myself.

I vaguely remember our first car – an A-model Ford. Dad was very proud of this car, and many of his friends did not yet have one. I have much better memories of the next car, a Ford Prefect. As I grew older

I was allowed to crank the engine for Dad when he wanted to start the car. Many people thought that cranking an engine was a very dangerous thing for a young blind boy to do. If you were not quick to pull out the handle when the engine fired, it could start spinning very fast. But Dad had showed me this, and soon realised that I used the sounds, and my quick reflexes, to minimise the risk. For him this was just a job that a family member with the right skills did, and it meant he could be at the wheel and in control of the car.

As I grew, I became intrigued by the clutch and the gears. Dad would let me put my hand on top of his on the gearstick to understand how it worked, and after a while he would let me change the gears on my own. At first he told me when to change them, but soon I was doing it automatically by listening to the sounds of the engine and the clutch. I was disappointed when – after the Prefect and a Ford Falcon station wagon – our next car, a Ford Fairmont, was an automatic and the gear changing was no longer required.

On long holiday and weekend trips the car was always a family place. We sang songs, Mum or Dad described what we were passing or we played endless games of Spotto or I Spy. I would often sit behind Dad with my window open, and he invented a counting game for me when I could not compete in certain games. I had to count the number of vehicles that passed us going in the opposite direction, separating out cars, trucks and motorbikes. He would regularly ask for reports on these numbers, and we would bet on whether I would pass a particular total before we reached the next town. It was great fun.

*

As well as Mum's relatives in Newcastle, we frequently visited Dad's relatives in Bathurst. The ups and downs of the three hills on the road that marked the approaches to their house always caused me great excitement. The McGregors owned land around Bathurst, Blayney and Kelso, and we would often stay for a few days or a week and help with farm activities.

Some of my fondest memories involved moving mobs of sheep from one paddock to the next along the road. This was a team activity, with four or five of us walking along and keeping the mob moving and on the side of the road. Uncle Keith usually drove the hospital ute behind the mob, picking up any injured or sick sheep that were walking too slowly. I worked with Uncle Keith, helping lift each sheep aboard and putting it back down on the road if the ute got too full or the sheep was recovered after its rest. Working with Uncle Keith in this way meant that I played a role and was part of the team doing the work.

On other occasions, often during dryer seasons, Uncle George would drive to the Edgell's factory and pick up a truckload of corn cobs to feed to the cattle. I liked to go with him, and feel the different pull of the two-tonne truck when it was loaded or empty. We would bring back the full load of cobs, and then drive around the paddock pitchforking them out to the cattle. Uncle George thought it was a bit dangerous for me to stand in the back of a moving truck full of corn cobs while using a pitchfork, and he was never satisfied that my distribution was even. So he got me to drive the truck instead.

After a few jerky starts I got the hang of the clutch and the gears. I would drive through the paddock with the window open, listening to Uncle George's instructions about turning left or right, or going straight. I could judge how close I was to the fence or a creek or dam by the way his voice would rise in pitch. The cattle were more interested in what was coming out of the back of the truck than in being at the front, and just got out of the way. The possible collisions so often talked about by others never occurred.

Uncle Allan, the oldest McGregor brother, used to take me with him to auctions – for cattle, sheep and many other things. He was always determined to get absolutely the best price, and his bidding technique helped me later in life.

Other memorable family holidays included visits to Chittaway Point, in a cottage that backed onto Ourimbah Creek and came with its own wharf and boat. I used to sit on the wharf for hours each day and listen to the river, the birds and the boat traffic going up and down. I learned to distinguish the sounds of canoe paddles and oars in rowlocks, and determine the size and type of boats by their motors. And I finally persuaded Grandma to let me climb down into the boat by myself. I loved to feel the different motions as the river flowed, and the wash as other boats went past, and it was only my great self-restraint, and the fact that Grandma had made sure that the oars were not aboard, that stopped me from letting off the line and rowing away to see what I could see. My imagination worked overtime, as only a young boy's can, and all the river sounds became part of secret sea journeys in my mind.

3
North Rocks

Essays were a weekly occurrence in Mr Grunsell's history class. He would give us the essay topic on a Friday afternoon, and expect the work by the next Monday afternoon.

Mr Grunsell never learned to sight-read Braille, as some of our other teachers did, so he asked us to read our essays aloud in turn so that he could mark them. Our desks were set out in a U-shape, and mine was at the top of the U furthest from the door. Mr Grunsell always started the essay reading at the other end of the U, so I got to hear five or six essays before it was my turn.

I enjoyed history, and studied it diligently, but weekends were often filled with family and other activities, and one weekend I ran out of time to write my essay. I waited my turn to read with some dread, knowing that Mr Grunsell would impose some form of punishment. Then, as the essays droned on, a happy thought struck me. I opened one of my geography folders, found last week's essay in Braille, and placed it in front of me. I then listened carefully to the other essays.

When it came to my turn, I composed the essay in my head, and spoke it out loud while moving my fingers across the Braille page in a reading motion. It was a little more hesitant than my usual text, but Mr Grunsell didn't notice, and I avoided the dreaded punishment.

I made this practice a regular event, saving me an hour or two of homework every weekend. It worked out well until, at the beginning of a new term, and with no prior warning, Mr Grunsell commenced the essay reading at the opposite end of the U. My trickery was exposed, and my dread of Mr Grunsell's punishment was confirmed.

*

The Victor Maxwell kindergarten in Woollahra, run by the Royal Blind Society, was my first place of formal learning. It was a kindergarten for children who were blind or vision-impaired, and I went there several days a week. I remember its highly polished, and therefore very squeaky, wooden floors, the glossy painted wooden toys and the severity of Matron Scott. Various medical and other experts were constantly looking at my eyes, and talking about me in words and tones that I neither understood nor liked very much. Mum or Grandma, with whom I had spent most of my life thus far, were usually not there, and this reinforced my sense of unhappiness. The environment was strange to me, and seemed to consist of large, open and noisy rooms and corridors. I didn't know any of the other kids, and don't remember that changing much while I was there. This kindergarten was a long way from home.

My first school was one for blind children in Wahroonga, again a long journey from Mountjoy. We were collected each morning and brought home each night by the teachers in a series of school buses. These were usually Volkswagen Kombi vans and, as one of the smallest children, I was often allowed or encouraged to sit in the boot on top of the motor, which meant that the floor was constantly warm. I was scared by the stories of older children who said that fanbelts regularly broke on the engines, and that the loose rubber belt would come up through the floor and whip me to shreds. It never actually happened, but the thought of it was my constant companion.

I didn't much like going to this school. I would wait with Mum at the front gate quietly until the bus arrived, and then run off to the large space of lawn that separated our house from the hospital. I remember Mum chasing me around this space and, when she caught me a few minutes later, bundling me embarrassedly onto the bus.

*

About six months after I started school in 1961, a new public school for blind children was opened at North Rocks. It was purpose-built by the Royal Institute for Deaf and Blind Children, as was the school for deaf children next door. My dad had been instrumental in encouraging the building process, and was president of the P&C for much of the time I went there. The institute also built facilities in which country kids could board, and a dining-room used both by boarders and day children at lunchtime. We referred to the school colloquially as North Rocks.

The school played a significant part in my life for the next ten or so years. It was staffed – in the main – by excellent teachers who were passionate about ensuring that children who were blind or vision-impaired received a great education. Keith Watkins, the school principal for much of my time there, had studied education for blind children throughout Australia and overseas. Don Hones, who also taught at the school for a long time, probably had the strongest influence outside my family on my development from a little boy into a young man. His work ethic, honesty, fairness and love of fun were values I learned and that have stayed with me throughout my life.

But the school was a closed environment, containing around 60 children from infants to Year 10, all of whom had a significant level of vision impairment. Views are strongly divided in the blindness community on whether education should be integrated or segregated – although integration is now largely the norm. The benefits of segregation are the passion and commitment of the teachers, the focus on Braille and other similar skills that blind children need to learn, and the less pressured and smaller environment. The benefits of integration are that you go to school with the kids where you live, you build lifelong friendships with your local community and you learn what living in the larger community is like. With the benefit of all the hindsight I now have – which of course gives you 20/20 vision – I support integration from an early age. But many people who are blind or vision-impaired would disagree with me.

*

We travelled to school by taxis, paid for by the Department of Education. I would leave around seven-thirty in the morning, and not get back to Ashfield until four-thirty in the afternoon. In contrast to the school at Wahroonga, my memories of North Rocks are quite positive. The school was built in a square shape with an area of grass in the centre. There was a concrete path around the four sides of the grass, with two sets of classrooms facing each other across the square, the assembly hall at one end and woodwork and craft rooms at the other. We would sit on the benches along the walls to eat our lunch or morning tea, and the rest of our playtimes were spent in games on the grass, or riding bikes or scooters round and round the square. The consequent noise was just like any other school playground.

We often played cricket at lunchtime. Blind cricket is played with a ball woven in a basket-weave fashion, originally from cane but latterly from nylon. The ball, somewhere between a sphere and a wheel shape, has bottle tops and a piece of lead inside it, to give it weight and to make it rattle. The ball is bowled underarm, and each team has some totally blind players, as well as some with partial sight. We used a metal garbage tin as a wicket as it made a satisfying ping when a batsman was bowled. Also, the person keeping wickets used to bang the lid on the tin three times to let the bowler know in which direction to bowl.

The other game we played was swish. This is a form of table tennis, again designed for blind people, which I am told is like air hockey in having goals at each end. The table has wooden sides raised about six centimetres above the level of the table and a wooden net. The round plastic ball – about the size of a tennis ball – is hit under the net, and again contains a bell or bottle tops to make it rattle. The game can be played in doubles or singles.

A further innovation of this game is swish cricket, where the bowler is at one end of the table and the batter at the other. Fielders stand along the sides of the table. A single is scored each time the ball is hit back to the bowler, two if it is hit into the net, and four or six depending on how far it is hit back past the bowler or over the side onto the ground. The batter can be out bowled if they miss the ball and it goes off the table. They can also be out caught by one of the fielders.

Many lunchtimes were spent on these pursuits.

*

As a child who was blind, I had various tools and equipment available to me to reinforce my learning – a large Braille library, wooden blocks and metal frames used to teach early mathematical concepts and the crashing sound of six or eight Perkins Braille machines all writing at once. Don Hones had a wonderful map of the world on the back wall of his classroom, made of foam rubber pinned onto canite board, outlining the shapes of every country in the world, and their relative position according to Mercator's projection. Rivers were cut in the foam, and topography represented by extra padding. Cities were marked with one type of pin, capital cities were marked with another. Borders were all marked as well. Don must have spent days and days of his time making and modifying this map. All the features were done to scale – geographical and topographical. And everything was labelled in Braille. One day he told the class that he had spent much of the previous weekend doing an 'operation' on Africa, because his geography lessons of the previous week had drawn an imperfection to his attention.

I loved looking at this map, and planning the travels I would take in future years. I sailed the seas of the world and imagined fantastic adventures. This work reinforced an understanding of geography and history that has stood me in good stead for the rest of my life. Sadly for me, although pleasingly for millions of people throughout the world, the rise of the Iron Curtain and the subsequent fall of communism has meant that my understanding is now significantly out of date.

*

Even though we couldn't see, as children we were not averse to a little naughtiness and advantage taking. On one occasion, when a music lesson being taught by Leah Wilson – who was also blind – became a little boring, my mate Charlie and I climbed out the classroom window. We stayed close by so that if Miss Wilson asked us a question we could pop our heads back in and answer, but were eventually caught when Charlie, enjoying the sunshine, lay down and went to sleep, and his snores drew her attention to our real whereabouts.

In my senior years, I was given the job of ringing the bell to mark various changes in the school day. I discovered that the tongue of the bell could be screwed out, and when I disliked a particular class, I would take it out so that the bell could not be rung. As well as shortening the class, it amused me greatly to watch the teachers trying to deal with the situation, while I stood there with the tongue of the bell in my pocket.

*

One of the regular end-of-year events for the kids at North Rocks was the summer camp run by the Royal Institute for Deaf and Blind Children. Senior students would go away for a week to a 'camp' (usually a collection of huts rather than tents) at the beach or in the Blue Mountains, for a mix of growing up while hanging out with their school friends, physical activity and life-skills training.

I enjoyed a number of these camps while still at North Rocks and was invited back a few more times as an ex-student. I was happy to attend, catching up with kids I had known and providing what I now know as peer support.

It's only as you grow older, and review events in your mind, that you recognise the critical role that peer support and role modelling provides in your life. When I was a younger child, my parents were good friends with David Hunter MLA, Member for Ashfield for 35 years and a man who was blind. I didn't talk to him much about his blindness, although we shared a love of reading and writing in Braille, but the fact that he could be a successful politician really confirmed for me that there were no limits to what I could do.

But at the time of the summer camps I did not appreciate the peer support and role modelling that I was providing to younger students. I just thought it was an opportunity to hang out with my friends for a week and indulge my passion of playing my guitar and singing around a campfire. I remember those weeks fondly, as we enjoyed a greater level of freedom away from our school and our parents, and learned more about the people that we were going to be. And at the same time it was of real benefit, both to me and to other students, to share our fears. By bringing them into the light, we could often show that their reality was much less scary than their imagining.

People's rights, too, started to feature in my life. Wayne Simpson, a few years younger than me at school, wanted to smoke cigarettes but, as a blind person who could not just model others' behaviour, he couldn't work out how to get the end of the cigarette and the burning end of the match to successfully meet so that he could light up. His family and the staff at the camp would not teach him, as they felt it was inappropriate for him to smoke. I strongly took up his cause, both arguing on his behalf and finding secret places where I could school him in the lighting technique, something I had perfected from lighting fires in my earlier years. I don't know if he still smokes (I hope not), but I know he smoked for some years as the result of my advocacy and teaching. People with disabilities have the same right as everyone else to take risks and indulge in foolish behaviours.

*

I learned many lessons at North Rocks, both from the official curriculum and the 'book of life'. A final one that I recall related to leadership, and the importance of taking people with you on any journey. It was during the year when I was house captain, and the annual sports day was coming up. Many of the school's best athletes were in the other house, and I knew that we had to come up with a different strategy if we were to win the competition. So I started to think about how the house points were awarded, and realised that winning the tug-of-war might just give us enough points to get over the line.

Cook house, our opposition, had the advantage in weight and strength. But we had one boy whose weight could be used as our anchor, if we could only get him to commit and try hard. He came from a disadvantaged background and did not have the benefit of the positive family encouragement that I had enjoyed. Expectations for him in school had been low, and he met those expectations.

I sat with him at lunchtime every day for the week before the sports carnival talking about the tug-of-war. I showed him the rope, and explained how he would need to tie it around his waist as the anchor, and how he could lean back on the rope and make a huge contribution to the team. I talked through the scenario of the actual tug-of-war, helping him to visualise the process, and encouraging him to think about it at other times during the day, because I had learned how that type of positive visualisation could make a difference.

When we lined up our teams for the tug-of-war, I placed myself just in front of him on the rope and kept up my positive talk. When we started it was a tense struggle for some time, but I could feel our team being slowly but surely dragged towards the line where we would lose. In a final desperate effort, I turned to him and yelled, 'Come on, anchor, remember what we talked about.' Suddenly, I felt the tension increase from behind me, and our losing slide stopped. Slowly, ever so slowly, as he leaned into the rope, we started to pull the other team backwards, until we were finally successful. I turned and gave him a huge hug, knowing that he had made the difference. He didn't quite believe me that he had done so, but I assured him again and again that he had.

He finally came to glow in the success of the moment. I learned a major life lesson about lifting the bar of low expectations. I've spent much of my life working to lift that same bar for many other people.

4
Ashfield Boys High School

One of the techniques I employed to make friends at my new school was to support the school sporting teams. I had been a rugby league fan all my life, but our school's best sporting work was done on the soccer field. The higher than usual migrant population in the area in the 1970s probably accounted for this. I knew nothing of the game, but a lack of knowledge had never stopped me in the past.

There I was, on the sidelines, knowing nothing of what was taking place on the field, except which goal Ashfield was defending, but cheering madly in support. Not playing any sport at school myself, I was a regular – and often the only – spectator. And I was loyal, even though we did not perform particularly well.

My loyalty was repaid when our Year 11 school debating team started to achieve results. Two or three of the soccer players attended a few debates, but I had to tactfully explain that the type of barracking I employed from their sidelines was not de rigueur from the back of the debating hall.

In spite of, or perhaps because of, those minor disruptions, we debated our way to the state final against North Sydney Boys High School. North Sydney Boys was a selective school, and arrived for the final with a cocky North Shore mentality. We were determined to knock them off their perch, and we proceeded to do so in a close-fought tussle. Our loyal soccer team supporters enjoyed the victory, and I'm not sure that the Hume Barbour trophy has had a humbler return to the winning school than it did that year – in the back of the ute with which George Kerrinakis's dad carried supplies for his Ashfield fish shop.

An entertaining coda to this story occurred some 25 years later. As the first chair of Vision Australia, I and several others interviewed – and appointed – Gerard Menses as our first chief executive officer. After he had signed his contract of employment, he admitted to me that he had been the fourth speaker for the North Sydney team, whom we beat. That would have been a happy reminiscence had he not also admitted that – unbeknown to me – he had led a protest by his team against our win. This was because I had read my notes in Braille rather than print, and was thus able to maintain eye contact with the audience. He felt that this had given Ashfield an unfair advantage. He hastily assured me that he had since revised his view of 'reasonable adjustments' for people with disabilities. We were able to laugh about this in hindsight (though I am not sure that I would have laughed at the time). It was the start of an honest and excellent relationship between me as board chair and Gerard as CEO, and a friendship that continues to this day.

*

More than anything else, the change from North Rocks to Ashfield Boys was reflected by the noise and the very different environment. Ashfield was a campus dotted with steps and odd angles. All of the buildings were two storey so, with steps in the playground and stairs in the buildings, people's concerns about me and stairs again reared their ugly heads.

For me it was not the climbing of the stairs or the finding of the steps that was the big issue. The new building had an external circular concrete staircase and, with a slight miscalculation in angles on the path of travel, the first contact I would make with the stairs would be with my head. That mattered to me much more. But, after a few bruised foreheads and the odd swear word, I learned not to make those mistakes. That was a good access lesson for the future.

My time at Ashfield, with 1,000 boys from years 7 to 12, provided a more robust environment than the one I had been used to from kindy to Year 10 with only 60 children. I spent my first few days wandering unknown corridors, trying to find my class. I used a white cane at Ashfield, which I had not done at North Rocks. This was partly to locate objects such as schoolbags dumped haphazardly in the corridor, partly to find the steps and the stairs, and partly to identify me to the other boys. The sight of the white cane did not prevent the bumping and jostling that only 1,000 teenage boys can create, but it certainly decreased it. So, with my white cane in one hand, my Perkins Brailler machine in the other, and a bag of books and a cassette recorder over my shoulder, I trundled through the busy, noisy corridors of Ashfield, constantly coping with the testosterone-fuelled noise and smells.

My next challenge was to make some friends. Most of the other students had friends they had made from years 7 to 10, so in Year 11 those friendships continued. But for me the first few days were a quite lonely existence. I gravitated towards the nerdy kids because of my inability to be recognised as good at sport, games or other physical activities. I didn't need to play sport though – all the walking and carrying that I did was a good fitness regime in itself.

The first friend I made was Peter Humphries. I think I was buddied up with him by one of the teachers, and he was prepared to wander with me to various classes and chat to me at lunchtime and recess. I kept that friendship throughout my time at Ashfield, but we were never close. Next was Stephen James, who shared my interest in speaking and debating, my preparedness to yarn and philosophise, and my passion for fairness and equity. As the days went on my friendship circles grew, as is usually the case, although my sporting team support technique didn't really have much impact until later.

One of the other differences for me between North Rocks and Ashfield was that, at Ashfield, for the first time in my life, I walked to and from school by myself. Most of the other kids at Ashfield caught the train or lived on the other side of the railway line, so I rarely walked with a friend. But I didn't mind. This was ten minutes of peace and quiet before and after the barrage of noise and hustle that was Ashfield boys. Most of the walk was in suburban streets, and the only busy crossing – over Liverpool Road – was supported by traffic lights. They did not have the audible traffic signals from which the whole community benefits today, but I learned to listen to the traffic patterns and cross safely.

I had not studied science at North Rocks as there were no facilities to do so. I presume this was because it was thought an inappropriate subject for blind children to study. I have never really understood this decision – some of the experiments would have been dangerous, but the theory would not have been a problem. This absolute lack of basic scientific knowledge has caught me out on occasions during my life. It also meant that I could not study science at Ashfield because I had no understanding of the basics of the subject.

My passion for reading (and writing) assisted with my study of English, and was not overborne by my dislike of grammar. I do not recall the texts we studied, except for *Hamlet*. I remember this because one of our teachers took us to a film of the play, which was entirely in Russian with English subtitles. I protested about this for the next couple of weeks by speaking loudly in a Russian accent, in made-up words that I thought sounded Russian, whenever I thought that particular teacher was nearby. I decided I had taken this far enough when he threatened to put me on detention for answering one of his questions in class in my Russian accent, much to the amusement of my classmates.

Ancient history was my favourite subject. I'm not sure whether it was the combination of mystery and history that were ancient Greece and Rome. Perhaps it was gaining further knowledge around *The Iliad* and *The Odyssey*, preferred reading in my youth. Or perhaps it was the teacher – Christine Lawler – who very clearly conveyed her love and passion for the subject, was an excellent teacher and on whom I had my first teacher crush. She probably never knew.

Outside school, my brother, Brian, was my companion through most of my teenage years. In fact, my parents' decision to send him to a different school from me was a very sensible one. If he had gone to the same school, it would have been assumed that he was my default support person.

We had grown up getting on together as a family, and we generally got on well. My four years' seniority in age somewhat compensated for my lack of sight, so we looked out for each other.

We were both in the Boys' Brigade together – following another one of Dad's traditions – which was a regular Tuesday and then Friday night activity, and included hiking, camping and other weekend activities. It provided some compensation for the lack of regular contact I had with my sighted peers at school.

Some of the others in Boys' Brigade became great companions of my teenage years. We hiked and camped together, and it didn't seem much of an issue for them that I walked next to them holding their arm, or behind them with my hand on their backpack. I worked hard to do my share of the work around campsites and, although my cooking skills didn't amount to much, I put up and struck camp, collected firewood and disposed of rubbish. Around the campfire or in the tents at night, my jokes and stories were well regarded. With their co-operaton, I managed to minimise the impact of my disability.

The highlight of my Boys' Brigade activity was also my first trip outside Australia – although it wasn't viewed as such at the time. Brian and I were sent to Rabaul, Papua New Guinea, for our first national camp. We flew to Port Moresby by Qantas jet and changed to DC-3s for the flight across PNG to Rabaul. This was one of the first times we had flown, and was certainly the greatest distance away from home Brian and I had been on our own.

The camp was great fun. We took part in the usual activities – sports and hiking during the day, and concerts and campfires at night. We climbed a volcano and clambered down inside the crater at the top. The smell of pumice stone was amazing and overpowering, and the slippery climb down into the volcano itself was equally exciting and scary.

I also experienced my first earthquake, and was one of the few on the camp to do so. Sports and outside games were often played late in the afternoon, when the day had lost its heat a little. I usually went with the others but did not play. So I, sitting on the ground rather than running around, felt the earth move. No-one quite believed me at first, but when I persisted the locals assured us that these tremors were a regular event.

The other stand-out experience for me was the regular afternoon storms. I had lived in Sydney, so thought I understood a thunderstorm – the humidity and heaviness of the air, the smell of the storm approaching, the lightning (which I heard usually through a radio) and the accompanying thunder. And then, of course, the rain. But storms in Rabaul were Sydney storms on steroids. The already humid air almost gained a texture and weight, clouds blocked the sharp heat of the sun and the thunder could be heard rolling around in particular quadrants of the sky. It was the only time I could point to where a storm was coming from.

The trip back to Moresby in the DC-3s was somewhat more exciting than the trip up. These were old army planes, not pressurised, with canvas seats along the sides and luggage stacked down the middle of the plane. Flying in PNG is done early in the morning, before the clouds come down too low over the mountains and make flying impossible. So it was an early start.

We boarded our three planes for the return journey, and learned from announcements by the pilot that there were two storms brewing that we would need to avoid. The first plane took a wide arc, making the trip to Moresby a lot longer but going around behind one of the storms. The second plane decided that the best course of action was to land in Lae until the storms passed.

Our pilot, in the third plane, was made of sterner stuff. He took a calculated gamble that he could fly between the two storms before they came together. He didn't make it.

Breakfast had just been served when we began to experience the consequences of his miscalculation. The plane went through some of the worst turbulence I have ever experienced, and I was told by other passengers that we were flying so low at times that you could see the coconuts on the palm trees – though this may have been more in the realm of travellers' tales than reality. However, I was a hearty eater, so polished off about four breakfasts that morning while others had none. I happily passed breakfast trays one way and sick bags the other.

*

I must have acquitted myself reasonably well during Year 11, because I won a prefect badge for Year 12 – although it was almost a very short appointment. At the same time we won the badges, Stephen and I had been appointed to the school magazine committee. We spent several sessions planning out the magazine for the new year, and were appalled when the principal told us that we could not call the magazine by the Aboriginal word we had chosen – the local name for 'message stick'. In one of my early social justice campaigns, I accompanied Stephen and a few other committee members into the principal's office, where we threatened to hand back our prefect badges in protest. After considering our position overnight the principal relented, and the name remained. I was pleased we had decided to go to him first before going public, learning the lesson that you avoid locking someone into a decision that you don't want them to make. That was one of the first milestones on my advocacy path.

I was a popular prefect with the students. Prefects had to take it in turns to do gate duty at lunch and recess. I staffed the narrow Liverpool Road gate, and regularly pleased students who preferred to buy their lunch at the Ashfield shops rather than the canteen by agreeing with them that I had not seen them go through. However, if I smelled them smoking before they had walked through the gate I would confiscate their cigarettes. This made me popular in the prefect room as well, as I obtained a regular supply for our consumption.

The routine rhythm of class, homework, debating and study continued as the Higher School Certificate approached. I am a solid performer at exams, having a good memory and always preparing fairly well, so I did not experience as much of the pre-exam stress of some of my fellow students. In no time at all, I found myself on my own in a separate exam room, bashing out my essays and answers on my Perkins Brailler.

The only small bump in the road was the morning I dropped and broke my Perkins 15 minutes before an exam was due to start. But, as regularly happened, a quick phone call brought Dad to the rescue, carrying my second machine to the school in the car, and leaving me with a comforting pat on the shoulder and a hearty wish of good luck.

School days were finished, and I waited with excitement for the next step in my life.

5
Social life

My brother, Brian, and I had just bought our first car. We had the perfect combination: I was about 22 and had saved a little money; he had just got his licence and was desperate to drive. So I paid for the car – he paid me back half the money later – and he drove. It was a blue Chrysler Galant, five years old, with a few miles (yes, they were miles back then) on the clock, but we thought it was the best thing ever. We never missed an opportunity to take it for a spin.

I had been asked by a social club in Wollongong to give a presentation on people with disabilities at their afternoon meeting. Brian and I decided to drive. For him, four or so hours behind the wheel of our little beauty was worth the tedium of listening to one of my presentations.

I spoke about the importance of including people with disabilities in all aspects of society. I encouraged people to focus on the person not the disability, and to ask if assistance was needed rather than making assumptions about what we couldn't do. During question time I commented how critical it was to talk *to* the person rather than about them.

At the end of the meeting we were invited to afternoon tea and were happy to partake of the excellent cakes and biscuits on offer. One of our hosts approached me and said to Brian, who was standing right next to me, 'Would Graeme prefer tea or coffee?'

I winced in disappointment, given the point of my presentation. However, 'coffee' was Brian's calm reply.

'Does he take milk?' she asked.

'Yes,' Brian replied.

'And what about sugar?' she continued.

'Two sugars, please,' was his calm response.

In contrast, my temperature was rising, steam was beginning to trickle from my ears, and I was planning the tongue-lashing he would receive during the drive home.

'By the way,' Brian said with a wry smile, as our host was about to leave with the coffee order, 'would you like me to drink it for him as well?'

Suitably chastened, she apologised to me, and my recompense was an excellent cup of coffee and an extra lamington. She had worked out the way to my heart.

This is a situation I have come to experience regularly in my life. The woman had switched on my invisibility cloak as she walked up to Brian and me. It happens in shops. I walk up to the counter with my wife or daughter, indicate to the sales assistant what I want to purchase and they immediately start talking to the person with me. Or, often, they will hand my goods or my change to that person, despite me standing there with my hand out.

It happens in restaurants – when the only advantage of my invisibility cloak is that the bill usually gets delivered to the person with whom I am dining rather than to me.

It happens on aeroplanes. On one memorable occasion, Maureen was scolded by a flight attendant for letting me use the business class rather than the economy class toilet.

And it happens to people with other disabilities as well. People who use wheelchairs often find themselves being discussed – in their presence – as if they were a package or simply not there. Many is the time I have heard airline passengers who use mobility aids referred to, in their presence, as 'a wheelchair'.

I'm told that this invisibility cloak is also worn by women of a certain age, who can stand in shops for ages waiting for attention, while men and younger women are served.

I wouldn't mind having an invisibility cloak if I could switch the damn thing on and off myself. It would be pretty useful when I wanted to walk between my family and the television screen, or to pop across to the bar or buffet table for that second cake or fifth beer. But I've lost the remote control. It's attached to the cloak somehow, and always seems to fall into the hands of the person with whom I am seeking to deal, rather than into my hands.

Why does this happen to people with disabilities? We're not any more difficult to talk with than the rest of society, once you get started. In fact, some of us are quite engaging people.

It's really a demonstration of the way people with disabilities are still viewed by society.

*

I took up cricket at a 'club' level in my mid-teens. There was only one club in Sydney, based at Campsie. We spent our Sundays during the summer playing RSL and sporting clubs throughout New South Wales. They were all fully sighted players, but they played to our rules, and we won as many games as we lost. While several of my mates from school also took up the game, we were largely playing with older men. This was a good experience for me as I moved into the adult world.

In the game of blind cricket, a score of 30 runs was the equivalent of a century, particularly for a totally blind player such as myself.

I remember the day I scored 27 in my first or second season, and became the proud owner of my own cricket bat as winner of the *Herald* Sportsman of the Week award. I carried that bat proudly to all my games and used it for many years, and the tradition of oiling it at the beginning of each season was one I looked forward to. I no longer have that bat, but I still keenly anticipate the first cricket game of the season. I remember crying with the pathos of an article about the start of the cricket season by Peter Lalor a few years ago.

I was first selected to play for New South Wales in December 1972, at the age of 17. I proudly acquired my blue blazer and baggy blue cap, and caught the overnight train to Brisbane where the carnival was to take place. By this time I had taken up the role of wicketkeeper, and was regularly crouched behind the metal cricket stumps that we used, wearing my big keeping gloves and baseball face mask. I had started wearing this mask after being hit in the face once too often with the ball. I still abhor and shy away from things hitting me there, even lightly.

We spent two weeks competing for the Australian championship, which we lost to Victoria – a regular event at that time. Each night we would go and find somewhere to have dinner, and most of us would enjoy a few beers. I thought that it was okay to drink alcohol as long as I was sensible about it, as I would be 18 the following August. It was only on the last night of our trip that I discovered that the drinking age in Queensland was 21 (I think that by now the statute of limitations would apply).

Bill Siddins was the manager of the NSW team, and the axle around which the club organisation revolved. He was a good man, very generous with the time and energy that he supplied to the club. His son Glen, a few years older than I, was one of the partially sighted players in the team. Bill encouraged team unity through not mixing with the players from other teams, and so New South Wales had a reputation in this regard. I was one of the few to challenge this approach, getting to know and like players and supporters from other teams and states. Bill discouraged this, but I persisted. It was a harbinger of things to come, as we disagreed significantly in later years.

*

One of my cricketing friends, Dennis Young, played the Hammond electric organ. We combined with another school friend, Ettorre Cippiloni, who played drums, and started a band, which we called Blue Moon, with the song of the same name becoming our theme. I owned the amplifier, which went with my electric guitar and had the only microphone. As the only one who could hold a tune, I was also the singer. We didn't get too many gigs, but the few ones we did contributed to my pocket money at university. However, as Ettorre and I could not see at all, and Dennis had limited vision, the cost of hiring a van to transport all of our equipment made a significant hole in our earnings.

We played one gig in a hotel at Kings Cross. Dennis had enough sight to see the red light that was shining in the building opposite. Perhaps his comments about once every half an hour to the effect that 'it's on' and 'it's gone off' meant we did not play to our best.

Our regular gig was Saturday night at the Rosnay Golf Club in Auburn. It was an older crowd, a little more tolerant of our less boisterous rock style. We developed a trick of encouraging the audience to write their requests on coasters and hand them to us in our breaks. We already had our playlist written up on coasters, so we would take the new ones home, learn the songs and play them the next week. It seemed to work.

6
Sydney University

Law at Sydney University used to be studied in King Street, adjacent to Phillip Street, the location of many barristers' chambers and the Supreme Court. Lectures took place on the first and second floors of the law school building, which were underground.

One lunchtime, I walked into a busy lift to travel up to the university canteen. There was already a crowd in there, so my white cane trailed slightly behind me, checking where I had been. The doors of the lift closed, and a pair outside caught the tip of my white cane between them.

The cane was made up of four hollow metal tubes, each slightly thinner than the last so that they slotted together. A piece of thick elastic was threaded through the centre of these tubes, keeping the cane tightly together when it was unfolded, but stretching slightly when it was collapsed. So I had the uppermost tube in my hand, and as the lift ascended the elastic stretched. My fellow passengers began to experience differing levels of panic on my behalf as the drama unfolded. One lecturer groaned with concern. Another of my quick-witted mates started taking bets on the floor at which the elastic would break. I just waited to see what would happen next.

As we reached our destination the doors on the floor we had left must have moved just slightly, releasing the tip. The elastic contracted, and the four tubes of the cane clicked back into place. I turned to the concerned crowd and grinned, and walked out of the lift as if this was a regular event about which I had never been concerned. However, the elastic in the cane was never quite the same.

*

From about my mid-teens I wanted to study law. I had a fairly unformed view of what I wanted to do with such a degree. But I wanted to do some good in the world, and thought a law degree was the tool I could use. As most people who have been to university know, it's a world away from school. So I jumped off the veranda at Mountjoy and strode across the grass on my way towards Ashfield Station with not much idea as to how the next few years were going to play out.

I was not the first blind person to study law in New South Wales, but I was one of the early ones. I was tentatively welcomed by the dean of the law school, Professor David Benjafield, who himself used a wheelchair. But no-one was really sure how it was all going to work out.

At our introductory lecture, we were encouraged to look around at the other students and understand that up to half of them would not be there at our graduation. This was meant to give us the incentive to study hard, but it was a pretty overwhelming thought to contemplate. No-one else in my family had been to university, so I had no support from relatives who understood what it would be like. And the friends I consulted didn't really understand how I would operate in that environment as a blind person. I was in very unexplored territory.

I was concerned, but not daunted. The law school was another new environment I had to learn. But at least I was learning at the same time as every other student, so it was not quite the challenge that Ashfield Boys had been. And it was all contained in the one building, which made it a simpler task.

The pressure of the first day was added to when my briefcase was stolen. This caused me a real problem, as it contained my cassette recorder on which I took notes, and a number of my new law books, painstakingly transcribed into Braille. I went straight to the canteen and asked for an announcement to be made over the PA system. Once we got past the issue that the books I had described in the case were Braille not brown, the announcement was made. Soon after, the miscreant, realising that there was not much in the briefcase of value to them, returned it quietly to the carrel in the library where I had left it.

I had been given a carrel in the library with a locked door, but this incident highlighted the uselessness of such a door when the partitions were only about five feet high. Any lock could be undone when all that was required was to reach over the top and turn it from the inside. So the law school gave me a locked room in the library where I could store my books, Braille machine and tape recorder.

This room, the lecture theatres on the lower floors and my bedroom at home became the places where I spent most of my waking hours for the next four years. I mainly commuted there by train, sitting with my briefcase between my feet, Braille book on my lap and my regularly-smoked pipe sticking out the side of my mouth. Those were the days when smoking was permitted almost everywhere, and I well remember the warm fug of the crowded train carriages on a cold Sydney winter's day.

I could not possibly read as widely as the other students, so I quickly recognised that I would have to know the books and cases that I could read better than most of the others if I were to survive the rigours of the course. Many volunteers had painstakingly transcribed books into Braille and read them onto tape. They continued to do this throughout my university studies. So I had shelves and shelves of books in Braille or on audio cassette. But it was still nothing like the range of material to which other students had access.

My days at university went something like this: I would attend lectures, whispering notes into the microphone plugged into my cassette recorder, or recording the lecturer directly. I would then either go home or to my room in the library and write those notes up in Braille. This was a tedious process, but definitely greatly reinforced the learning from the lecture. It was these notes, plus the Braille and taped books that I had, that were my study aids before exams.

As my now colleague Professor Ron McCallum – who studied law in Melbourne – has often said, I did not have much time for social life at university. I was resolutely determined to succeed and spent much of my time in study. I played cricket on the weekends, and started to participate in the disability advocacy movement, but that was about it. Four years of my life were committed to obtaining the holy grail of a law degree.

*

Partway through my university course Dad spotted an advertisement in the paper for mediators. I applied and was accepted into the first Community Justice Centre course for mediators. After ten weeks' training we began mediating neighbourhood disputes from the centre in Surry Hills.

This was excellent skill development in mediation, and I was pleased that I was the only lawyer accepted for the course. It was also excellent training in life skills, as we heard the stories of many disadvantaged people in the community who could not afford to take their neighbourhood dispute to court.

I got a real buzz out of working with people to resolve their problems themselves, and it is something I have enjoyed since. It reinforced in me the view that a dispute resolved between parties, even with the assistance of one or more mediators, is usually going to bring a better and more sustainable resolution than one handed over to the courts for decision.

*

A number of my friends from North Rocks went on to high school and university, and there were other blind people older than us who were studying as well. We got to know each other and compared notes regarding the services then provided to us by the Braille and audio transcription department at the Royal Blind Society (RBS). Student material was dealt with in the same way as recreational reading – 'we are working through our list of requests, and will get to yours as soon as we can'. A number of us thought that student and vocational material should have some priority, and that connecting with universities may mean that reading lists became available earlier. Also, we were keen to encourage better resource-sharing, as some texts could benefit more than one student.

As a student group we got together and lobbied the RBS for an improvement in services. Our joint action resulted in the creation of a separate department for student services, with a greater focus on working with universities and lecturers to obtain earlier notice of textbooks to be used, and increased availability and professionalism of volunteers preparing these books. Our aim of better services was achieved. But it was also a great lesson in the value of collective effort, and the strength to be gained by a united voice.

It also benefited me financially. As quality improved, Braille proofreaders were employed by RBS, and I was able to gain some part-time work. I also got to know the head of Braille production at the RBS, Joan Leddermann, a blind woman herself who – as well as reinforcing for me the value of high-quality Braille – introduced me to the Association of Blind Citizens of NSW, the state organisation of blind people advocating for better services and rights.

Through cricket I was also introduced to a newly forming national organisation, the National Federation of Blind Citizens (later Blind Citizens Australia, or BCA), with which I became heavily involved. This organisation's leaders, all from Victoria, reinforced the lessons I had learned about united voices. Many of them had completed university courses and were excellent role models. They also introduced me to the cut and thrust of debate at BCA conventions, where arguments around many and varied policies relating to blind people and the blindness sector were energetically discussed. My organisational and advocacy skills were finely honed in BCA, which prepared me for my later participation in the advocacy sector.

*

After four hard years of study, I walked onto the platform in the Great Hall at the University of Sydney and received my degree, to a sustained round of applause. Gareth Johnson, next in line after me, has never quite forgiven me. He claims that everyone remembered and applauded when I, walking with a guide, received my diploma, and that he – coming next – was just an afterthought. I don't remember him receiving his degree either, which has just reinforced the issue in his mind.

Mine was not a brilliant law degree – fifteen passes and just two credits. But I had my law degree, and after six or 12 months, who was going to look at the results of each subject? I had found a way to achieve my goal.

I reluctantly accepted the official advice to wait to complete my College of Law course – required for admission as a solicitor in the

Supreme Court of New South Wales – in the second half of 1978. Staff at both the college and the RBS were not sure that the course materials would be available in time for the first half of the year. Instead, I spent time working, collecting debts for the Masonic Hospital and proofreading Braille for the RBS, and preparing to take on yet another new environment, the College of Law at St Leonards.

The college course was intense, and we were divided into teams of four or five students, acting as law firms and handling matters and cases against each other. This gave us some sense of what law in the real world would be like, although one of the pretend firms, MacDonalds, did have to undergo a name change during the course as many of us persisted in using the internal telephone system to call them with our hamburger orders. The monotony of quasi-legal practice had to be broken somehow.

During my career, I have crossed paths with many people from my university and college days. I remember many of them, but some I don't. I used to wonder why I did not remember them as well as they did me. I think that it is partly because of the public profile I have had, but also because I was the one who was different, the only student at university and college who was blind. It is only when you come from such a minority that you can appreciate that difference, and the impact it can have on you. This is another lesson I have shared with many in my career.

7
Finding work

If you were at school in the seventies like me, you may have spent time wearing a denim jacket and listening to Status Quo. They were touring Australia back then. They're still going: one tour some years ago was titled 'Famous in the last century'.

Recently, an interviewer pointed out to them that their work over the years displayed a remarkable thematic unity; or, putting it more bluntly, that whatever the title it all sounded the same.

'Course it does, it's a Status Quo album, innit,' they replied. 'It's gotta do what it says on the tin.'

Sadly, this is also true about jobs for people with disabilities. The policies may change, but the high unemployment rate stays the same.

*

Dave changed his attitude, which changed my life. This is how it happened.

I roared out of the garage of Sydney University and the College of Law a shiny new lawyer. My social-justice engine, fuelled by its knowledge of unfair dismissals and unconscionable contracts, was ready to drive people from the back roads of disadvantage onto the freeway of life.

Then reality kicked in. I spun my wheels for 12 months while I went to 30 job interviews. I know that doesn't sound like much to today's unemployed. You might submit 100 resumes today and not get an interview. But in the seventies a young person, particularly a law graduate, could get a job relatively easily. I didn't get any of those jobs, mostly because employers could not comprehend how a blind person could work as a lawyer.

The question of whether or not to disclose one's disability to a prospective employer is a vexed one. Do you risk the no-calls-returned response by being open and honest, or just not mention it and at least get to the interview stage? I adopted the second course, and achieved the dropping jaws at interview rather than the telephone handset remaining at rest on its cradle.

That was a hard year for me. My focus while at university had been to get through my course as quickly as I could. I have never loved study as a process in itself – just as a means to an end. And I never once considered the possibility that there would not be employment at the end of my studies.

I don't think my family anticipated the problem either. If they did, they certainly did not raise its prospect with me. Perhaps they shared my naivety, or perhaps they did not want to lower my expectations. As always, they were supportive. Mum never let me go to an interview without checking that the shirt, suit and tie were perfectly clean, and all matching, and that my shoes were polished. She constantly reminded me about how well I had done at school, university and college, and expressed surprise at the foolishness of the employers for not snapping me up.

Dad gave me a job as a debt collector at the hospital, and paid me 10 per cent of whatever I could collect. My legal-sounding letters, and firm-but-friendly approach on the phone, certainly decreased the hospital's bad-debt register. But the small amounts that people could afford to pay off each week or fortnight, combined with the inevitable irregularity, minus the 90 per cent to the hospital, didn't make my wallet overflow. Dad spoke to members of the hospital board about my skills, and put the word out among his colleagues in business.

But the opportunity never came, and I experienced for the first time the pain of discrimination, and the diminishing level of hope that I would ever achieve my dream.

The actions of one potential employer particularly hurt me. He was a solicitor with a thriving inner-city criminal law practice. I discovered from some of Dad's friends that he used a prosthetic leg. This should be a guy who understands, I thought. I talked with him about disability and discrimination at the interview, thinking that his lived experience would give him an acute appreciation of my problem.

'Oh, that's not a problem for me,' he said. 'I can get around quite well. But you wouldn't be able to read the files, and look up the law books. And you've got to be able to read the face of the magistrate in court. For that matter, how would you find the courthouses?'

'Well, I found the university and the college, and your office didn't present any difficulty,' I said. 'I've been reading books and files all through university and college. And you'd be surprised what I can draw from someone's voice, rather than their face.'

I couldn't change his mind. The disability advocate in me thought that, as well as us having much work to do on progressing the rights of people with disabilities, we could also improve in empathy across the disability sector.

*

I thought long and hard about my lack of success and decided that I needed to find another way to approach the problem. I would need to get into an organisation and show them how I could perform, rather than just telling them at an interview. This was an excellent lesson for me. Many times later in my life I have recalled this experience and gone around, over or under the obstacle, rather than trying to push through it.

So this shiny new baby lawyer took a job as a clerical assistant at State Lotteries, the first step in the NSW public service. I used to joke that I was the only clerical assistant in the NSW public service with a law degree. Mostly the job consisted of answering the telephone and telling people the winning Lotto numbers, which did not tax me a great deal. It was a job, so I was not complaining; particularly when the pay envelope was put into my hand every fortnight.

Next was a short stint at the Land Titles Office, where I brushed off my knowledge of property law and conveyancing. I worked in the legal section, answering telephone enquiries. I learned much about the intricacies of property title and at least got the feel of a legal department. But there was little opportunity to do more than talk to people on the telephone.

Then I found a job in the Department of Consumer Affairs, again answering the telephone. At least I was providing advice to consumers, but I was still the only clerk with a law degree.

The Department of Consumer Affairs was a great place to work. Syd Einfeld was the Minister for Consumer Affairs in Neville Wran's Labor government, and change was in the wind. Sure, I was only taking telephone calls; but I was part of a department and a culture focused on looking out for the rights of consumers.

Michael Chesterman was in charge of this section when I started. He was a friendly guy whom I got to know well, and apparently a bit of a hunk. He was a supportive supervisor, but called a spade a spade. When I was introduced to Michael, his first response was friendly but to the point. 'Great to have you here, Graeme,' he said as he shook my hand. 'We always need extra staff. Now you can't see at all, right? So how the fuck are we going to make this work?'

I sat down at his desk, and we tossed around some ideas. I had a sheaf of Braille notes I had made during training, a basic understanding of consumer law and a tongue in my head to ask questions if I didn't know. Sure, I could start giving advice to consumers. What could possibly go wrong?

So ten minutes later, I was on the phones. The questions came thick and fast.

'How long is the warranty on my fridge?'

'I've bought a second-hand car that is a lemon – what can I do about it?'

'I've paid my bathroom renovator all this money and never seen him again.'

'My baby just swallowed part of the toy she got for Christmas – what should I do?'

Day after day I listened to the advice of others, checked my notes, jumped up and asked Michael, and became more confident. His idea of calling a section meeting was – 'Put the phones down and get over here, you bastards. I've just got a media release from Uncle Syd's office I need to tell you about.' But he always answered your questions, laughed at your jokes and helped out with the phones when he could.

Once I had gained my confidence in the department, the brasher side of me often came out. One morning I was there answering ten telephones with about three of my workmates, and we received a high number of calls asking questions about skateboard helmets. Around nine-thirty, a woman walked up to our table and inquired if we had received many calls about helmets. 'Oh, yes,' I replied. 'Some bloody idiot in Public Affairs put out a media release about them, and the phones have gone crazy.'

'Is that right,' she said equably. 'I haven't introduced myself. I'm Helen Wellings, the head of Public Affairs.'

'Hello, Helen,' I said with a grin. 'I'm Graeme Innes, one of the blokes who gets the phone calls when you guys put out media releases.' We got on famously after that little exchange, and it taught me several lessons about communications.

Consumer Affairs did not fit the often mythical mould of a public service department. People in the department worked hard and late, gathering evidence to support legal actions, some of which were never taken, and others that were unsuccessful. But many did succeed, in support of a disadvantaged consumer. I was enrolled in this cause and became part of the team culture. I learned about operating as a small cog in a large organisation, about the culture that ensues and the support that occurs.

The Burdekin Hotel across the road on Oxford Street was our favourite watering hole. In fact, it was rumoured that when Jack the publican's sales were a bit slow he would make one of the numerous bomb-hoax calls our department received, to guarantee his regulars would come over. The downstairs 'dug-out' bar had the code name of 'the other office' from which people sometimes worked during, and after, lunchtime.

*

I was in my mid-twenties before I was safely established in the Department of Consumer Affairs. For some time I had wanted to assert my further independence by moving out of home – I loved my family, but felt it was time for life on my own – but without a job this had been impossible.

So when a unit came up for sale in Queen Street, Ashfield, about three blocks closer to the railway station than Mountjoy, I decided to try to buy it. This was one of the few occasions when I did not take my dad's advice – while he saw the benefits of me owning property, he saw no reason for me not to continue to live in Mountjoy.

He refused to come with me to the auction. Mum came, and showed me where I could stand just next to the auctioneer before retiring to the back of the room.

Uncle Allan's cattle auction technique was of great value to me that day. I leaned nonchalantly against the wall of the unit, and as Mum later described it, 'I thought you had gone to sleep.' I listened intently to the whole process, learning the auctioneer's technique and sizing up the competition.

I held my nerve, not putting in a bid as others did and then dropped out. As the auctioneer was about to bring the hammer down for the third time on what he thought was the only remaining bid, I quietly bid $1,000 above it. As Uncle Allan had taught me, you make one bid, high enough above the last one to knock out that bidder, and you should win. His technique worked, and with a shaking hand I signed the contract on my first property.

My next challenge was how to pay for it. I knew, with the salary I was earning, that I could get a loan for about 85 per cent of the cost. But because I had not been working that long I had not yet saved the other 15 per cent. So I went to my main bank and had the loan approved with the assurance that I had the deposit in an account at a different bank. I then went to the different bank and borrowed the deposit as a personal loan.

I am not sure that I would get away with this today, but I did back then. Every second Thursday when I collected my pay envelope, I would walk the two blocks to the personal loan bank and pay off as much as I could. I repaid the loan in 11 months, grabbing meals at Mountjoy when my groceries ran out before payday, and not having much for drinks at the Burdekin. But I was in the Sydney property market and I was living independently.

*

It was in the Burdekin that I got to know Dave Turley, the senior legal officer at the department. I kept talking to him about how I wanted to be a lawyer, and how I would do the job if I could get it. He wasn't absolutely convinced, but eventually agreed to give me a try. I worked first as a clerk in the legal section, and then as a legal officer. I contributed to the department's work on bicycle helmet regulations, and then the National Uniform Credit Code. I was still a small cog in a large government machine, but I was at last using my legal knowledge and qualifications to change the lives of people who were disadvantaged. I was living the dream.

I made it because I was determined, and because Dave changed his attitude. He was definitely not convinced that a blind person could operate as a lawyer, but he had seen me successfully working in the telephone group, and he decided to give me a try.

People with disabilities in Australia are limited by the soft bigotry of low expectations. We don't get appointed to jobs that we know we can do, because others think that we can't. We are not offered the careers that we want; we are told what limited careers we can have. We don't do things because people assume – usually incorrectly – that we won't be able to.

As a result of this, we don't have the opportunities to enjoy fulfilment in our lives, and the broader community misses out or does not value the contributions we make. Everyone loses.

This was the employment situation I faced in the early 1980s. Sadly, little has changed. Jobs for people with disabilities became a major focus for me as my life continued.

8
The disability rights movement

As an activist in the disability movement, I travelled around the country to various meetings and conferences. On one occasion, I was travelling back to Sydney from Wagga Wagga in a car full of my mates and our various mobility aids – a couple of wheelchairs, a walking stick and my own white cane. We decided – as you do – to stop for a meal at the Dog on the Tuckerbox café near Gundagai.

We had found a table and ordered our hamburgers and milkshakes when a group of bikies arrived. Now, these weren't bikers – that gruff, rugged bunch who look tough in their leathers and helmets but underneath are just your average suburban boys with the need to blow off a bit of extra testosterone. These were bikies – the sort who live outside the law, and communicate with grunts and rattles of the chains they wear around their necks. And their idea of fun that day was to harass the young woman managing the hamburger joint.

Now in those days I was a fighter for equality on the front line, not using the more conservative legal tools that I use today. And I was offended by the crass and sexist behaviour they were demonstrating.

Their lewd comments, urged on by the support of their mates, were causing her a lot of discomfort.

But what could I do? I was one bloke with a white aluminium cane, whose pecs needed a lot more work, up against half a dozen tattooed gym-junkies with chains at the ready. So, I came up with a cunning plan.

They had parked their machines on either side of our car. Borrowing the car keys from my mate in the wheelchair, I proceeded to walk to the car, white cane prominently on display, in full view of the marauding horde. I tapped my way to the driver's door, got in, started the engine and revved it a couple of times.

Balancing the opportunity to have some fun at the expense of the female café manager against the potential terminal damage to their prized modes of transport from my driving, they made a prompt and absolute retreat. I've never known a group of motorbikes to leave more burned rubber in the car park of a hamburger joint. Which just goes to show that brains can sometimes outwit brawn, and disability can have some advantages. At least, that's the way I've told the story since.

*

The National Federation of Blind Citizens of Australia, which later became Blind Citizens Australia (BCA), was first established in 1975, and has for some time been the premier national voice of people who are blind or vision-impaired. I participated in its first Sydney convention in 1977.

BCA had a different national structure to the existing groups, which were all state-based and formed a loose federation of organisations. BCA's membership was for individuals across the country, who could participate at national conventions and/or at branch levels. Given the greater role federal governments play in policy-making, this seemed a better structure to me. BCA also contained many more people of my own age with whom I had played cricket.

The organisation has had many successes in its 40-year history, including the introduction of audible traffic signals, radio reading services for people with print disabilities, better standards for Braille and audio production, and fundraising practices that do not demean and disempower people who are blind or vision-impaired.

The huge consequential benefit BCA continue to provide both formally and informally is role modelling and mentoring for blind people, by other blind people. This is not something that other blindness services across Australia can provide because their staff, in the main, are professionals trained in how to support the needs of blind people. Most service providers or agencies employ some blind people, but it is rare that they are employed in such mentoring roles.

As a student, job-seeker and employee, I was incredibly empowered by my involvement with BCA. I honed my debating skills at BCA conventions, and I gained a place on the executive of the organisation where I learned much about management and leadership.

I also saw many other blind people living independent and productive lives. BCA members were employed as computer programmers, lawyers, salespeople, physiotherapists, public servants and at blindness agencies, to name a few. Those horizons, which had been opened wide for me by my family and my involvement with David Hunter MLA, were expanded even further.

In return, as I progressed in my study and my career, I put much back into the organisation. I drafted policies and resolutions, spent time on the executive managing the organisation, and participated as part of BCA delegations in lobbying governments and blindness agencies on numerous issues. BCA, and those involved with BCA, became a significant part of my life.

*

No one person builds a rights movement. Initially I was part of the specific movement for the rights of people who were blind or vision-impaired. But, particularly as the International Year of Disabled Persons (IYDP) approached in 1981, I became drawn into broader disability rights activities.

As with many other civil rights movements, the disability rights movement began in North America. The number of people with disabilities was increased significantly by veterans returning from the Vietnam War. Their voices were strengthened by the support for what those veterans had done, and the fact that the veterans had the experience of life before the war when they were not people with disabilities. They sought to return to as similar a life as possible, but this was just not available.

People with disabilities were often corralled in institutional settings, and were cared for as an act of welfare or charity rather than being supported in their right to be part of the broader community. Our independence was very limited, and most of us did not have jobs, or were significantly underemployed. So in the seventies and eighties we began to demand a much more independent life.

The blindness rights movement was in the forefront of the development of disability rights. There are a range of reasons for this. People with physical, intellectual and psycho-social disabilities (mental illness) were far more institutionalised than people who were blind or deaf, so we were already on the way to more independent lives. This meant that blind people had lessons in organisational development and advocacy to share with the broader disability rights movement, and I was one of the people who began to share those skills.

Organisations in this area, as with other organisations or movements of disempowered groups in Australia, initially developed differently in the various capitals around the country. We lived in the days before internet, and interstate telephone calls were relatively expensive. It was also before mobile phones, so there was no texting. The fax machine – yes, remember those? – was the height of modernity, though of course it produced material in a format to which I did not have access.

As IYDP approached, people with disabilities were beginning to gain a voice, and small activities and organisations began to develop. A number of people, including Rhonda Galbally, have written about the development of the disability rights movement in Victoria. Others, such as Geoff Heath, wrote about activities in South Australia. And people such as John Roarty and Joan Hume wrote about events in Sydney. My much briefer perspective will start in Sydney, but quickly progress to the nationalisation of the movement during and following IYDP.

*

My first involvement with the broader movement was with the Handicapped Persons Union, the first cross-disability organisation in New South Wales. Our membership consisted of people with various disabilities, and the first challenge we had was with our name. Barrie Unsworth, then with the NSW Labour Council but later to become NSW premier and be famous for his cardigans, led the opposition. They asserted that we could not call ourselves a union because we were not employees. It always disappointed me that the trade union movement, who should and could have been our allies, were our first opposition. But this probably reflected the society-wide lack of recognition that people with disabilities had any particular rights or voice. The unions were intransigent, despite our arguments and entreaties, and we changed the name to the Handicapped Persons Alliance (HPA).

One of our early challenges was raising money to keep the organisation functioning, and one of our members proposed that we purchase a consignment of red and white wine, label it with HPA labels and sell it. I had just moved into my unit in Ashfield and was the only person with an empty garage, since I didn't drive a car, so we decided to store the wine there.

The day the truck of wine arrived, Arthur – one of our members with an intellectual disability – was on hand to help. This was lucky as most of the other HPA members, with physical disabilities, were not of much assistance. As a young, fit bloke I thought I would be able to do my bit in the unloading. But my contribution was quickly dismissed.

'You might be a good lawyer,' said Arthur, 'but you've never worked in a warehouse, have you?'

I shook my head.

'Just leave it to me. If you stack the cases one on top of the other like that, it will not be stable. You have to interweave them,' he said.

I recognised that day that a law degree did not make me the font of knowledge on everything, and that there was little correlation between intellectual disability and not being smart. I would remember this often in my future advocacy work.

Over time the cars of various members and friends came and went, taking two or three cases of wine at a time, most of which I loaded. We drank some and sold most, and the money gradually trickled into the organisation. And eventually, I got my garage back.

As the HPA grew in issues and numbers, we took on a range of challenges. We protested outside the then Spastic Centre's Miss Australia Quest – we were opposed to the use of beauty and bodily perfection to raise funds for people whose bodies would never be considered for entry in the contest. We blockaded a Sydney street with people – mainly in wheelchairs – because the buses were not accessible. We protested at the opening of the Eastern Suburbs railway – again an inaccessible mode of transport. We were learning as we went, and some of our activities were perhaps not as strategic as they could have been, but we were doing our part in promoting our cause and building a movement.

*

IYDP certainly raised the profile of disability across Australia. I was asked to participate as a member of the NSW IYDP committee. We had many meetings and a few events and campaign activities to raise the disability profile. Disability rights was not really what the year was about, but wherever we could we did our best to raise the rights issues.

Prior to that year, the late and great Ian Dury, a man with a physical disability as a result of childhood polio, had been commissioned by the United Nations to write a theme song for IYDP. Instead of something worthy but forgettable, he gave them 'I'm Spasticus – Spasticus Autisticus'. The song builds on the moment in the film *Spartacus*, where all the members of the defeated army of Roman slaves rise in turn to say, 'I'm Spartacus!' – to claim their humanity, and to reject oppression and exclusion. It was a raw look at the unglamorous sides of disability, and a triumphant affirmation that disability is a universal part of human experience; that disability is, in fact, about everyone, everywhere, everyday.

The UN could not cope with the song, and they rejected it. I can't remember what was used instead, which tells you something in itself. But I do remember thinking that this failure, of imagination or courage or both, was not a big surprise. Rights for people with disabilities were just not on the radar of most, except for people with disabilities ourselves.

December 1981 was the date for the first world congress of Disabled Peoples' International, an organisation that people with disabilities had formed after not being given a voice at the Rehabilitation International conference the year before. The congress took place in Singapore. Some insightful state government bureaucrats in New South Wales, Victoria and South Australia used money from their IYDP budgets to fund delegations of people with disabilities to attend. This was a great way to give the rights movement a little more momentum.

Twenty-seven of us with disabilities went to the conference, with our various guides and attendant carers. Deidre Ward, my colleague from Consumer Affairs, came as my guide, although it was the tourist delights of Singapore rather than the conference sessions that kept most of her attention. At the beginning of the conference we were a rabble. Many of us did not know each other, and lots of us thought we should be leaders. But our daily morning meetings by the pool, where the strong smell of chlorine was overlaid by the other scents of coffee, clove cigarettes and open drains, helped us to form a coherent delegation. I don't think that our international contribution was strong, but we came back determined to form a national rights movement.

It was incredibly exciting for me to be involved. Apart from Papua New Guinea, I had never been overseas before, so the international experience was amazing. The tropical feel and smells, and the noise of Singapore traffic and voices as we walked out of the airport, was incredible. Even the bird sounds – when you could hear them over the noise of a busy thriving city – were different.

I sat through all of the sessions, faithfully recording them for my later use. I did not participate much but learned a huge amount. I took in the intellectual content, the broad range of worldwide experience, but most of all the passion for change. At night we would all talk and enjoy the tropical delights of Singapore. Physical accessibility was not great, and the cultural differences were many, but most of us revelled in the challenges and the learning.

After the conference, on the last day we were there, we visited Sentosa Island. Back then you could only travel there by ferry.

The quay at Singapore was not easy to access for those in wheelchairs, but Sentosa was altogether a different matter.

The swell caused by the wash at the wharf was significant, and the ferry would drop at least a metre in the trough, and then rise up on the swell and bump against the pontoon. I waited to board while our attendants (including Deidre and Ian Cooper's very strong and fit attendant Chris Larn) – with the assistance of willing but less skilled Singapore ferry staff – got those using wheelchairs on board. Because I was not involved in this task, I was given the job of minding the cameras, and had three or four around my neck.

Finally, Deidre said it was our turn. I took her arm with my left hand, and prepared to step on board when the ferry rose on the swell and bumped against the pontoon. Unfortunately, I moved a little more slowly than I needed to, and missed the ferry. Gripping tightly to Deidre's arm with my left hand and holding the wrist of the ferry attendant who had reached out to grab my right, I was suspended – hanging by my arms – between the ferry and the pontoon. My feet did not touch the water, but they must have been very close.

Much flashes through one's mind when one is in imminent danger. I knew that, if I stayed where I was, within a second or two the ferry would rise on the next swell and crush me between it and the pontoon. So, combining strength and the adrenalin rush, I lifted myself up with my arms (and the help of Deidre and the attendant), and threw myself onto the deck of the ferry at her feet.

As I hung between the ferry and the wharf, I have a graphic memory of the tortured voice of Chris Larn coming to me from the ferry's deck, saying: 'Oh no, not the cameras.' His lack of concern for me cost him more than a few beers that night, as I reminded him whenever it was my turn to shout.

*

One of the more practical results of IYDP was the establishment of the Disabled Persons Resource Centre, which became somewhat of a hub for the rights movement. Based in Castlereagh Street, near Central Station in Sydney, it provided some much-needed financial resourcing for the advocacy side of the movement, and a plethora of books and other material detailing activities and progress of the movement both in Australia and overseas. In those pre-internet days it was a very useful source of information, and a place to plan our broader activities. I joined the management committee.

Funds from IYDP and continuing grants for a while gave us the capacity to employ staff. Margaret Tucker began as our librarian, and Karen Healey became our resource officer. I spent much of my after-work early evening time there, attending committee meetings, helping to manage the centre and using it as the base for our activities towards building a national organisation.

I became the chair of the committee established to form a Disabled Peoples' International (DPI) branch in Australia, and its first national president when it was formed. This job entailed travel, negotiating our way through the politics of disability organisations, and persuading other people with disabilities about the importance of having our own voice.

Most of the time early on was spent forming the organisation and keeping it together. We were working with people with a range of disabilities, significantly different skill levels, and the big egos that people who are going to succeed and rise to the top need to have. The task was made more difficult in those pre-internet days by the lack of easy communication, and having few resources.

We worked on the development of many policy positions, but the reality of what we achieved in terms of real change was small. But what we were doing was growing a national movement. It failed financially some years later, but morphed into People with Disability Australia, which is today the country's most effective national peak advocacy organisation, so the work was all worthwhile.

*

Perhaps because of my disability, perhaps because of the time I had needed to put into study, or perhaps because of my focus on getting employment, being involved in the rights movement and playing sport, relationships had not been a feature of my life to this point. I was sometimes attracted to women, but my initial advances had – in my mind at least – been rebuffed. Beginning relationships is definitely trickier if you cannot see those subtle signals – smiles, eye and body movements, etc. My inability to see those signs, added to my lack of experience and somewhat tentative approach, meant that not much had happened.

I have always been attracted to strong, assertive and energetic women who are prepared to challenge my statements and assertions, and to be agents of reality. I always throw myself passionately into activities once I commit to them, and I looked to partners who would share that approach. Karen Healey was such a woman.

I recognised this soon after she started work at the Disabled Persons Resource Centre, and tried to find opportunities where we could work together. I would give her what I thought were special looks and smiles, and sense from the warmth of her voice that they were being returned. I contrived opportunities to enjoy meals with her and others, and finally worked up the courage to ask her out to dinner. She accepted my invitation, and we seemed to get on well.

She had just moved into a terrace in Summer Hill, within walking distance from my unit in Ashfield. We visited each other's places several times, sharing meals and helping each other with maintenance and related tasks. Our relationship was consummated in her house in Summer Hill, and I remember my walk back to Ashfield late that night. I felt as though I was floating, and my personal life took a significantly positive change thereafter.

When her lease ran out in Summer Hill, she moved into my Ashfield unit, and we spent a very happy year or so there. I fondly remember our regular visits to her grandma in Parramatta, who clearly loved Karen and was very kind to me, and who reminded me a lot of my own grandmother. I also remember family dinners with her parents in Strathfield, where her mum was very chatty, and her dad clearly thought I was not good enough for his daughter.

I thought our relationship was going well, and would last a long time, but for Karen there was another love in her life. After our year or so together, and against my strong protestations, Karen moved to a share house in Balmain, and soon after married Dave, her former partner. I don't think she fell out of love with me; she just never really fell out of love with him. I never quite appreciated her internal struggle.

This was pretty devastating for me, and I took some time to come to terms with it. Ending a relationship is hard for both people involved, but the person who makes the break is usually further along the path to recovery.

Karen and I have stayed in contact since, however, and her warm laugh and ability to bring me down to earth when we talk always makes me smile.

9
Cricket

Some life lessons are relatively easy to learn – particularly if you observe and listen carefully. Others, in my experience at least, require a mistake before you start to get it right.

I was a member of the first Australian blind cricket international team. We toured Sri Lanka in 1981. One of the ways in which cricket was played differently in Sri Lanka is that totally blind players ran for themselves; so, when we played Sri Lankan rules, I was running for myself for the first time. My mate Chris Stewart, a player with some vision, stood beside the bowling umpire calling for me.

My first ball arrived at a good pace, just outside my leg stump, so I flicked it away through square leg and sprinted off to score my first run outside Australia. Unfortunately, having pivoted as I played the shot, I sprinted more towards mid-wicket than towards the other end of the pitch. The Sri Lankan captain, Simon, who was also totally blind and a bit shorter than me, was fielding at mid-wicket.

I must have realised what was about to happen just before it did, because instinctively – coming from a rugby league state – I dropped the right shoulder and caught him neatly under the jaw. We both fell, and my nose hit the top of his head as we did so.

Immediately mortified by what I had done – I'm sure these days it would have constituted a code-of-conduct breach – I bent to help him up, and make sure he was okay. Chris, clearly somewhat more of a competitor than I was, yelled from the other end, 'Don't worry about him – finish your bloody run!'

Both of us were bleeding so, while the game continued, Simon and I were taken to the local hospital. This was nothing like the hospital experiences I had had in Australia. On arrival we spent some time talking with someone I presumed to be the receptionist through what seemed to me to be an open window.

Picture the scene. I was the only Australian with Simon, and two other Sri Lankan volunteers, none of whom spoke much English. I was guided into a waiting room where quite a few other people sat. I was somewhat shocked when someone – without saying anything to me – grasped my arm and started to roll up my sleeve. I pulled my arm away and started to protest, but on her third or fourth repetition of the word I realised that she was saying 'tetanus', and agreed to the jab.

Then I was ushered in to see the doctor. 'This will be tricky,' I thought. 'I need to explain what has happened.' As the door closed, I stood up from the seat I had been shown. Accompanying my words with dramatic gestures and much pointing, I said, 'Cricket ... batting ... running ... cannot see ... hit other player ... shoulder ... nose ... blood.'

Thinking that I had done all I could, I sat down to hear the results. He had waited calmly through my part-mime, part-verbal ejaculation. Then he quietly said, 'In Sri Lanka, before we go to medical school, we study English. I did my medical training in London.'

I desperately sought a hole in the ground so I could disappear, but it just did not show itself. I had made the classic tourist assumption. I hope that my cultural awareness has improved since then.

*

Blind cricket was first played by staff at the Royal Victorian Institute for the Blind (RVIB) factory in Melbourne. As radio became more prevalent in Australia, its obvious benefits in providing both information and entertainment were quickly grasped by blind people. Blind people used the knowledge they gained about cricket from radio as a conversation point, both within the blind community and, more importantly, as a way of interacting on an equal basis with the broader community.

A strong cricket following developed at the RVIB factory, and the question of whether the employees could play as well as follow the game inevitably arose. Much of the work done at the factory involved the making of cane or wicker baskets and furniture, so the first balls were made of cane, woven around a small metal or wire frame. A piece of lead was put inside the ball to give it weight, and four or five bottle tops gave it sound. The dream became a possibility.

The rules were modified so that the ball was bowled underarm. This meant that it made regular contact with the ground, thus creating a noise. Most of the other rules were not much different. In Australia the game developed with one batsman at a time rather than two, which reduced the likelihood of mid-pitch collisions. A batsman could not be caught out, but apart from these changes the game was very similar.

From a fun occupation at lunchtimes the game became more formally organised. Rules were clarified regarding the number of players and sight-level classifications, and a competition began in Victoria. Inevitably interstate challenges were offered, and by the time I arrived at senior level in the early seventies the system of interstate carnivals every two years had been in place for some time.

Ivan Molloy, a prominent Victorian blind cricketer, had some involvement with blind people in Sri Lanka, having travelled there previously. Cricket in Sri Lanka was even more popular than in Australia, and he floated the idea of an Australian team visit.

The idea was discussed in Melbourne and volunteers sought, a little like the early English and Australian cricket touring teams. Most of the players were from Victoria, but Rod Mills and I were encouraged to participate to give the event a more national flavour. We did some fundraising for the trip, but most of us paid our own way.

*

So, just a few weeks after my return from my DPI trip to Singapore, I was off again. We overnighted in Singapore, and flew the next day to Colombo. We left a few days after Christmas in 1981, and I celebrated my first new year overseas.

But just when I thought I had this overseas travel thing mastered, Sri Lanka came along and showed me that our world is filled with many different and fascinating cultures and experiences. Just as Singapore was tourist-oriented, efficient and governed by quite strict rules, Sri Lanka was wonderfully chaotic. Most people, apart from my doctor, did not speak English that well, so communications – particularly when the visual component was removed – were often complex and sometimes problematic.

Probably my most frightening experience was our first Sri Lankan suburban train trip. We visited a facility for blind people, and (perhaps unwisely in hindsight) decided that we would return to our hotel by train. Travelling on a foreign suburban transport system can be challenging for anyone, but it is even more so when only one person knows where the group of twenty or so others are going, and that person cannot easily read the signage. After some hesitations and deviations, we boarded what we thought was the correct train. But when it arrived at our station, the carriages in which we were riding had not reached the platform.

After some hurried consultation, we began to jump off the train onto the side of the track, with the plan of walking the 20 metres or so to the platform. This must have been an amazing spectacle for the locals. I was the last to get off and, before I could alight, the driver, whose patience must have been sorely tried by our activities, decided that the train needed to move.

I was left with a Hobson's choice of significant proportions. Did I jump from a slowly moving train onto ground that I could not see? Or did I, the one remaining Australian – dressed in shorts, t-shirt and sandals, with no form of identification as my passport and wallet were locked in the safe at the hotel, no mobile phone and a non-existent grasp of Sinhalese or Tamil – remain and test my fate? I jumped.

Such decisions are made in a heartbeat. And it is amazing how fast our brain can process consequences and decide. But as I leaped, the last thing I remember hearing over the increasing noise of the train was the voice of Rod Mills shouting, 'For God's sake, roll forward.'

This was a quickly provided and excellent piece of advice. What I had not appreciated was that the ground sloped steeply down to the train tracks, so rolling back would have put me under the wheels of the train. I stood up, brushed the dirt off my hands and knees, and followed my teammates onto the platform. We did not catch the train again.

*

We played two tests and a number of one-day matches during that trip to Colombo, Galle and Kandy. Our trip occurred before the escalation of the war in Sri Lanka, and my memories are of an incredibly warm and friendly people, always welcoming, fascinated by a group of blind Australians visiting their country, and ever-ready for a conversation about cricket.

Honours were about even in the various contests. The skill level of the Australian side was probably slightly higher. But this was balanced out by us playing in different conditions, the need to adjust to the slightly nuanced Sri Lankan rules and the somewhat more relaxed approach used in Sri Lanka to the vision classification levels.

One of the amazing phenomena about our matches in Sri Lanka was the number of spectators. In Australia we were lucky to get ten spectators to a match, and most of them were parents or partners. In Sri Lanka the tour received excellent coverage in the local press, and we had up to 5,000 people at each game. Good shots or wickets were followed by applause and cheers, and we were clapped on and off the ground. I recall one particularly poor piece of out-fielding, where the ball stopped as I was chasing it. I could not find it and was at first greeted with a soft ripple of laughter, followed by some helpful advice as to where the ball was. I discovered it, threw it back and turned to wave my thanks to the crowd. I then pointed to myself and smacked myself on the wrist. I quickly learned that self-deprecating humour was a good method to keep the crowd on my side.

Our time in Sri Lanka passed quickly. We improved the skills of those playing cricket, and left some equipment as legacies. We supported schools for blind children throughout the country, and also provided to the broader Sri Lankan community some positive role models of people with disabilities, in a sport that they loved. Sadly, the war that occurred later set much of this back. But not the love of cricket – I understand that there was always an unspoken truce between government troops and the Tamil Tigers whenever Sri Lanka was playing a test match.

*

While the waters of cricket in Sri Lanka were pleasant, the waters of cricket back in New South Wales were more turbulent. This was caused by the tension between the parents of players, who had controlled the game for many years and wanted to retain control, and the younger players such as myself, seeking a greater voice. Not an unusual situation.

Bill Siddins, who had been the club secretary from well before the time I started to play, liked to arrange the draw, the games and the associated activities in the way he had always done. Some of the younger players, of whom I was one of the leaders, sought change and more independence. We wanted to start a competition between teams of players who were blind or vision-impaired, rather than just playing social matches against RSLs and sporting clubs. We believed that this would raise the standard of the game, as it had in Victoria, but Bill remained unconvinced.

While Bill had been secretary, the club had for many years had a blind person as president. But they had largely played a figurehead role, with Bill calling the shots. When I was elected president prior to the Sydney carnival, I decided that this needed to change.

I had not run a carnival before. But I had enjoyed what took place in other states, and I wanted the Sydney carnival to meet or surpass those standards. So I started to bring issues, which had always been Bill's province, into discussions at the committee table, and draw other people into the organisation who would assist with the process.

At this stage of my life, I had not appreciated how much I – as a change agent – needed to take other people with me. I had not learned how graduated change needed to be, and how it was often better to plant ideas and have others run with them rather than running with them all yourself. If I wanted things to happen, I took them by the scruff of the neck and shook them until they did.

This was in direct opposition to the way Bill operated. The committee continued to plan the carnival and run the early part of the season, but the tensions increased. I am not sure which lump of coal made the whistle blow – to use an old metaphor – and I did not expect the crunch point when it came. About seven weeks out from the first ball of the carnival, Bill resigned as secretary and took almost half of the club members with him. The committee was advised of this when it was a fait accompli, through a letter he read at the end of one of our fortnightly meetings.

Bill's pre-emptive strategy was clearly aimed at wresting back his control by having us come to him pleading for his continued involvement, when he would then set the terms of that involvement. But, while during the next week or so we requested him to reconsider his decision, we did not accept his terms. I, and a number of others, were absolutely determined not to do so.

We played that carnival with six or seven players of the required 11. We had no back-up players and were beaten in every match. On top of that, most of us were there at six every morning marking pitches and setting out boundary flags, putting up tents and arranging catering. And because we were young, fit and determined not to be seen to flinch, we were usually the last to leave the bar at night.

By the end of the carnival we were all totally worn out, and the administration of blind cricket in New South Wales was significantly changed. Bill and the players with him had formed a new club, and we formed a state association to run cricket. The two Sydney clubs were joined by one in Newcastle. Bill eventually returned as association secretary, but the players were now in control.

So the game I loved to play was firmly in the hands of the players, and my learning about change and change management was significantly increased. I would put this experience to use in my time with Vision Australia, and my work at the Australian Human Rights Commission.

*

Sri Lanka was my third trip out of Australia, if you count my New Guinea experience. And I certainly had the taste for more; a taste that has been well satisfied during my life. Many people are surprised by my love of travel, thinking that a person who is blind would not gain much from the experience, and would find the process so stressful that it would not be worth the effort. For me the absolute opposite is the case.

I have enjoyed all the travel I have done, by myself and with others, and still yearn for more. The plane environment is not a problematic one, as they are all designed in much the same way, with things such as bathrooms in relatively predictable places.

Airports and other countries are different. Particularly when I am travelling alone, I have learned to be very organised and patient. Airlines and airports around the world make some of the most negative assumptions about what people with disabilities cannot do. These assumptions have to be pleasantly – or sometimes less pleasantly – challenged and overcome. So when my requested guide turns up with a wheelchair for me, I usually thank them and place my carry-on luggage on it, as the thing I most want to do when I get off a plane is walk.

I never let go of my passport or boarding pass, and never agree to wait anywhere without knowing why I am waiting. If I am concerned that the wait is too long, and I am likely to miss my next connection, I just get up and start moving. This normally brings me back to people's attention.

In countries where I know English is not the first language, or where it may not be frequently spoken, I have a printed copy of my itinerary handy, so that I can support my verbal input with visual information. The process is made much easier if I have my guide dog with me, but this is usually not the case, as the quarantine processes – although easier for guide dogs – still cost significantly in time and money.

A recent incident highlighted this difference for me. I travelled back from Melbourne and had what I thought was a standard experience. Several days later I received an email from someone who was outraged at the way I had been treated while going through airport security. I had received little positive assistance to find my way through the retractable barriers that form the queuing system, been physically pushed through security, had both of my bags opened without either my knowledge or permission, and had my white cane put in a place where I could not find it.

My fellow traveller took the trouble to find an address and email me to offer a statement in support. And until I received her email I had forgotten the whole incident. As Australia's first disability discrimination commissioner, the late Elizabeth Hastings, said, 'People with disabilities swim in a sea of discrimination.'

One good friend once said to me, 'I don't know how or why you do it. It must be incredibly hard.'

'What would be the alternative?' I replied.

'Not doing it,' he said.

For me, that is definitely not an option.

10
The bowlo

I'm not quite sure how I came to be the conciliator who specialised in bowling club complaints when I started to work at the NSW Anti-Discrimination Board (ADB). Perhaps the president, Carmel Niland, thought I had a nice way of dealing with the older men and women who tended to be the main protagonists. Perhaps I showed a tendency to enjoy the reading of club constitutions and rules. Or perhaps, through random allocation, they just landed on my desk.

Whatever it was, I got to spend a lot of time talking about the disparity in costs and value of memberships, and how 'the girls preferred to play on their own, and didn't really have time to come to the club on a Saturday'. Since sexism was rife in these organisations back in the eighties, many of the women were quite happy with that situation.

I also got the chance to travel quite widely, both in Sydney and regional New South Wales, conducting conciliation conferences. And, as I had cleverly negotiated to cover the north coast of New South Wales, I got to travel in some of the most pleasant parts of the state. Tweed Heads was one of my favourite places, and I recall a conciliation conference up there lasting two days.

However, one destination eluded me. I had been negotiating for many months on a complaint against the Lord Howe Island Bowling Club. I knew it would require a conciliation conference, and that it could be complex. I started researching Lord Howe Island and planning my visit. I had always wanted a trip in a flying boat which, at that stage, was the only form of transport to the island.

As we often did, I went into Carmel's office to report on the progress of that and other complaints.

'When is the conciliation conference coming up in this complaint?' she asked innocently.

'Oh, it's set for a fortnight on Monday,' I said. 'I'm about to book the airfares.'

'Umm, it looks complex,' Carmel replied. 'I think I had better do this one.' What could I say? She was the president!

*

Carmel was a great person to work with. As president of the ADB she had been involved in negotiating amendments to the NSW *Anti-Discrimination Act 1977* to include disability as a ground of discrimination. So had I, representing both BCA and DPI.

Carmel thought it would be good to employ someone with a disability at the ADB when the amendments were passed. When she discovered my background as a lawyer, my committed disability rights advocacy and my passion for social justice, she thought that I fitted the bill. She encouraged me to apply for one of the four conciliation jobs that were being advertised, and I moved to the ADB in 1983.

It was hard to leave Consumer Affairs. It had given me my break in the public service, I had good friends there, and I was committed to the work. But for similar reasons to those in Carmel's mind, I was keen to make this move.

Carmel shared my social justice passion and was a smart political operator. I was pleased with her decision not to make me a specialist. She expected me, and other conciliators, to deal with complaints on all grounds of discrimination. This gave me the chance to gain a deep understanding of those grounds – race, sex, pregnancy, sexual orientation etc. – and the specific impacts of those areas of discrimination.

Carmel recognised from the start that I would need to have reasonable adjustments in my role. She expected me to carry the same caseload as others, but facilitated a way for me to read the handwritten and printed material in the files I was handling. She assumed that I would do the same amount of travel as other conciliators, and just accepted that, where it was necessary to drive, I would arrange an alternative form of transport. It was great to have this level of support from an employer. I paid her and the ADB back with loyalty and hard work.

The types of complaints with which we dealt were many and varied. While I did not handle them, this was the time of the complaints by the Wollongong women against Australian Iron and Steel for the impacts of the last-on, first-off system, which meant that – because they had been employed later at the steel works due to their gender – they were dismissed first when a downturn occurred. The successful resolution of their complaints was a huge case on the journey towards equality for women. I loved seeing this occur, both for the women involved and the other women who would benefit. I also saw the implications for disability discrimination. At the other end of the spectrum, I conciliated sex and race discrimination complaints against small employers running fish and chip shops and three-person accounting businesses.

I saw the negative impact of these complaints on all of the people involved, not just the complainant, and became determined to reduce such discrimination. I learned that – particularly for employment complaints – the outcome was usually that the complainant would need to find another job. But I also saw the positive benefits in the lives of the complainants when their complaints were upheld. I saw the empowering experience that a conciliation conference, where complainants told the respondent in a controlled and neutral venue how the discrimination had hurt them, could have.

I particularly enjoyed the change that sometimes occurred for respondents in this process. Hearing someone lay out how a respondent had hurt them with conscious or unconscious discriminatory behaviour could be life-changing. My ADB experience confirmed my view that both mediation and conciliation were very positive and beneficial processes for all parties most of the time. It was pleasing to know that I had played some small part in change through the use of the NSW *Anti-Discrimination Act 1997* and my conciliation skills.

*

Mum and Dad retired to Gerringong, and I often visited them, working out of the ADB's Wollongong office. They needed to sell the house in Petersham to build their new house, so I took the opportunity to leave my Ashfield unit and buy the Petersham house. I returned as a man to that place of wonderful boyhood memories, and the experience was a positive one.

For a while I lived in the house on my own as I had done at Ashfield. The house had been rented out for some time, so I spent some effort painting, carpeting and generally refreshing it. I enjoyed the space and having my own piece of dirt rather than being a part of a body corporate. It was great to have a backyard, and I installed a barbecue and got myself an old mower from Mum and Dad to mow my two small pieces of grass.

One Sunday afternoon, after a long day at cricket and a few beers, I returned home around seven at night and immediately noticed something different in the house. I had the sense that someone else had been there and, when I investigated further, I discovered that the back door was open. I was certain I had not left it that way.

I thought that someone may have broken in, and my suspicions were confirmed when I touched the outside of what I discerned to be my full laundry basket on the dining-room table. I knew that I had not left it there. My thought was reinforced when I discovered the sharpest knife from the kitchen sitting on the table beside it. It was time to call the police, but I did not want to touch the contents of the basket in case I destroyed fingerprint evidence.

I explained my situation, and two officers arrived about 20 minutes later. They followed me through the house as I pointed out what I had discovered. They agreed that a burglar had been in the house, and said that the fact the basket and knife were still there suggested that I had disturbed them at their work. That cold finger of fear crept up my spine as I thought through other possible consequences.

'Sir,' one of the officers said, 'this basket is full of electrical equipment and kitchen groceries, but there is a bong sitting on top of it. Are you able to explain that?'

Thinking quickly that my good luck in missing the intruders had just turned bad in a serious way, and wondering how long I would keep my highly prized admission to legal practice, I replied confidently, 'Well, it's not mine. They must have left it here when they hurried out.'

'Yes, that's probably it,' said the officer, and I detected a smile in his voice. They completed the necessary formalities and were on their way.

I decided that I needed a stiff scotch to recover from the close shave I had had on a number of fronts. Deadlocks were installed the next week.

*

My work with BCA continued, with Chris Stewart – my competitive, partially sighted cricket colleague – and I deepening our working relationship and friendship. We represented BCA in an Australian delegation looking at services for people who were blind or vision-impaired in China. The delegation was led by the then president of the Australian National Council for the Blind (the organisation of service providers), Peter Blockey. We were also accompanied by the then CEO of the Braille and Talking Book Library of Victoria, Jan Smark Nilsson and her husband, Bertil.

When I woke in Beijing on the first day of our visit, I was surprised to find that, although we were in the middle of a huge city, all I could hear from our open hotel-room window were bicycle bells and the sound of walking feet. The occasional truck rolled past, but no cars were in evidence.

We spent ten days travelling to four cities in China, visiting many services (schools, massage hospitals where mainly blind people were employed as masseurs, workshops and offices), but also visiting some of the key tourist attractions. We climbed the Great Wall, visited the entombed warriors and trekked around the summer palace in Beijing. The sight of four or five white Australians, two quite tall and Chris with his curly red hair, attracted small curious crowds. This visit occurred before China was opened up to tourism, and we made a very unusual sight. Two blind people moving about confidently on their own was also a quite unusual thing to see.

Jan has a way with words – spoken and written – and is an excellent audio describer. So my memories of the sights we saw, and the general Chinese landscape, are much enhanced by her word-pictures.

On one of our numerous flights during that trip I asked Peter – as a former air-force pilot – to describe the landing experience. I did this in an effort to minimise Chris's fear of flying, but for that purpose it was a dismal failure. However, Peter's running commentary from about 20 minutes before touchdown taught me a great deal about the workings of aeroplanes, and has certainly enhanced my knowledge of flight. His explanation of the thrill and wonder of the experience of reverse thrust is a fond memory for me, recalled frequently when my plane hits the runway.

*

As the chair of DPI Australia I travelled to the first meeting of the DPI Asia-Pacific council in Manila in the Philippines. Chris was my guide for this trip. The meeting was an important one in establishing DPI in one of the world's largest and poorest regions. However, the meeting itself is a bit of a blur, punctuated by my frequent exits to deal with the stomach bug I had picked up somewhere during the trip. Chris represented Australia well during my absences.

On the day prior to the meeting we decided to make contact with the local blindness organisation in Manila, and exchange views and experiences. It was an interesting and valuable visit, and we gained a much greater insight into the real disadvantage experienced by blind people in poorer countries with virtually no social-security system. We were invited to a meal at the end of the day and happily accepted. One of the courses consisted of a raw egg containing the partially formed foetus of a baby duck – it was the delicacy of the meal. As a confirmed non-eater of eggs I was able to justifiably decline. But as a farm boy, and a proud upholder of our quasi-diplomatic Australian status, Chris felt that he should accept. His voice quavered and went up about an octave as he answered affirmatively when asked if he was enjoying the delicacy. But his frequent coughs into his hand afterwards, and his unusual keenness for a prompt post-meal departure to the hotel, suggested otherwise.

We experienced an instance of disability discrimination on our way home. When we arrived at the airport, Philippines Airlines informed me that – as a blind person – I would need to sign a document before boarding. It was a waiver, removing their liability for my injury or death due to any event that occurred during the flight, including an event for which they were responsible. Not surprisingly, given my legal training, my advocacy and the nature of our trip, I refused to sign. We were not allowed to board.

The indignity increased when a more senior airline official, called into resolve the matter, suggested that as a blind person I would not be able to sign, so Chris could sign on my behalf. I was further affronted, but Chris saw this as a possible solution. He turned to me and asked, 'If I sign a document with my name, which is made out in yours, will it have any legal validity?' I confirmed that it would not, he signed, and we boarded the flight. We did not draw the irony of Chris's legal blindness to the attention of the airline until we had safely landed in Australia.

*

In 1987 I did a lot of soul-searching. I was 32, and seeking more responsibility in my life. My twenties had been great fun, I had played and worked hard, but I did not think that this was all there was.

My friend Leigh Baker had lost her partner Rod to cancer in about six weeks. I did not know Rod well, but I knew he had been a fitness fanatic, running and bike riding regularly. He had also never smoked in his life. He was about my age. I did my best to contribute to the support of Leigh through her grief. The experience affected me greatly, and made me think much more about what I had achieved and where I wanted my life to go.

Some of my friends at the ADB gained much from meditation, and were involved in the Brahma Kumaris sect. I decided to join them on a retreat on a mountain in Rajasthan.

Travel to India was an experience that overwhelmed my senses. I had been to Asia before, but India was different: the heat and humidity, the smell of petrol fumes, food cooking, rubbish on the streets, the chaotic buzz of activity all around, many voices speaking many languages, and the constant roar of cars and motorbikes.

We landed in Bombay, now Mumbai, and travelled by train and bus to the Rajasthan retreat. The mountain was an island of peace in the sea of busy chaos. We spent a week there, eating vegetarian food, drinking no alcohol and spending much time in lectures and meditation. I didn't continue with the Brahma Kumaris's meditative process after the retreat, but I took the sense of inner calm, which has got me through many situations of stress. I learned to focus on the big strategic picture, and not get caught up in a lot of the smaller issues. And I came to appreciate much more the value and contribution I could make in my life, and the value and importance of lives around me. I learned a deeper love for my fellow humans.

My relationship with Karen had ended, but I yearned for what that had provided in my life. I loved the work that I did, but wondered if I would do it more effectively in a different environment. I'd gone on holiday to Perth with Chris and his family, and it had given me a positive taste of the city. So when some colleagues at the ADB told me of a job going as a conciliator at the Western Australian Equal Opportunity Commission, I knew it was the right opportunity.

11
Going west

Chris and I had visited Perth in January 1987 as part of a trip his sister Viv made to introduce her young daughter Elise to Elise's father, John Hopper. John had moved to Perth when he and Viv had separated some years before.

John held a number of parties in Viv and Elise's honour while we were there. He assembled an interesting and motley group of guests to whom he always introduced Viv as his very first wife, and Chris and me as 'not looking too good'.

One of John's guests was an iridologist. She stood in the backyard looking for a long time into Chris's eyes, and telling him about what she saw of his life, to the strains of Dire Straits. Chris was obviously sceptical of what he was being told, but happy to play along as he was enjoying the female attention.

Finally she turned to me, but told me it was difficult to assess much from my eyes as it was getting darker now, and she could not see well by the torchlight. After a few beers and in a playful holiday mood, I whipped out one of my artificial eyes, popped it on the palm of my hand and said, 'There you go. Have a closer look.'

She almost fainted with the shock, staggering into Chris's

accommodating arms. She finally forgave me, but that was the end of all diagnoses for the evening.

*

Relocating more than 3,000 kilometres away from Sydney was a big move. My parents and family, who had always provided major back-up for me, advised against it. Many of my friends thought that, even for an adventurer such as me, it was perhaps a step too far. But I knew it was the right step to take, and my time in India earlier that year had convinced me to look into myself and trust my instinct. That same trust of instinct has served me well throughout my life in a few challenging situations. So I found a tenant for my Petersham house, packed my things, and headed off.

I had resigned from the ADB, giving myself a week to find accommodation and acclimatise, before starting the conciliation job at the WA Equal Opportunity Commission. My truck of possessions was on its way across the Nullarbor, so I didn't have a lot of time. But I have always found that I operate more effectively with tight deadlines.

Changing environments, let alone cities and states, is a significant challenge for a person who is blind. I had built up the maps of Sydney in my head over almost 30 years, and I had to adjust to a new city in just days. With the sun setting rather than rising over the ocean, everything in the maps in my head was the wrong way around.

Chris came over to help out for the first week, and Steve Moore, an orientation and mobility instructor at the Association for the Blind in Western Australia, was also a great help. Steve spent some really useful time with us, acquainting me with the map of Perth, and sketching in the river, topography and transport options.

I decided that I wanted to live on a train line, and near the beach or the river. I also decided to break my habit of a lifetime and rent rather than buy. I have done this only twice in Australia, on my arrival in Perth and on our return to Sydney, and did not enjoy either experience. I like to be in control of where I live, and being restricted by the decisions of a landlord does not sit well with me.

I finally settled on a two-storey townhouse on Canning Highway in Applecross. It had a sunny aspect, was close to bus transport with routes to the city, near shops, and available. We signed the lease in the morning, and the truck full of furniture rolled up to the door that afternoon.

*

Chris and Steve had shown me the environment around the Canning Highway house, including relevant shops and the local hotel, and they had also caught the bus with me into the city, so that I knew where my office was. Everything else I built more slowly as I reached out from my points of knowledge. At this time the commission was in offices at 5 Mill Street, across the road from the Parmelia Hotel. The bus dropped me on St Georges Terrace, just a short walk away.

I learned landmarks in the city as I visited them – other government offices on the terrace, shops in Hay Street and Murray Street, as well as the hotels and restaurants. I could always catch a taxi from the Parmelia if I needed to, and as my mum had often said: 'You've got a tongue in your head, so put it to good use.' I learned, I wrote myself notes, and I reinforced my learning with visits.

Not only had I changed my environment, but I had to go through the physical separation from my friends and family. This was made worse by the time difference, which began as two hours but quickly changed to three when the eastern states went to daylight saving. My phone bill certainly increased for the first few weeks.

The only people that I knew in Perth, apart from Peter Blockey, worked at the commission. June Williams had worked as the director of Equal Opportunity in Public Employment in Sydney before she took the job as commissioner at the EOC in Perth. Luba McMaugh, the senior conciliator in Western Australia, had been recruited by June from the same office. I knew them both from my time at the ADB. They were both of great assistance to me, making sure that I was adjusting to the environment, and finding me some new friends.

I had also met several of the WA conciliators at the national conference in Canberra earlier that year. I remembered Maureen Shelley from the conference because she and her husband owned a yacht on the Swan River. She had since left the commission, and was managing a small chain of hotels. But I decided to get in touch with her as I had liked her when we met. I wanted to build a broader circle of friends, and the idea of sailing on the Swan was particularly attractive.

The work at the commission was quite similar to the work I had done in New South Wales. WA government was smaller and you had to learn its inter-relationships; the state was bigger, so travel took longer and was less frequent; and the resources sector drove the economy. I arrived just after the America's Cup, when Alan Bond had transformed Fremantle, and before the crash, so corporate excess was running rampant. It was a fascinating ride, but with excess and power comes discrimination and sexual harassment, so we were kept busy.

I loved my work, had a supportive and smart boss to work with, and my personal life took a huge turn for the better. Moving to Perth had been absolutely the right call.

*

I soon phoned Maureen Shelley to see if she wanted to catch up. She readily agreed – admitting later that she remembered admiring my bum in tight jeans at the conciliators' conference – and I was pleased when she chose the restaurant and arrived to pick me up after work in her red BMW. First impressions were good, and it continued that way.

We enjoyed an excellent dinner, and she told me that she was now separated and close to divorce, and that her husband, Rodney, had moved up to Broome with their four-year-old, Leon. The excellent food and WA wine, both Maureen's choices, were accompanied by stimulating conversation. Her genuine warmth overlaid a quick mind and wit – hard for me to keep up with – a real determination to succeed, a care for humanity and social justice and a real zest for living life. Her separation was recent and still raw, and she lamented the loss for Leon and herself, but was determined to move on and continue to build her life.

Her offer to drop me home after dinner was appreciated, and she accepted my invitation to coffee and port. She parked the BMW in my garage and, as she later told me, was a little shocked when I locked it in. This was just normal procedure for a Sydney person, to keep it safe, but in Perth it suggested to her that I had closed off her escape route.

However, the coffee and port led to something more, and we didn't need to unlock the garage door until the next morning.

Getting together with Maureen happened very quickly for both of us. I really only lived in my Canning Highway house for about six weeks before moving into her house in Menora. I made occasional visits to my furniture for about another six weeks until my three-month lease ran out, and we decided it would be financially better if I paid my rent to Maureen. This I was pleased to do. And when Leon returned from Broome some weeks later, I was happily ensconced in my new life.

I knew from early on in our relationship that my love for Maureen was very real. My commitment felt solid and long-lasting. As well as finding a lover, I had found a friend, a mentor and a soulmate.

As with any relationship we went through our tricky periods after the first three months or so of bliss, but I always had the sense that we would find a way through them.

I wouldn't tell Maureen that I loved her for some time after we got together. I had been through the experience once before, and those words meant a lot to me, so I was determined to use them carefully. By the time I did say them, I was absolutely sure that I was right.

For Maureen, our relationship really came too soon after her separation. But for me, after just a few weeks, I was absolutely sure. I have never had any doubt about that, and it's now been almost 30 years.

*

Leon's return from Broome marked a change in our relationship. We had lived as two single people getting together, but Leon's arrival meant that Maureen – who had a very busy full-time career – had responsibility for a happy, independent four-year-old, with an inquiring mind of his own. I wanted to carry some of the load of that responsibility, but always regarded my role as that of Leon's second dad. Both Maureen and I have always worked to ensure that Rodney continued his place in Leon's life. On his return from Broome later, Rodney lived on his boat in Fremantle, and we often went down there during the weekend to drop Leon off or pick him up.

Leon seemed quite relaxed about my approach and was ready to participate in some of the games I initiated. He used to lead me on merry chases around the house and gardens, but soon worked out that the quieter he kept, the harder it would be for me to find him. He was intrigued by the television I had brought from Sydney. 'Do all people in Sydney watch green TV?' he asked me one day. Not understanding, I asked Maureen to tell me what he meant, only to discover that the picture tube in my television had not been functioning properly for some time. Leon told me that he preferred all the colours, and did not want to watch green TV again.

Even as a young boy Leon was pretty self-contained. He could play with Lego or other toys for a long time and keep himself happy. He didn't avoid people's attention, but he did not crave it either. He also had a clear view about his world and the way it should be. When challenged one day about something that Maureen said was against the rules, his quick response was: 'But you don't know the rules of me.'

*

Maureen was the youngest of a family of six who lived throughout Western Australia. So drives down to Australind became a regular event, where we visited her sister Patricia. I also got to know Maureen's sister Susan and her seven children. Susan's husband, Joe, had died the year before my arrival, and during the years we lived in Perth I became one of the kids' important male influences. I have really enjoyed my contribution to their growing-up process.

Maureen's nanna lived with her daughter Monica (Maureen's aunt) in the house across the road from Susan's house in Tuart Hill. We visited them regularly as well, and I came to appreciate the strength and capacity of the female dynasty from which Maureen had come. Nanna and Mon's acceptance of me was somewhat grudging as I was the unmarried partner of Maureen, who – in their minds – still had a husband. But we managed to get past that and I really enjoyed their company.

I also met Maureen's parents, who had been travelling Western Australia for some years, living what appeared an idyllic lifestyle of working in the north of the state during winter, and coming south in the summer months when it became too hot. They ran hotels and roadhouses, took care of properties, and had other similar itinerant activities. Maureen's mum, Molly, or Mopsy as she was known, was a wonderful storyteller with a quick wit and ready laugh, and accepted my presence with equanimity. Her dad Tom was a little less talkative, but an interesting man to converse with when you got to know him.

Maureen had a chance to meet my family as well. My brother, Brian, married Sue in January 1988, and we both went back for the wedding. Maureen's introductions to my family were a little tentative, as Mum and Dad were not comfortable about me living with a woman who had been divorced. Yet we enjoyed a great time at the wedding, and met many family friends.

So I had a new job, which I really enjoyed, and a new love who very effectively filled that place in my heart which had been empty for a few years. Along with the new love came a wonderful extended family, and the challenging but very satisfying share of responsibility for a quickly growing four-year-old. My life was pretty complete. But in September 1988 that all changed.

*

Maureen promised me early in our relationship that it would be many things, but never boring. As usual, she was right. But her announcement one day in August that I was the last person with whom she wanted to spend her life, and that she was selling her house and going overseas with Leon, hit me as an absolute bolt from the blue. Our relationship, and all that came with it, was exactly where I wanted to be. But it had come too quickly for Maureen, and she still needed time on her own. I railed against her decision for some time, but inevitably started to come to terms with it, although never accepting its permanence.

Maureen sold her house in Menora. I decided that I was staying in Perth, and started looking to buy property closer to the city.

Maureen did not get involved with my house-hunting, until she rescued me from buying a very dark house in North Perth. Instead, she found me a much better option at a cheaper price in Highgate, a neighbouring suburb. She joked that – while she was leaving me – she was setting me up in a good house, and leaving her sister to keep an eye on me.

On the day in September when Maureen put her car on the train, and she and Leon flew to Adelaide to meet it, I tried to be happy for them, smiling and waving and wishing them a great trip, but my tears were always close to the surface. I swung between despair and the little spark of hope that I was determined to change her mind.

Maureen had provided me with her itinerary, so I organised for Qantas to provide her with champagne on her flights, sent chocolates to her hotel in Melbourne, and flowers to her apartment in Hawaii. I planned on a relentless and lengthy campaign.

Patricia, Maureen's sister, visited regularly while Maureen was away. I think she secretly barracked for my efforts in trying to re-establish my relationship with Maureen, but she was very careful not to say that. What she did do was provide me with great and entertaining company when she was in Perth, and happily embarked on a determined shared quest to find the best Vietnamese restaurant within walking distance of my house. I suspected Leon was a barracker for me, also.

It was the early days of email, when you connected a modem to your computer and plugged it into a telephone line. When the modem connected, it made a very satisfying scratchy and then eerie whistling sound. I regularly wrote long emails detailing my activities and telling Maureen how much I loved her, and how much she was missed. She sent wonderful and well-written replies (not surprisingly, as she was an experienced journalist), beautifully describing all of her and Leon's activities, but not reciprocating my passionate entreaties.

We also spent long (and in those days expensive) hours on the telephone chatting when I could get the time-zone calculations right. I enjoyed much of that trip vicariously, but missed her and Leon terribly. But I was determined to find a way to have us all back together.

Maureen's itinerary indicated that she planned to spend Christmas with her great-uncle and aunt, Tom and Marie, in Dundalk, Northern Ireland. I planned a surprise visit, but my surprise was spoiled when Maureen told me on the phone in mid-December that she was seriously considering a proposal of marriage from a Baptist preacher in North Carolina. I told her that I had bought my airfares and pleaded with her to fly to Ireland. She reluctantly agreed.

*

Ireland was another adventure for me – stepping off into the unknown with no idea of how the future was to play out. Some of my family and friends told me that it was the craziest idea that they had ever heard – going halfway around the world to meet the woman you love, with every expectation that she will gently reject you. Others told me to chase my dreams. And that's what I did.

I landed in Heathrow for the first time, and negotiated immigration and the transfer to my Dublin flight. When I arrived in Dublin, I was jet-lagged but incredibly excited about seeing Maureen and Leon for the first time in three months. Their flight arrived at about the same time, and we arranged our travel to Dundalk, about an hour's drive away. They were both pleased to see me, but Maureen was clear that her position about living with me had not changed. Still, she seemed happy enough in my company, and I was ecstatic to be in hers.

'Where are you going to stay?' asked Maureen on our way there.

'I don't know. I haven't booked anything. As close as possible to you,' I replied.

But Tom and Marie were not fazed by my arrival, and welcomed all of us into their home. I should have expected nothing less from an Irish family.

We had some trouble finding their house because the numbers in their street did not run in order. They appeared to us completely random.

'How are the houses numbered in your street?' Maureen asked the next day.

'Oh, by when they were built,' replied Marie with equanimity.

'Then how does the postie know where to deliver the mail?' asked Maureen with astonishment.

'Oh, well, he's lived here all his life,' Marie said.

We spent Christmas day with the family, and the rest of the first week visiting with relatives, and going out some nights to Irish pubs with Tom and Marie's adult children, Lorchan, Bronagh and Oonagh, with Tom and Marie happy to look after Leon. Pubs in Ireland, I quickly discovered, are very different to those in Australia. They are small, friendly, welcoming places, and contain much of the social life of the community. While Kalgoorlie in Western Australia had as many as 32 pubs, Dundalk, a town of similar size, had 230. The music – usually played by two or three live musicians – was fantastic. And the conversations, easily struck up, were fascinating.

On one occasion Lorchan told us we were going to a 'Brothers' pub. We were uncertain how to behave as 'the Troubles' were a significant part of Northern Irish life. The place went very quiet as we walked in, speaking in our unusual accents, until Lorchan said, loudly enough for most people to hear, 'They're Australians'. As soon as the fact that we were not English was established by us saying loudly, 'G'day', all returned to normal.

We decided to spend the second week touring Ireland. So I borrowed Tom and Marie's phone, and put myself to work renting a car. This was a far more difficult experience than I had imagined, firstly because we only had Australian passports and no Irish address, and secondly because – in comparison to Australia – the cost of car rental was exorbitant. I joked that we would have been better to rent a car in England and put it on the ferry.

I finally succeeded in doing a deal, and we headed south, through Dublin and into the 26 counties that constitute independent Ireland. We visited the Dublin tourist places, and were driving across the Liffey on the Penny Farthing bridge, when Leon asked how the bridge got that funny name. I immediately went into storytelling mode, making up some fantastic tale about how the lords who built the bridge did not think that the peasants should benefit from it for free, and so charged a penny to go across one way and a farthing to come back the other. Maureen indicated how impressed she was with my knowledge, and started asking further questions. The story, upon more rigorous journalistic examination, crumbled into the tissue of lies and fantasy that it was. Ever since, whenever I start telling a story in the family about which people are in some doubt, I am hit with the accusation that it is a 'Penny Farthing' story.

Some way out of Dublin headed south we needed to fill the car with petrol. It was pumped by hand, and I got out of the car to stretch my legs, chat to the attendant and pay the bill. I commented to him that petrol was much cheaper in the North than it was down here in the South, to which he happily replied: 'Oh, to be sure. But they're not shootin' at you down here.'

We enjoyed the soft green Irish countryside that Maureen beautifully described to me as we drove along. Leon was constantly searching for knights' gravestones, so we visited many cemeteries. He was also intrigued by the castles in which they had lived, and we stayed in one that had been converted to a hotel.

We drove along single-lane country roads, where other drivers saw no problem holding up the traffic behind them while they wound down their windows to have a quick chat with someone who they knew passing the other way. We saw quaint road signs indicating the seriousness of bends with the words 'slow', 'slower', and 'dead slow'.

And, of course, we visited and I kissed the Blarney Stone. I described it in an article I later wrote for *London Australia Weekly* as 'leaning precariously backwards, having your ankles held by a superannuated Irish public servant, while you touched your lips to the face of a rock soiled for centuries by the lipstick of other tourists'. Many have suggested that there was no need for me to kiss that stone, since I'd already been blessed with its gift of the gab.

When the time came for Maureen and Leon to fly back to London, and me to Australia, Maureen did not give me any new hope of resuming a permanent relationship. But as I flew from the misty chill of an Irish winter to the baking dry heat of Perth in January I was buoyed by our time together, and making plans for my campaign into the future.

12

If at first you don't succeed ...

Three or four months later – having persuaded June Williams to give me three months' leave without pay from the ADB – I was on my way back to Europe. Part two of my campaign of being closer to Maureen involved doing something I had wanted to do for some time – studying Italian for three months at the Università per Stranieri or University for Strangers in Perugia, Italy.

I thought that, before embarking on such an adventure, I should visit Mum and Dad. So I found myself, after a few pleasant days with them in Gerringong, in Dad's company checking in for my flight to London.

My bag was 11 kilograms overweight, primarily due to the amount of Margaret River wine and champagne I had crammed in for Maureen. The woman behind the check-in desk pointed this out to me, and quoted the exorbitant amount of money I would need to pay to get it through.

I half-turned to Dad, looking at them both with a sad face, and said: 'Oh, well, I guess I'll have to leave my Braille Italian notes for studying at the university at home. I can't afford to pay that amount.' Dad said nothing, and I could feel the reluctant shake of the Qantas staff member's head as she sent the bag down the chute. Kissing that Blarney Stone had paid off after all.

*

Studying Italian was a shared dream for Maureen and me. I had decided to put my part of the dream into effect, partly because I was again becoming restless, and partly because I thought if I visited Maureen in London for a few days, tantalised her with the prospect of Perugia, and then headed off, she might actually follow me. I was wrong about that, but being in Perugia meant we could visit each other on weekends.

So I flew to London, where Maureen was working as a nanny for a family who had separate accommodation out the back of their house for visiting relatives. They had no-one using it at the time, and agreed I could stay for a couple of days. I spent my time happily with Leon and Maureen in London, doing some sight-seeing and catching up. I marvelled at the smells, noises and traffic of the huge city about which I had read so much. The diversity of accents that I caught as I moved about was amazing, and the Tube was a train-lover's dream, as well as an excellent way to get around.

Maureen was allowed to have friends over to the house to dinner when the owners were away, and did so on the night before I was to leave for Perugia. Six of us enjoyed a convivial night of food, conversation and good WA wine. And my hopes were raised when – after the guests had left – Maureen accepted my invitation to join me in my outside accommodation for a few hours.

Early the next morning I left for Perugia, tired but very happy.

*

I boarded the Rome flight with a tinge of fear and sadness in my heart. Maureen and I were apart yet again, and I was taking another step into the unknown. I was going to live for three months in a country I had never visited, and whose first language was not English. I had no accommodation, and just a letter offering enrolment in my pocket. Was this a challenge I would not be able to overcome, or could I find a way? But the sun was out when I landed in Rome, and the excitement of being in Italy helped to burn off the mist of hesitation and fear.

Maureen had persuaded me, against my tighter budget-management judgment, to book a driver and car for the trip to Perugia. She had also counselled that I book a hotel for my first night in Perugia, and not ride my luck as I had done in Ireland. This was very good advice and, once I had negotiated the airport and found my driver, the trip to Perugia was pretty relaxed.

When I say that the trip to Perugia was relaxed, this is a relative term. Perhaps it was the amount of Margaret River wine I had drunk the night before, the flight to Rome or the mixed emotions, but that drive was one of the scarier ones of my life. We seemed to constantly weave in and out of traffic, horns blasted and people yelled, straight stretches were completed at breakneck speed, and windier sections not much slower. Driving in Italy takes some getting used to.

The next morning I caught a taxi to the university and joined masses of other enrolling students. Thankfully the process, which seemed to take an inordinate amount of time and form-filling, was carried out largely in English. Not so the negotiation of a room to stay, known as a pensione.

The university recommended to me a Signora Rossi who regularly accepted students. One of the tutors agreed to walk up the hill to the town with me, and show me the address. It was a great location, in a block of apartments one street back from the main street. However, the tutor handed me my suitcase – which he had insisted on carrying – at the door and left, saying pointedly to me in Italian, 'This conversation is your first lesson at the university.'

I climbed the stairs, my first month's rent in my pocket, wondering how I would be received. The door was answered at my knock, and I was greeted with: 'Ah, *Signore Nonvedemente* (Mr Blind Man), come in, come in. My uncle is blind. I am used to you.'

Signora Rossi spoke no English. '*Solo Italiano* (only Italian)' was her rapid-fire reply to my first question. She guided me to the room, and explained its features and benefits in eight or ten sentences of which I got about eight or ten words. I knew there was a bed, the bathroom was down the hall, I could not bring girls back to my room, and meals were not included. I am sure there were many other excellent facilities, but my preparatory Italian classes in Perth had only gone so far. The apartment smelled of good cooking and cleaning materials, and the welcome had been positive if hard to understand, so I decided to stay. My Italian immersion had commenced in earnest.

My rudimentary grasp of the language was quickly enhanced by the necessity of communication when I was in situ. As a blind person, smiling and pointing did not work. This actually assisted my learning, as I was forced to explain what I wanted or sought. Italian people seemed pleased at anyone seeking to learn their language, and they were very patient. Also, people in Perugia were used to university students arriving with little knowledge of the language. One who couldn't see was a little more unusual, and *l'Australiano Nonvedemente* (the blind Australian) was the way people referred to me once they got to know me. I thought this a long title, and tried to teach them my name. But Graeme was too much of a challenge for most of them – so they just called me Signore.

I had taken an early-model computer with me to assist with my studies. It was a Eureka, invented by an Australian, Milan Hudecek. It was the size of an A4 sheet of paper, with a Braille keyboard that mimicked that of the Perkins machine I had used most of my life.

Its output was in speech rather than on a screen, but it did not have a Braille display. I remember proudly telling people that it had 64k of RAM, a minuscule amount compared with the capacity of smartphones today, and it used floppy disks.

This computer could be connected via a modem to send emails, but most of my friends did not yet have email accounts. So I devised an ingenious way of communicating my news to friends and family. Before I left Australia, I arranged for about ten envelopes to be addressed to each of the dozen or so family and friends with whom I wanted to keep in touch. I marked these envelopes in Braille with the initials of the person to whom they were addressed. I had purchased a writing guide from the Association for the Blind in Perth. This consisted of a clipboard, which held a pad of paper. Across the board were stretched thick pieces of elastic to mark the lines on the page, and all I had to do was hand-write between those lines.

I had learned printing at school many years before, but it was not a skill I had regularly practised. So I spent evenings in my room, when I was not studying Italian, laboriously drafting notes, letter by letter, trying to remember what I had already written, and where I was up to on the page. I could not see the results of my work, and I knew that I would not be able to read any of the answers I might get, but at least people in Australia would know what was going on in my life.

I was told later that these long scrawled missives would arrive in people's letterboxes, and they would open them with a degree of excitement. They would then spend the next ten minutes or so trying to decipher my scratchings, and glean some glimpses of my life in Perugia from the words that they could understand. Most of them gave up eventually, and the feedback I received was that I should either buy a printer to connect to my computer or give up corresponding altogether.

*

The weather got warmer, and I adjusted happily to the routine of university life in Perugia. This consisted of getting up in the morning and heading into town. The coffee shops, which doubled as bars, had high counters at which one stood or sat on stools. Coffee was consumed, cigarettes smoked and a quick pastry eaten for breakfast, among morning chatter. My preference quickly became *caffe corretto* (corrected coffee). Mine was usually 'corrected' with a shot of Sambuca. This seemed to be quite a normal practice, and I found that it loosened my tongue nicely for the lessons to come.

We would walk off the cobblestones of the town and down the bitumen hill to the university, where lessons took place all morning. We would then adjourn for lunch, and in the afternoons our tutors sent us out into the town for *conversazione*, which translated to going and sitting in bars, coffee shops, or wherever else took our fancy and talking Italian. We were to do this with other students or locals. While on its face this sounds like a bit of a cop-out for the tutors, such immersion in the language and culture of Italy was really the best way to learn about it. My conversation in Italian went ahead in leaps and bounds, and the desperate reversions to English became less and less frequent.

I met students from the Nordic countries, Germany, France, England, the Netherlands and Poland, the United States and Canada, and also several other Australians, and a couple of Kiwis, all there for the same purpose. I was humbled when I met students who already spoke two or three languages, and who were adding Italian to their repertoire. We spent time studying and talking together, drinking mainly coffee during the day, and mainly beer and wine during the night. I enjoyed many excellent Italian and other meals in the local *trattoria* (family or cheaper restaurants).

I did not really get to know the local Italians very well. Signora Rossi was friendly enough, but my room was really a place for sleep and study. She lived with her adult daughter, and they watched much

Italian television when her daughter was not at work. We shared pleasantries but, because meals were not included with my room, opportunities for conversation were relatively few.

Prior to leaving Australia I had purchased a quite complex and expensive Swiss Army knife. These were the pre-9/11 days, when there were no security checks at airports, and you could carry such devices. Early one evening I was studying in my room, and took a short break to eat some fruit I had purchased that day. My knife slipped when I was cutting the fruit, and I cut my left hand quite deeply. The flow of blood quickly told me that this was too serious an injury for me to deal with. I sought the aid of Signora Rossi.

Her daughter came to the rescue. My grasp of Italian started to slip due to my stress, but she quickly scolded me for using such a sharp knife so carelessly, then bundled me downstairs and into a taxi, which she instructed to ferry me to the hospital. My approach to the doctor was far more circumspect than the one I had used in Sri Lanka, and the cut was quickly dealt with.

They summoned another taxi, and I returned to my pensione, to a further scolding and regular dressing of my cut for the next few days. I was very appreciative of the support.

*

I really enjoyed my time in Perugia, but I had not forgotten the other purpose of my visit. I rang Maureen several times a week, and we planned my weekend visits to London, and her return visits to Rome, which occurred about once each month. Every time we spoke, I asked her to marry me. And every time she either refused or in some other way parried the question.

After a month at the university I travelled to see her in London, bearing gifts of a very large box of Baci – chocolate kisses made in Perugia – and a bottle of Sambuca. These were well received, and we enjoyed a happy weekend exploring more London tourist sites. Maureen was contemplating changing her nanny arrangements, and getting a flat in London.

On the way back to Perugia from Rome, I missed my train connection, and had to spend a few hours waiting at Rome Station. So, carrying my heavy leather satchel and an overnight bag, I found a café in the terminal and settled down to while away the time drinking beer and listening to people speaking Italian.

I started to make my way to the platform about 15 minutes before the train was due to leave, not wanting to miss another connection. It was about nine at night, and there were not many people around. I don't know whether it was immediate opportunism, or whether two men had picked me out as a vulnerable target. But on the way to my platform they approached me from behind, each one grabbing one of my bags.

My immediate reaction was driven by adrenalin rather than clear thought. I was not prepared to lose my possessions. I quickly folded my collapsible white cane in half and, using it as a baton in my right hand, and my heavy leather satchel as a club in my left hand, started spinning in circles, hitting out wildly, and shouting profanities at the top of my voice. The ferocity and unpredictability of my attack must have surprised them, coming from someone who they thought should be an easy target. I have no idea to this day how big or strong they were, or whether they had weapons that could have done me real harm. But after a few seconds of my whirling dervish performance, they fled.

My noise brought a small crowd to the scene, one of whom identified himself as *carbinieri stazione* (railway police). He wanted to take a statement, but when he realised I could in no way identify my attackers, he guided me to the platform and assisted me to catch my train. He also spoke to the guard, directing him to make sure that I alighted in Perugia. Which was just as well, because what I had not realised was that the train I was catching would spend four or five hours in a siding on the way, and not arrive until 4.45 am.

Signora Rossi scolded me again on my late return, reminding me that I was here to study Italian not to be out all night. 'What would your mother think?' were some of the words I understood.

I explained that I had been visiting my girlfriend in London, and what had happened on the way home, and she was quite mollified.

I further explained that I needed lots of *gettone* – the tokens to make phone calls – because I called Maureen regularly to ask her to marry me. And when Maureen called and spoke to Signora Rossi (using the number I had given her for emergencies) to change our weekend visit plans, the one message that managed to pass between Signora Rossi's Italian and Maureen's English was that Maureen should marry me, as that I was a good man who studied hard. Also, blind men needed wives to look after them.

I did not necessarily share these last sentiments, including as they did an assumption that I could not look after myself. But the complexity of that explanation, and the benefit of having her on my 'team', dissuaded me from challenging her position.

*

My next weekend with Maureen was a month later, and we met in Rome. We spent a wonderful day exploring Rome's tourist attractions – the Spanish Steps, the Colosseum and the Vatican. Maureen's excellent and detailed audio description confirmed the pictures I had in my mind from studying Roman history at Ashfield Boys High School all those years ago.

We travelled to the Vatican by taxi, and when I was lost for the Italian translation I simply said, '*Il Papa*'. The driver happily complied, telling me that my accent was excellent but my Italian vocabulary needed lots of work.

On the Sunday we enjoyed a wonderful long lunch at an Italian café near our hotel, where I had arranged for flowers to be delivered and for three musicians to arrive on their bicycles and serenade us while we ate. After the performance I got down on my knees and proposed to Maureen for about the twelfth time. She did not agree that day, but when I called her the next Tuesday night she accepted. I immediately started to make plans to return to London and organise the wedding, in case she changed her mind. If at first you don't succeed …

The grin on my face was a mile wide when I walked back into my pensione after that phone call, and Signora Rossi intuited what had happened immediately. She quickly baked a cake, got some red wine out of her cupboard, and the celebrations commenced. She was almost as pleased as I was.

The phone lines to Australia ran hot the next day, and my pocket quickly emptied of those heavy *gettone* as I shared my news.

13
A London wedding

In May 1989, I said goodbye to my tutors and classmates, and the man who made the best *caffe corretto* in Perugia, and headed back to London. Maureen had found a one-bedroom flat just off Green Lanes in North London, in the midst of a Kurdish community. Life was sweet. I was again living with Maureen and Leon, my wedding was occurring soon, it was a warm English summer, and the Australians were on their way to challenge for the Ashes. What more could I ask for?

I had a few challenges. First, I had to convince June Williams to extend my leave without pay. Second, I had to negotiate a tenancy for my house to pay the mortgage. And third, although Maureen was now working full-time managing a temp agency, we were paying London rent for a flat, and I had to contribute some money. But these were minor blips to be sorted out on the way to what I had most wanted in my life – marrying Maureen.

June reluctantly agreed to my request when I explained that love had finally won out. Maureen's brother Tom needed somewhere to stay, so he happily rented my house. And I got some work with George Bell, demonstrating the Eureka computer I had brought with me from Australia. George was the agent for them in the United Kingdom, and needed a competent user to staff his stand at several major upcoming exhibitions for blindness products.

George's employment arrangements were novel, to say the least. He paid an agreed, and very reasonable, sum for each day I worked at the exhibitions. He also transported me in his car, and paid for all my accommodation and food, and as much beer as I could drink. When travelling with George, a Scotsman, and his Welsh assistant Oggie, that proved to be quite a lot. But I regularly accepted this casual work.

I also wrote some articles for *London Australia Weekly* at 50 pounds each if accepted. Another job was training local authority library staff to use Kurzweil Reading Machines. These machines scanned a printed page and read it aloud in synthetic speech and were funded and installed in many council libraries. It wasn't regular income, but it supplemented Maureen's. I also took Leon to and from school while Maureen was at work.

Taking Leon to school reinforced my awareness of him as an independent and determined little person. We had to catch a bus and then the Tube, and I was concerned that a six-year-old for whom I was responsible could easily become separated from me. So I purchased a bright yellow curly cord, with a handcuff arrangement on each end – one to clip to my left wrist, and the other to Leon's right.

We tried to pass this off as a game, but Leon was having none of it. 'I won't get lost, and I'm not wearing that,' he said. Maureen and I discussed his trenchant opposition, but decided that we would need to enforce the decision. So Leon found another way to deal with the problem.

As we waited at the bus stop on the first day of our combined school travel, he quietly walked around a lamppost two or three times. When the bus arrived, we were effectively attached to the post, and could not move. I unclipped the strap from both of our wrists, and let it fall to the ground, where I left it. I knew defeat when I saw it. And Leon never left my side when I travelled with him to and from school. I had learned a salutary lesson of life – confidence and trust will beat enforcement every time in parenting.

*

The first exhibition working for George was in Glasgow, five days before our chosen wedding date. I am not sure if it was the features of the computer or the attraction of my Australian accent, but George's sales went well. I was starting to like this work, and to regret that I had not proposed he put me on commission rather than a flat fee.

Each night for the three days of the exhibition, we adjourned tired but happy to an Italian restaurant near our hotel. They cooked excellent Italian dishes, waved them over the garlic, and then served the garlic and threw the food away – or at least, that's what we used to joke.

George, Oggie and I, as participants, failed to notice that we took the aroma with us. But the cloud of garlic that wafted through the door of our flat on my return was so palpable that – as Maureen and Leon described – they could taste it from across the room. I was banned from entering the bedroom until the smell improved, as Maureen and Leon asserted that they could not breathe. All of my clothes were immediately washed, and I spent the night before my wedding sleeping on a two-seater sofa in the lounge room.

*

Smelling somewhat less of garlic, I bounced out the front door of our flat the next morning – 5 June 1989 – to collect our wedding cake from the Kurdish bakery. This was the start of the next phase of my life, and the enormity of it struck me as I walked down Green Lanes, past the 'chippy' (fish-and-chip shop) and the 'offie' (off-licence liquor store), to the bakery itself. I actually stopped in the middle of the pavement, pondering the wondrousness of it all, and my biggest step in the adventure of life. I was brought back to my senses by the chirpy cry of a Londoner who said: 'Come on, mate, I know it's a beautiful day but I can't get past and I've got work to do.' I apologised and walked on.

We had ordered a lamington cake, Maureen going to much trouble to explain the recipe, in the shape of Australia. The ceremony took place at the Old Finsbury Town Hall, with several of our friends as witnesses, and Leon as photographer. He did a great job with the photos, but the elevation is a little unusual given his height as a six-year-old. We adjourned to our flat for champagne and cake, to which we invited the neighbours, our landlord and a few other friends. Then the wedding party went to a restaurant for dinner.

We bought each other Russian wedding rings – three intersecting bands of different colours. Maureen had given me one set of these as a friendship token in June the previous year, while we were in Adelaide at the BCA convention. I had lost the election for president that year, and she said it was an expression of friendship and a form of consolation. I wore that on my right ring-finger, and my wedding ring on my left. They have remained there for more than 26 years.

My wedding day is etched in my memory. I was sad that it occurred overseas, away from friends and family, but exultantly happy that it had occurred at all. I wasn't sure where life would take us, but I couldn't wait to embark on the journey beside Maureen.

*

So what do you do for your honeymoon when you are living in London and are responsible for a six-year-old? Maureen visited the travel agent a week or two before, and set out two possible options – a three-day trip to Paris and a babysitter for Leon, or five days in Disney World in Orlando, Florida. They both cost 99 pounds each for Maureen and me, and Leon was free if we chose the Disney World option. Leon's and my reactions were prompt and unanimous. So the next morning, after another drizzly London taxi ride to Heathrow, we boarded a jumbo pointed for Miami.

We had a great time at Disney World, the Epcot Center, and SeaWorld. We went on ride after ride, I pretended to be shot by the Pirates of the Caribbean, and tried to frighten Maureen in the haunted house. It was lucky she was there, really, as she had two kids – one big and the other small – to look after.

We also experienced three challenges on the honeymoon. First, we lost our car for more than two hours in the SeaWorld car park. At the end of a long hot day, when we were all tired, this was an incredible frustration, made even worse by the fact that I could make no contribution at all to the searching process. We vowed to never again rent a white Ford sedan, as the car park was almost full of them. And I developed another rule of life – always ask Maureen to tell me where the car is parked, and memorise it.

The second challenge was for Maureen. I had omitted to tell her that I had agreed to give a report to the BCA convention via telephone during our stay. She was a little surprised when – looking at my watch – I rejected her offer of an early cocktail by the pool, and returned to our room. Coming back to the room herself ten minutes later, she discovered why I had sneaked away, and spoke sternly to me about my wedding vows and changed priorities. She was right.

The last challenge was mine. The third day of our honeymoon was the first day of the first Ashes test at Headingley in Leeds. I had brought my short-wave radio, expecting to be able to enjoy sections of the game while lying in the Florida sunshine. I was horrified to discover that the best I could get was two five-minute reports each day. But, despite my lack of support, Australia won that test, which was the commencement of our march towards reclaiming the Ashes, which we held for the next 16 years.

*

I had always wanted to go to a test match at Lord's, the home of cricket. My wish came true in 1989. I bought tickets for the five days of the match myself, and even persuaded my new wife – probably against her better judgment – to come with me on the first day.

The sounds and atmosphere of an English cricket ground were very different to those of the SCG or MCG. This was first because the Australian grounds are much smaller, and so is the crowd. Second, although the Barmy Army has changed this a little in more recent years, there is a somewhat more genteel approach to the following of cricket by the English than by Australians.

So when I yelled out a piece of friendly advice to one of the England players, probably something about 'having a go' or 'see that red thing, your job is to catch it', I heard mumblings in the crowd around me to the effect of: 'Don't worry, he's an Australian.' The surprise by the English at my behaviour was returned by me when, about ten minutes before the lunch break on the first day, I could actually hear the sounds of the teaspoons being put on the saucers in the dining room at the back of the stand. As a regular cricket-goer this shocked me: first, because it would never be heard above the noise at an Australian ground; and second, because we would drink our tea from polystyrene cups rather than china cups with saucers.

*

The summer of 1989 in England was one of drought and heat waves, with the temperature sometimes getting as high as 26 degrees Celsius. We regularly visited one of the many London parks. Leon and I cooled down by just climbing out the window of our flat and sitting on the roof, where I might enjoy a quiet beer or glass of Hungarian wine (bought cheaply at the offie), while Leon played happily.

Maureen was working full-time as the coordinator of a personnel agency. I did some part-time work, but spent most of my time taking Leon to and from school, and listening to cricket and the plethora of other great programs on the BBC.

As the weather cooled and we headed towards Christmas, we wondered where life would take us. Maureen was well placed in her job, with opportunities beckoning. I applied for a senior conciliation role, and was down to the final few for interview. Leon was settled at school, and enjoying new friendships. Our lives in London were becoming well established.

Then Australia began to call – literally. My unpaid leave was coming to an end, and I had to make some decisions. I had been approached to chair the Disability Advisory Council of Australia (DACA), and was drawn to this opportunity. My friends and colleagues in the disability movement were also keen for me to accept the role.

On the other hand, adventure beckoned. Maureen was keen to stay in London, and I was certainly open to persuasion to take that course. Should we choose further uncertainty and excitement, or return to families and life in Australia?

In the end, I decided to return to Perth and the Equal Opportunity Commission (EOC), and accept the DACA role, and Maureen decided to stay in London. I felt incredibly torn by this situation. I loved being married to Maureen and enjoying my family life. Our marriage would not end, of course, but we would be living a long way apart again, and I was not sure I wanted to go back to that.

On the other hand, I had a secure job in Perth, and the opportunity to make a real contribution in the disability field at the national level. I did not want to pass that up.

As she has done a number of other times in our lives, Maureen solved the problem. About five days before I was due to leave, Maureen decided that she was coming as well. So, after a flurry of phone calls to book airfares and end our London tenancy, we arrived back in Australia just before Christmas. We didn't have much money, but we had our house in Highgate, and our friends and family around us after our return from the lengthy overseas adventure.

14
Landmark legislation

When Maureen's first husband, Rodney, decided to sell his wooden Van de Stadt yacht *Serenity*, it was obvious what I should do. Leon and Maureen loved *Serenity*, and I wanted a boat. So I bought her. I used to joke that *Serenity* was part of the package when I married Maureen.

Maureen and I, and often Leon, spent lots of fun times on *Serenity*, moored at Applecross. We lovingly cleaned piles of seagull guano off her decks, maintained her as best we could, and occasionally took her sailing. The fact that we did not sail her more often was only due to Maureen's lack of confidence in her helming, and my lack of sight. I was happy to sail the boat, but slightly concerned about running into other things.

On one of these rare occasions we had Maureen's sister Susan and most of her seven kids on board as well. We sailed along happily for a while – well, I was happy and Maureen was somewhat tense – until we ran aground. This can be a common occurrence in the Swan, with an average depth of ten centimetres. I knew that we would need to lean the boat over to get her off, so most of us climbed into the dinghy or the water and pulled on a rope tied high up the mast. We were unsuccessful.

Then someone pointed out that there was a mooring in the water about 20 or 30 metres away in the deeper water. I decided to swim to it with a rope, tie *Serenity* to it, and haul us off.

This sounds like a simple operation, but it is no easy task swimming while towing 30 metres of rope. Once wet it is quite heavy. I thought it was too risky to ask any of the kids to do it, and Maureen and Susan were sensibly not up for it, so the task fell to me.

By the time I had reached the proximity of the mooring I was quite tired. It was not far, but the rope was heavier and harder to tow than I thought. And then came the challenge that I had not considered: as a blind person, finding the mooring – a floating and moving target. My swimming – or perhaps by that stage unproductive splashing – kept pushing it away just as I was about to touch it. And not knowing which way I had pushed it, I could not easily chase it. The slight slap of water against it was quite hard to pinpoint, and all I could hear were the incredulous yells of the children who could clearly see the thing: 'It's right in front of you,' and, 'You've missed it again.'

This went on for several minutes, and my tiredness and frustration were beginning to increase. Finally, a wavelet going in the opposite direction gave it more momentum than my movement pushing it away, and it hit me in the face. I happily wrapped my arms around it, stuck a thumb up at the kids, and tied on. I followed the rope back to *Serenity*, we hauled her off 'the putty' as it was known, and sailed back to our own mooring for a well-earned picnic.

*

Coming back to Perth was far tougher for Maureen than for me. I had my job at the EOC, and the excitement of chairing a national disability advisory body, which took me to the eastern states for around a week each month. I also had the strategic challenge of leading DACA, and through it the government to the extent that we could, towards improved outcomes for Australians with disabilities. The Hawke government had been in power for more than six years, and Don Grimes was the minister to whom we reported. I was new at this game, and on a steep learning curve.

Maureen, on the other hand, did not have a job to return to. She decided to build a business selling computer equipment to enhance learning in schools. This was rewarding, but also hard and lonely work, and she did not have a lot of resources with which to start it. We had our house, but we had pretty much drained our savings during our time in London.

Leon settled in to school at Highgate Primary, just a block or two away, and enjoyed the benefits of schooling in a diverse community. English was not the first language for about 80 per cent of the children, many of whom were from families of Vietnamese origin. The school dispensed with a siren to mark the start and end of the day and playtime and lunchtime because of the negative reactions of many of the children attending.

*

Laurie Alsop had been the first chair of Australia's disability advisory body when it came to fruition after the passage of the *Disability Services Act* in 1986. Before that time, government had talked about, rather than with, people with disabilities. This changed under Minister Grimes, and the committed and very strategic advice of Patty Warne. People with disabilities now chaired the council and led most of its work. Service providers were represented, but were in the minority.

I had been in Western Australia, and overseas, during the first term of DACA, so I was not across the detail of its activities.

However, I knew that Laurie and her council had worked hard to change perceptions around disability, and to move people with disabilities more into the centre of the conversation. I wanted to build on that work.

Margaret Ward was my deputy chair. A parent of a daughter with disabilities, she had cut her teeth on challenging the role of service providers that completely controlled the lives of people with disabilities and their families. Families who did not accept gratefully what services they were offered, or did not make adequate 'donations' to the service providers, were regularly punished by withdrawal of, or exclusion from, those services.

This had not been my experience. People who were blind had been treated this way in the first half of the twentieth century, before I was born, but examples of punishment and service withdrawal during my lifetime have been rare. So Margaret's tough experiences were both educative and valuable for me in my new role.

With the rest of the council members, we worked in, and advised on, many areas of policy – education, employment, double disadvantage experienced by people with disabilities who were women, Aboriginal people and people from culturally and linguistically diverse backgrounds. Our crowning achievement was our role in the passage, in 1992, of the *Disability Discrimination Act*.

I had learned, both from my experience in BCA and DPI, and my work in discrimination in New South Wales and Western Australia, the value of such legislation in changing the lives of communities who experienced discrimination. So when Brian Burdekin, the then human rights commissioner, and his team at the commission indicated their interest in pushing for such legislation, I was immediately on board.

After Chris Ronalds, already well known for her legal work in the area of discrimination, prepared a report in this area, DACA conducted a period of Australia-wide consultations with the disability sector to seek their views on the importance to them of disability discrimination law.

The legislative drafting was led by Kym Duggan in the attorney-general's department. Kym provided me with a confidential copy of the draft for my comment, and I persuaded him to breach departmental regulations and give me a copy on disk, so that I could produce it in Braille with my embosser. The machine pounded away in the office in our Highgate house for several hours as I excitedly waited to get my fingers on the draft.

The draft legislation contained some innovative concepts in discrimination law. First, the definition of disability did not follow the US model, which required a person to demonstrate the limiting impacts of their disability before they proved discrimination. This broader definition of disability was seen by some as risky. It meant that the first 'gate' for people to get through was much wider, including more than 20 per cent of the population – if they could show that they had been discriminated against. But the concern has been ill-founded, and people with disabilities have not had to go through the disempowering experience of showing what they cannot do before arguing for what they believe they can.

Second, the law covered past, future and imputed disability. Yet again, this broadened the definition of disability, and placed the emphasis for making out a complaint on whether a person had been discriminated against.

Third, the law included coverage of readers and assistants, aids and equipment, and assistance animals. The last of these has been somewhat problematic, but only because governments have dodged their responsibilities to regulate further in this area.

Fourth, unlike sex and race discrimination laws, the law dealt with discrimination only against people with disabilities. As well as protecting the existing benefits that people with disabilities had, it did not prevent positive discrimination.

Fifth, the law included the concept of standards or further regulations in a range of areas. While hard to develop and enact, these have proved incredibly beneficial in achieving removal of discrimination in areas such as transport and access to premises.

Finally, as with other discrimination law, it allowed for the Human Rights Commission to grant exemptions. This negative power was used in a very positive way later on to support broad systemic change in areas such as captioning on television and in cinemas.

By the time the legislation arrived in the federal parliament, Paul Keating was prime minister, and his deputy, Brian Howe, was responsible for disability issues. Heather Butow, with whom I worked a lot on the legislation and other matters, was Howe's adviser. The time for the crucial briefing arrived, at which the deputy PM would decide to take the legislation forward to Cabinet. I was part of a delegation to brief the minister, which included Chris Ronalds and myself, as well as Human Rights Commission representatives and others from various departments.

The government was not travelling well at that time. It was early 1992, and Howe was under a lot of pressure about the proposed introduction of the Medibank co-payment. As the briefing continued, the signs were clear that the minister was not going to take the legislation forward. He was under too much pressure in other areas of his portfolio, and wanted to minimise risk.

Towards the end of the meeting Chris Ronalds tapped me on the arm and quietly said: 'I'll take the rest of this lot away. You stay here with Heather. You have to change his mind. It's the last chance we've got before the election.'

I knew she was right, so I stayed with Heather and we strategised while the deputy PM continued with other meetings. After each meeting he would come out to the office foyer, and each time Heather and I would nod and smile at him. He would say things like: 'You two are still here.'

At about nine-thirty that night, after our four- or five-hour vigil, his last meeting finished. Again, he saw us in the foyer. 'Come in while I have a cup of tea before I leave,' he said.

We sat down and his first words were: 'You're not leaving until I change my mind, are you?'

'That's right, Minister,' we said in unison.

'All right,' he said. 'Go home. I'll take the Bill to Cabinet.'

The grin on my face must have been a huge contrast to the way I had looked earlier in the day. As I walked out of the office with Heather, he put his hand on my shoulder and said: 'It's nice to see you smile. I haven't seen much of that for the last few weeks.'

The Bill gained the support of Cabinet, and progressed to parliament as the election loomed. Passage of the Bill in the House of Representatives was fairly predictable, as the government had the majority. Timing and elections were the only worry there, as the general expectation – later proved wrong by baked products and the proposed GST – was that the government could not win another term. The Senate was trickier, and Telstra's lobbying at this point to get a complete exemption from the law was almost successful. But, thinking that they may not be in government much longer, several influential Labor senators decided to hold the line on 'doing the right thing', and the Bill went through.

I had been in the reps chamber during some of the debate. But I was back in Perth by the time the Bill passed the Senate, so I was not part of the celebrations that occurred for those closely involved in Canberra. However, for some time I enjoyed the warm inner glow of knowing that I had participated in something really important for people with disabilities in Australia.

That glow was not lessened by the sadness that touched me some weeks afterwards, when Heather rang to tell me that I was not going to be appointed as Australia's first disability discrimination commissioner. Many people had assumed that I would be, and it was certainly my hope at the time. But, as is often the case with the benefit of hindsight, I realise now that this was the best outcome, as the lessons and wisdom I gained during the next 12 years served me well when I was eventually appointed.

*

My friend Peter Luckett and I met through the WA Association for the Blind, and Radio for the Print-Handicapped. Peter came from London, and had been a tour bus driver before he lost most of his vision. He met his partner Jo in that industry, and Maureen and I became good friends with them both. Peter has a very positive attitude towards life, and is always ready with a joke or two. He is also a hard worker on any cause to which he decides to commit.

He and I both ramped up our sailing activity, and became part of the WA team to compete in the first World Blind Sailing championships in Auckland in 1992. Western Australia entered three boats, one in each of the sight categories (determined by the vision of the person at the helm). B1 had a totally blind person at the helm, B2 had a person steering with up to 5 per cent vision, and B3 (our category) had a person at the helm with up to 10 per cent vision. This was Peter.

We had two sighted crew on the boat as well as Peter and myself, and our tactician David Lightfoot became a firm friend. His calm and thoughtful approach, combined with his sailing experience and keenness to succeed, made a big contribution to our success.

We travelled to New Zealand and met teams from most other Australian states, New Zealand, England and Sweden. We competed in a fleet of equivalent Farr-designed boats kept in Auckland for just such competitions. This meant that it was all down to sailing ability. We managed a silver medal, beaten only by the English crew. We were pretty happy with this result.

The Auckland experience reinforced, for Peter and me, our love of sailing. Peter bought his own boat on our return, and we have both enjoyed sailing ever since.

*

I had returned to the EOC as a conciliator, but soon moved to working as a legal officer representing complainants in the Equal Opportunity Tribunal, where commissioner June Williams had a responsibility to provide complainants with representation. I did this work under the tutelage of the senior legal officer Helen Versey. Legally trained in the United Kingdom, she came to Australia with great experience, and a real commitment to equality and social justice combined with a shrewd strategic brain. She went on later to the commissioner's role, and then to become privacy commissioner in Victoria.

I learned much from Helen about legal practice and broader policy approaches. She criticised constructively, had confidence in my work and was always ready for a glass of wine at the end of a hard day. You can't ask for much more than that in a boss.

I acted in some cases that broadened my knowledge of both litigation practice and discrimination law. My first case was representing a woman sacked from her job as a barmaid in a suburban hotel when she became pregnant. I was nervous throughout the case, and keen to perform as well as I could for my first client. Helen honed my cross-examination skills, showing me that often less was more in the number of questions one asked, and how not to ask that one question too many. I think I was happier than my client on the day that the verdict came down in her favour.

I also acted for a number of women refused service, or dismissed from their jobs, because of their Aboriginality. One woman was returning home from the committee meeting of an Aboriginal support organisation and was abused by the taxi driver with whom she travelled on the grounds of her race. He acted for himself against me in that case, and employed the rather idiosyncratic argument that he had not abused her on the grounds of her race, as he abused all of his passengers irrespective of race. He even called his best friend to confirm that this was the way he behaved. Pleasingly, the president of the tribunal was not persuaded by this argument.

This work grounded me, and reinforced what I already knew – the damage that discrimination, on whatever ground, could do to individuals; and the empowering experience that could be provided by a tribunal recognising the wrong, and publicly calling it as such.

Towards the end of our time in Perth, I was also recruited part-time by Jane Brazier to the newly established Bureau for Disability Services to assist with the drafting of Western Australia's first *Disability Services Act*. Jane guided, tempered and encouraged rather than directed me, and taught me how a collegiate approach and the sharing of knowledge could provide for a far better outcome.

One Wednesday night, Maureen, Leon and I had gone down to Fremantle to sail in a twilight race with Helen Versey and her partner, Peter. We were way behind the rest of the fleet at the second mark, and Helen jokingly proposed that, rather than completing the rest of the race, we should just take advantage of the Fremantle Doctor, and sail straight on to Rottnest Island.

Peter and I took up the idea with fervour, and we enjoyed a good sail across to the island and a drink at the Quokka Inn. The sail back on the gentle breeze of a warm, moonlit Perth summer night was one of the best I have enjoyed, but we did not get home until three in the morning. When I turned up late and bleary-eyed for work at the bureau the next morning, Jane's mild rebuke was: 'Isn't that taking work-life balance just a little too far?'

Late nights, or early mornings, were clearly a thing at the bureau. The draft legislation passed the WA Upper House at 2.45 am on the last sitting day before the election. I remember Jane waking me from my sleep on a bench outside the chamber when the Bill came on for debate. We got the result we wanted, and I celebrated my involvement in the passage of another law that would set the groundwork for change in the disability space. For a long time afterwards, Western Australia led in its service delivery to people with disabilities.

15
Qantas flies me to Sydney

DACA had lobbied government about jobs for people with disabilities, and an initiative taken in response to this was the establishment of special employment project officers (SEPOs) in major companies to try to increase the numbers of employees with disabilities. I strongly supported this initiative, as the increase was needed in the public and private sector. It still is.

However, it was with some surprise in mid-1993 that I received a phone call from Maria Walsh at Qantas. She was responsible for setting up this program, and wondered if I might apply to be the SEPO. It was a position based in their Sydney Jetbase at Mascot.

Maureen and I were pretty happy in Perth, and I had moved the family four years before to come back to Australia. I was not keen to do it again. But, as Maureen pointed out, there was an opportunity here for me. My family lived in Sydney and we had not visited for some time. Qantas would fly me over for the interview, I could see the family, and then we could consider our options if they offered me the job. We did our planning and settled on a large package of salary and benefits that we did not think they would accept – but it was a place to start the negotiations.

I flew over for the interview, which went well. At the end of it they offered me the position, and asked what it would take for me to come on board – they were already talking to me in aeroplane language. I set out my proposed package, and suggested that they may want to think about that and come back to me.

'Oh, no,' they said. 'We're happy with all of that. When can you start?'

Damn, I should have asked for more, I thought. I prevaricated, and went back to my hotel to call Maureen. We talked it over and decided to accept. It was a one-year contract with a year's extension, and we could come back to Perth afterwards. We are still in Sydney more than 20 years later.

*

I had friends all over the city, but Maureen's only Sydney friends lived on the lower North Shore. They were just moving out of their rented house in Willoughby to one they had bought in the same suburb, so we moved straight into the rented house. I knew I would settle in most places in Sydney, but it was Maureen and Leon who would need to make the adjustments.

Qantas was a very different work environment to the Equal Opportunity Commission. The merger with TAA, the Australian government–owned domestic airline, had just occurred, and I learned a great deal about moulding two corporate cultures. Much of my time was spent educating and persuading, so it was moving very much from the helicopter-level policy of the EOC or DACA to being down on the ground doing hands-on implementation.

Qantas had decided that its SEPO program would deal with customer service as well as employment, so I had a broad canvas on which to work. The program had much potential, but one major flaw. With almost 30,000 employees, and a strong place in the

Australian psyche, Qantas was a great vehicle to change the negative view in Australian society of people with disabilities. However, while I gained support to achieve change in various small areas of the company, I was never successful in achieving broad-ranging change. The main reason for this was that there was little or no commitment to the change from senior management.

Some positives did come out of the program for both Qantas and me. I met my now very good friend Sharon Young, who managed an employment agency for people with disabilities. We immediately got on well, sharing a deep love of cricket and a passion for social justice. We have attended and enjoyed the third day of the January Sydney test match every year since, and reached our twentieth year in 2014. The company employed a number of people with disabilities, particularly at the Mascot Jetbase. Most of them were people with intellectual disabilities, and some of them remained with the company for lengthy periods of time. John Macdonald, a long-term TAA employee based in Melbourne, and I teamed up on some customer-service projects. We attended several conferences of the US initiative Access to the Skies, and persuaded Qantas to introduce the US innovations to carriage and transfer of wheelchairs. Onboard toilets were made more accessible, and onboard wheelchairs began to be carried on international flights, making the journey to the toilet possible. I also worked on the development of safety videos that were more inclusive of people with disabilities. Captions were included on the videos, and safety instructions were made available in Braille.

But the problem then, as it is now, was that – unlike in the United States and Europe today – the detailed obligations of airlines to assist people with disabilities has never been regulated in Australia. While Qantas is probably leading the field in the adjustments it makes, airlines and airports are still well below the mark in providing an equal travel experience. Safety and cost are often used as arguments not to act, and while this is true in some cases there is usually a solution to be found once negative attitudes are changed.

The project ran its course, but at the end of the two-year funding period Qantas decided not to fund and continue with it. However, they must have been happy with me, as they kept me on as the equal employment opportunity coordinator.

*

Leon settled into his new school, and we began to establish new friendships. Maureen's keyboard technology business, which she had worked hard to establish in Perth, floundered after the move. However, she had completed a number of consultancies in the disability sector and, combined with her experience as a conciliator, she soon became the first convenor of the Disability Discrimination Legal Centre in Kingsford. This centre, an offshoot of the University of New South Wales's Kingsford Legal Centre, was funded to represent clients in their disability discrimination claims. Maureen found accessible premises for the centre, set up all of its policies and protocols, and appointed staff and volunteers. It has gone on to become one of the leading centres of its type in the country, and is now known as the Australian Centre for Disability Law.

Maureen worked on with other initiatives. She was appointed as the first CEO of the Australian Council of Businesswomen, building that organisation to become a strong national representative body.

I was never really happy in our rented Willoughby house, so we decided to find a house of our own. Maureen has a great eye for finding properties with potential. This usually means that we have a lot of work to do on renovations, but both of us have been happy to do that. She found a narrow three-storey house in Elizabeth Street, Artarmon, which fitted this description.

It was right on the train line, and three minutes' walk from the station, which I loved. It had easy access to shops, but was run-down and needed lots of work. So we bought it. We lived in it while renovating, and when we left it in 1998, to move to Roseville, it was in excellent condition. Sadly for Maureen, we seem to have a history of fixing houses and then leaving them before we can properly enjoy them.

*

We also brought *Serenity* to Sydney by truck. As she was a wooden-hulled boat, I was very worried when the prime mover on the truck broke down, and she was parked in a truck stop in the dry South Australian heat for a week while she was repaired. I had visions of timbers shrinking and cracking, and her sinking to the bottom the first time she was put in the water. But when the crane at Woolwich lowered her into Sydney Harbour, she floated as well as she ever had – full marks to Van de Stadt design and hull-building.

The next question was where we should keep her. Maureen and I decided to visit some of the local sailing clubs to find out about moorings and the processes involved. The first on the list was the Greenwich Flying Squadron (GFS), an unprepossessing white shed hiding quietly at the bottom of Bay Street. We walked in one Saturday afternoon as weekend racing was coming to an end. The welcome we received was so warm and friendly, and the setting and view so perfect, that we did not continue down the list. We knew that this was the right place for our boat, and it has been right ever since.

As well as working and playing on my own boat, I started to sail in GFS twilights and on Saturday afternoons. GFS became a place of solace for me. The surroundings, the water and the friendly atmosphere made it a place where I could slough off the stresses of my work, and really relax. In fact, on occasions when I used to get grumpy, Maureen would suggest that it was time I went down to the sailing club.

I was keen to be able to reach my boat independently so that I could carry out work and maintenance on her by myself. I approached Technical Aids for the Disabled for a solution. One of their volunteers constructed two battery-powered and salt-resistant boxes, controlled by a garage door opener, which made a loud bird-whistling noise. I left one on the boat, and placed the other on the club pontoon, and rowed happily between them.

This worked well on most occasions. On one day, when the wind was blowing dogs off chains and I probably should not have rowed out to the boat in the first place, I could not hear the club beacon when I wanted to row back. Based on the direction of the wind, I worked out where the shoreline was, and rowed directly towards it, on the theory that I could then row along it until I heard the noise. After travelling along the shore for some time, avoiding rocks and overhanging jetties, I realised that I must have been swept past the club, and turned around before being swept out of the Lane Cove river and into the harbour proper. After a lot of hard paddling against the wind I heard the sound I was seeking and, tired but triumphant, reached my goal.

'We wondered if you were coming back,' said some of my new clubmates. 'We've been watching you, and were about to get a motorboat out and come and pick you up when you turned around. All that rowing against the wind will have done you good, though,' they said.

I loved crewing on other boats in twilights and Saturday afternoon races, and made a number of good friends in the process. But I yearned to have my own boat competing. Maureen's university friend Sher Guhl had moved to Sydney some years before, and married a barrister, James Kearney. James had done a lot of sailing earlier in his life, and I persuaded him to come and sail with me on

Serenity. He brought his school friend Peter Hamilton, who was also a good sailor, and the three of us formed a crew to enter *Serenity* in the twilights.

We have sailed together ever since, become good friends, and now co-own our third boat. James jokes that it is the only partnership he has known where there has never been a disagreement. If one of us does something on the boat that the others regard as a little extreme, the others just smile and shake our heads, and learn from the experience. I view our success as the product of the joy we all gain from sailing.

16
Tribunals and babies

One warm Saturday afternoon Maureen and I were browsing for boat equipment in the ship chandler's, a place you could never walk out of without spending at least $100. We walked up to the counter and placed our purchases next to the till.

'I know you,' said the young woman behind the counter. 'You heard my case in the Residential Tenancy Tribunal.'

My reaction must have been clear on my face, as she quickly said, 'Oh, no, it's all right, you found in my favour.'

I sighed with relief.

'It was a funny day, that,' she said. 'I'm a student, so I usually get around in jeans and a t-shirt. But my dad warned me that appearances in court were important, and that I should make an effort. I sent my best dress to the drycleaner, and spent at least an hour on hair and make-up. My dad and I walked into your hearing-room, and he tapped me on the arm and said: 'Sorry. That's a couple of hours of your life you just wasted.'

We laughed, she gave me some further positive feedback on my hearing technique, and we left with our purchases.

*

Maureen has given me many gifts during our time together. Some have been physical objects that I have appreciated, used and treasured. My long-case chiming clock is second only to Grandma's mantel clock in my chiming clock collection. But the three most important gifts are not physical objects.

The most important has been her love and support in the time we have been together. As well as lovers we have been great mates, sharing experiences and mostly enjoying each other's company. We have worked together on particular projects, spent family time together and time on our own, dreamed together of what we could achieve, and achieved much of it.

The third-most important gift has been the gift of advice. Maureen has always been prepared to share her views with me, and I have benefited from them on many occasions. As well as constructively criticising, she has always sought to build my confidence and encouraged me during those times of self-doubt.

The second-most important gift is our daughter, Rachel. When Maureen and I married, it was clearly on the basis that Maureen did not plan to have more children. I had accepted that, and gained a great deal of enjoyment from playing my part as Leon's second dad. But as the biological clocks ticked down for both of us, once we were settled in careers in Sydney, Maureen changed her mind, and I could not have been happier.

By the end of 1996 I had been appointed as a part-time hearing commissioner with the Human Rights Commission. Then my old friend and mentor Dave Turley came back into the picture. He had moved on from the Department of Consumer Affairs to become senior referee of the NSW Consumer Claims Tribunal, and he encouraged me to apply to become a referee, which I did successfully.

I had felt for a while that my time at Qantas was running out. My role as equal employment opportunity coordinator was on a contract basis, so my future was not certain, and I was by no means sure that

I wanted to stay with the organisation long term. So I came home one November evening and told Maureen that I had resigned from Qantas. I had decided to put together a tribunal portfolio, and earn my income in that way. This had been a matter for discussion between us for some time, but until that day I had not made the final decision.

Instead of what I had expected – Maureen's slight trepidation, but then absolute support of my decision – she burst into tears. She had confirmed that day that we were having a baby, and she saw two income streams coming to an end.

My approach, however, proved to be a quite successful strategy. I applied for, and achieved, roles on a number of tribunals. I also obtained some consultancies with Westpac, Sydney Water and others on employment of people with disabilities – which I achieved as a result of my reputation and my SEPO role. For the next eight or nine years my diary was mostly full for six weeks ahead, and completely empty after that. But once I got past worrying on that score, life went along quite well.

*

Westpac and the other consultancies were quite productive for me. I helped Westpac build their knowledge and awareness in the disability space, and they are now a leading employer of people with disabilities in Australia. Their initiative of employing Paralympians in and around the time of the Sydney Olympic Games was creative and groundbreaking. People with disabilities now make up around 13 per cent of their workforce, a great figure when around 15 per cent of working-age Australians are people with disabilities. They have also led other financial institutions, and organisations of similar size, on this journey.

A few years later I did some work with Employers Making a Difference, which changed its name to the Australian Network on Disability. The brainchild of long-time disability employment practitioner and advocate Suzanne Colbert, it became the national organisation of employers committed to employing people with disabilities. One of its many initiatives in this area was its Stepping Into program, and I did some work convincing legal and accounting firms to take part in it. The program is now one of the most successful entry paths for employees with disabilities.

*

While my consultancy work played to my knowledge and experience in the disability field, my tribunal work took me in different directions. The Consumer Claims Tribunal built on my work for the department in earlier years, as well as my experience appearing before the Equal Opportunity Tribunal in Western Australia. As the name suggests, it dealt with claims by consumers against traders and retailers in a number of professions. Hearings were conducted informally, and most of the time parties were not legally represented.

I met all sorts of people in these processes, and for most of them my blindness was of little relevance. I would spend the time when I was not conducting hearings getting one of the clerks to read me the files, while I took detailed notes on my Braille computer. If parties produced documents or other evidence at hearings, I would simply get them to tell me about it, or have them hand me the exhibit so that I could feel it. The process of having them tell me about the evidence and exhibits provided them with the chance to set out their concerns, and allowed the other party to hear those concerns. Matters were often resolved as a result of those discussions.

I remember the thousands and thousands of dollars being spent on wedding ceremonies, and the despair when the photographs were lost by the photographer, or did not turn out as expected. I remember the wedding dress where three or four fittings had taken place, but when the final product was presented the day before the wedding it could not be worn. I recall the inedible wedding cakes, flawed catering arrangements, and the mothers and daughters who came before me to tell the stories. I could provide them with a sympathetic ear, and a fair award of damages in compensation, but I could not make the most important day in their lives the perfect experience of which they had dreamed.

There were also men, clearly falling into the more vulnerable of groups in our society, who had their hopes cruelly raised by the glowing stories of successful and happy relationships achieved by dating agencies. These men poured much of their savings into the process of finding the right partner, only to be bitterly disappointed again and again. I recall one in particular, a dirt-poor western NSW farm labourer, who pawned his mother's prized and valuable engagement ring to seek the happiness his mother and father had shown him in their marriage. I was unable to help him achieve that dream of happiness, but my termination of the contract and award of damages at least meant that he could redeem the ring and return it to his mother, who was dying of cancer.

I recall the young married couples, or single parents, whose struggles were made worse by the purchase of questionable second-hand home appliances or cheap and nasty kitchen installations, and the poor or non-repair of these same appliances. I kept a box of tissues in all of my hearings, and both women and men used them as the retelling of their stories brought back the pain. It was sometimes hard for me not to use them.

But I also met consumers clearly trying to take advantage of traders, when the product they had bought either exceeded their budget or just did not meet their expectations because they had made a bad purchasing decision. And I met some honest operators who, sometimes hearing the consumer's story for the first time, offered compensation – before I had made my decision – that exceeded that which I would have awarded.

The Consumer Claims Tribunal reinforced for me the value of a free market, but the important need for some regulation of its excesses. It showed me a somewhat disappointing side of humanity, but certainly provided me with some opportunities to determine the fair and equitable result that I had sought during the hard years studying at Sydney University.

Another place where the market needed some intervention was real estate, and the Residential Tenancy Tribunal dealt with tensions between landlords and tenants. Because it was about people's homes, highly valued in Australian society, it was often fraught and energetically contested. Its hearing processes were more formal than those of the Consumer Claims Tribunal, with a set-up much more like a court. Landlords were usually represented by their real-estate agent, and these agents – while not lawyers – became regular participants with much more understanding of the procedure than tenants. While this gave the landlord a little more power in the dispute, it also meant that often one side of the dispute had a real appreciation of the range of likely outcomes, so the process became more efficient.

I arrived at the tribunal at the time when conciliation was increasingly coming into play. As conciliators, we would quickly gain an understanding of the views of both parties and assist them towards a fair agreement. We would usually help write up an agreement, ensuring that there had been no undue pressure by any of the parties and that the agreement was within the law. If the matter could not be settled then it was sent for hearing, always before a different member of the tribunal. I enjoyed this process because I have always been of the view that the resolution of a dispute is far more sustainable if the parties to that dispute are involved in finding a resolution. Because I enjoyed it, and because I had a fair degree of mediation experience, I had a higher than usual conciliation rate, and therefore was preferred as one of the members nominated for conciliation.

Some of the extreme cases in this tribunal dealt with landlords or caravan park operators who chose to terminate long-standing tenancies at very short notice, or to enforce significant rent increases on quite vulnerable or disadvantaged people. But most cases dealt with smaller arguments over whether a tenant could have their bond returned or to what effect a landlord had carried out needed repairs.

The third of my tribunals was the Commonwealth Social Security Appeals Tribunal (SSAT). People came before this tribunal if they were refused a benefit, or if a benefit was removed or suspended. We were seeing vulnerable people, living in the most disadvantaged strata of society. The social security benefit that they received – or sometimes did not receive – usually only just sustained them. I remember seeing perhaps one or two examples of people 'rorting' social security benefits, but all of the studies in this area indicate that such examples are very rare. Yet those vulnerable members of society are regularly pilloried as 'bludgers' or 'leaners'. It's a myth created by our politicians and some of our senior bureaucrats, to support their continued limiting of such systems, and they are supported in this work by the shock jocks and the tabloid press. However, as a society we are complicit because we continue to demand lower taxes. During the time I was on the tribunal, social security laws were tightened, and provisions were reduced. I did not seek reappointment because my conscience would not allow me to continue to administer a law I regarded as unfairly harsh and punitive.

My fourth tribunal was the NSW Equal Opportunity Tribunal, which heard complaints lodged under the NSW *Anti-Discrimination Act 1977*, on all grounds of discrimination, whether race, sex, pregnancy, disability or same-sex attraction. Many of the parties in this tribunal were legally represented. This meant that there was a greater understanding of legal procedure, although surprisingly many lawyers would appear before the tribunal with only a passable appreciation of discrimination law. There were several occasions when I suggested that a representative should perhaps go and read a certain precedent overnight, and then reconsider the submissions they were making to us.

*

My final tribunal was the first one to which I had been appointed – as a hearing commissioner with the Human Rights Commission. This dealt with complaints lodged under federal discrimination law, so was limited to complaints on the grounds of race, sex, pregnancy and disability. Decisions were unenforceable, and had to be confirmed by a Federal Court decision, although they carried significant weight. Several race discrimination cases I heard gained significant prominence in the media. Two in Western Australia dealt with the provisions in the *Racial Discrimination Act 1975* relating to racial vilification, which have more latterly gained political prominence.

The first was lodged against well-known Perth shock jock Howard Sattler, who allowed a talkback conversation to go to air in which Aboriginal people, and their traditional laws and cultures, were insulted and humiliated. A number of elders and others gave evidence about how they had heard this conversation broadcast, how it had hurt them and damaged the reputation of their people. I found against Sattler in that case.

Another case related to the then editor of *The West Australian*, Paul Murray. He had written an editorial about the redevelopment of the Swan Brewery site on the Swan River. He referred in a demeaning way to the Wagyl, the serpent recognised by Indigenous Australians as forming the river many, many years ago. Again, many members of the Aboriginal community testified in that matter. I found that, although vilification had occurred, he and his newspaper were able to make out one of the defences in the section, so a breach of the law had not taken place.

I was visiting family in Perth some five or ten years later when one of the elders who had testified stopped me in the street. He just wanted to shake my hand. 'I know you found against us in the WA Newspapers case,' he said. 'But I just wanted to thank you. You may not have found that the law had been broken, but you treated us with respect, and believed the story we told you about our traditional law. That was very important to us.'

I also heard some of the early disability discrimination cases under the *Disability Discrimination Act 1992*. It was a privilege to be part of the interpretation of a law that I had assisted to develop.

I was involved in two early cases about education. In the first of these, six-year-old Scarlett Finney was refused enrolment at The Hills Grammar School on the grounds of her disability, spina bifida. The school argued that it would incur significant costs in making modifications, although much of the necessary ramping was already in place. It also argued that it would be too expensive to build a lockable cupboard in an already existing accessible toilet where necessary equipment could be stored for Scarlett. Third, it asserted that school excursions would be difficult, and would require extra assistance and supervision, even though Scarlett's mother was happy to provide this.

This case was similar to hundreds of others in the commission that were successfully resolved by conciliation. But the school board were not prepared to conciliate. I found that the school had discriminated against Scarlett on the grounds of her disability. By the time the decision came down she was already happily attending another school, and I awarded her significant damages for the discrimination that had occurred.

My decision in this matter was upheld on appeal to the Federal Court. It was also one of the stories featured in the *Twenty Years:*

Twenty Stories series made by the Human Rights Commission in 2013 to celebrate 20 years of the *Disability Discrimination Act 1992*. In the film, the school is shown to have changed its practices, and kids with disabilities now attend there successfully and happily. It was great to play a part in that systemic change.

The result of the second education case was not so positive. Daniel Hoggan was expelled from his local primary school in Grafton, and alleged that it was due to discrimination on the grounds of his disability. Daniel had multiple disabilities, including significant intellectual disability. He had attended the school for some time but, after several suspensions for behaviour regarded by the school as inappropriate, he was expelled. He was offered a place at another school on the other side of town, but his parents wanted him to attend his local school, just over their back fence.

The case involved lengthy hearings, and complex factual and legal argument. I finally found in Daniel's favour, but my decision was overturned all the way to the High Court. The particular area of the law involved has now been superseded by amendments to the Act. For me, the saddest part of this case was that, due to the length of time that all of these cases took, Daniel completely missed high school. Irrespective of my views on the decisions of the higher courts, this seemed to me a perverse result.

*

Our family life continued in Artarmon. Leon progressed to high school at St Pius X College in Chatswood, and pursued the usual teenage activities. Despite strong pressure from the school, his career in sport did not blossom. Maureen jokes that he is the only person who competed in school running races with his hands in his pockets – whatever Leon does, he does it with style.

Maureen's workload seemed to increase at the Australian Council of Businesswomen as Rachel's arrival approached. But we still had time to paint the room and spend happy Saturdays deciding on prams, cots and hammocks, and collecting masses of baby clothes and toys that we had either bought ourselves or were given to us by generous friends.

I had a phone directions hearing set down in the Human Rights Commission for 4 pm on 21 August 1997. Susan Roberts, then the senior legal officer, knew of Rachel's imminent arrival, so had some idea of what was going on when I completely forgot the hearing, and just did not call in. She softly chided me later, but agreed that it was the best excuse that I would ever come up with for such a mistake.

Rachel's birth, for which I was present, is one of my most amazing memories. Maureen's sister Patricia, a midwife, came across from Perth to ensure that all went well. When she passed Rachel to me to cuddle for the first time I could not have been happier. And I cried tears of joy when the doctor told me that Rachel's eyes looked quite normal, and that in all probability she could see.

I had been worried about this for the whole pregnancy, but not shared my concern with Maureen or anyone else. It was a shame that I had not, because they would have quickly pointed out to me that it was a worry completely without foundation, as my blindness was not hereditary. I knew this myself, of course, but just had not put the knowledge together. Our minds can sometimes be strange places.

Maureen did not allow the arrival of our daughter to lessen the impact of her work at the Australian Council of Businesswomen. Three days after Rachel's birth we were off to Canberra, where Maureen successfully coordinated the first national summit of businesswomen in Parliament House, while I sat outside and minded the baby. John Howard, then prime minister, observed and favourably commented on the skill sets that Maureen and I were demonstrating. Rachel received her first prime-ministerial kiss at three days old.

We took Rachel back to our house in Artarmon, where she spent the first eight months of her life. She sometimes did not sleep well, and I recall late nights walking up and down the stairs with her on my shoulder. The hammock with spring suspension we bought for her often helped, as did late-night broadcasts of cricket from the 1997 Ashes series in England. Despite using this technique for her as the years went on, I was not successful in raising another cricket tragic.

Maureen soon moved to the NSW Office of Small Business, where she initiated and coordinated the first mentoring program for women in business. It was a great success, and we have gained many good friends from the process.

Rachel commenced day care for one or two days a week fairly early, but both before and during her time at day care Maureen and I took her to our workplaces. Having a mum bring her baby to work at a place like the NSW Office of Small Business was relatively acceptable. However, having a dad bring his baby to work, particularly a dad who was blind, was a far more unusual occurrence. I received very positive support for this action from all of the tribunals on which I sat, although some of the parties at hearings were a little more surprised. I found her presence, on my chest in a Kapoochi baby carrier, very conducive to successful conciliation in the Residential Tenancy Tribunal. It's hard for parties to shout at each other when there is a baby in the room, particularly a sleeping one. I was often encouraged by other tribunal members to take on the particularly difficult conciliations, a challenge that I regularly enjoyed.

One incident saddened me, because – although an extreme on the spectrum – it reflected the significantly negative view that the Australian community has towards people with disabilities. I was standing on a platform at Central Station, waiting for my train, with Rachel in the backpack I used, and my white cane in my hand.

A woman walked up to me and, without preliminaries demanded, 'What is your name?'

'Why do you want to know?' I asked in some confusion.

'Because I am going to report you. People like you should not be left alone in charge of a baby.'

I told her to leave immediately, or I would report her to the police for harassment. But I was amazed that this view could be expressed at the end of the twentieth century. Sadly, it was not an isolated experience. One of the health professionals to which I took Rachel when she was little asked me on several occasions quite intrusive questions about Rachel's mother, and why she was not present. The message she gave me was clear – a blind man is not competent to be looking after this child. Not surprisingly, I found a different health professional on subsequent occasions.

The Kapoochis changed to backpacks as Rachel got bigger. I found it easier while using a white cane to have two hands free, and Rachel thought it was lots of fun to steer Dad where she wanted to go by pulling on either the left or right ear, or tapping me on the head to either make me stop or go along more quickly. I never quite worked out the tapping sequence for each.

Being a blind parent created new and different challenges for me. As Rachel started crawling, and then walking, I needed to monitor her location when I was the only one in our family around. Yet I did not want to mark her out as the daughter of someone who could not see, so we had to develop a relationship of trust. She had started this early, working out that she did not get a reaction from me by using visual cues. So she started using verbal cues, and it was quite obvious that she made more noises in my presence than she did with Maureen. It may also be why she started talking at eight months. I learned a great deal from friends in Blind Citizens Australia who had raised children. The *Kids Are Fun for Everyone* book, brought out by BCA for parents who were blind, was also a constant reference. And Maureen's previous experience, and innate capacity, were also a source of very valuable thoughts and advice.

As with other challenges I have faced in my life, I was determined to find a way. I was not missing the chance to have an equal role in the parenting of my daughter.

Reading has always been one of the great pleasures in my life. And I have never been averse to reading aloud, as demonstrated by my success in Braille-reading competitions as I grew up. Maureen and Leon shared my enjoyment of books, so from early on in our relationship I had read, often to Leon and sometimes to them both. As Leon grew, so did the books we read. I read my favourite book, Tolkien's *The Lord of the Rings*, to him, as well as *The Hobbit*. I read John Wyndham's *The Day of the Triffids*, and Frank Herbert's *Dune*. This reading, usually just before Leon's bedtime, was a wonderful part of our family time together. And Maureen's entreaties of: 'Just one more' when I came to the end of a chapter were as loud as those of Leon's.

So when Rachel was born, one of the first things I did was to start buying stories in Braille. I regularly read her bedtime story, and I can still recite the words of *Looking after Sarah* (a guide dog story), *Julius* and *Goodnight Moon*.

As Rachel has grown, we have passed these books on to other blind parents to read to their children. But she has kept a few of her favourites locked in her special books box, and I have kept memories of stories, bedtime cuddles and pats to sleep locked in my heart.

17
The proof is in the pudding

In September 1998, I ensured that the annoying question about getting a guide dog was one with which I would have to deal no longer. Soon after the arrival of my first guide dog Jordie, I had to spend a couple of days in Melbourne, and stayed with my good friends Chris and Trish Stewart. Naturally, Jordie came with me. The travel to Melbourne was uneventful, and I enjoyed Trish's excellent cooking and their good company. When it came time for bed we decided to lock Jordie in the laundry for the night. I toileted her outside, and then closed the door.

What I didn't know was that Trish's carefully prepared family Christmas pudding was hanging above the laundry sink in a muslin bag, proving. Trish had thought about this but, since it was about two metres off the ground, she thought Jordie had no chance of reaching it.

The rich smells of Christmas pudding were just too much for my new guide dog. During the night Jordie achieved the new high-jump world record for labradors, grabbed a mouthful of pudding plus muslin bag, and hung on until the combined weight of pudding and dog pulled the hook from the ceiling. At least, that was our reconstruction when we discovered a very empty and chewed muslin bag, and a very sluggish and unwell (probably drunk) guide dog the next morning.

Her normally jaunty walking pace slowed to a crawl, and we had numerous stops while Christmas pudding remnants were evacuated from both ends. The old saying 'as sick as a dog' gained real meaning for me that day.

*

One of the questions I have been most frequently asked during my adult life is: 'Why haven't you got a guide dog?' My flippant response, coming as one of Leon's numerous clever and quirky ideas, is that I'm training a guide parrot, which will sit on my shoulder. The evocative image of a parrot sitting just below my right ear squawking, 'Left a bit,' 'Go right,' 'Steps down,' always makes me think of Leon and smile.

The idea that all totally blind people use guide dogs must rate very highly on the chart of community misconceptions. The facts are quite different – in New South Wales there are around 250 to 300 guide dogs, and about 60,000 people who are blind or have low vision, so the percentage is small. However, as with any situation that is a little bit different, blind people and their guide dogs stand out, and are remembered.

I applied for my dog through the Guide Dog Association of NSW/ACT. They are based in Sydney, and I had been very satisfied with other orientation and mobility training I had received from them over the years. That was the right decision – they have given me great support ever since, and provided me with two excellent guide dogs so far.

The Guide Dogs Association estimates that the cost of training one of their dogs is $30,000. I recommend them for support, and thank the many puppy-raisers who train and socialise the dogs for the first 12 months of their lives. Their efforts are much appreciated by me and many others, particularly knowing how hard it must be to give up the dog after that 12 months of work.

I have always been a good independent traveller using a white cane. So while not dismissing the value of dog guides for those who choose to use them, I have never placed myself in that category. However, I came to appreciate that my independent travel had been at a cost – it takes a lot of concentration and causes a degree of stress. At the end of a long working day this was the last thing I needed.

I was also often frustrated when trying to find a particular place, or navigate through new or less familiar areas. This meant that I tended to avoid visiting such areas on my own, or when I couldn't avoid it I walked more slowly and hesitantly. If I was running late, the extra stress was only increased by the frustration of having to slowly and carefully navigate through an unfamiliar street or building. My work as a member of a number of state and Commonwealth tribunals was done in many different venues, and required me to be fairly mobile, so this was a frequent occurrence.

At the end of a long day, I tended to catch a taxi rather than use public transport and walk, which was sad, as all of my life I have gained much pleasure from train travel and a relaxing stroll. If I was out with my family or friends, I tended to stay with them all the time, holding one of their arms when we moved around.

So, was there an answer to the ever-increasing taxi bill, and the complaints from family that I was always too tired to do things? Could I remove some of my frustrations while travelling, and make family outings more enjoyable for all by having just a little more independence? Perhaps the answer was a guide dog.

I have outlined the positives, and on their own they are persuasive. But I had a few other issues to consider. My independence and recognition as a competent and capable member of society are things that I highly prize. I also work hard to have people interact with me, not with my disability. I have observed many people with guide dogs over the years, and seen that often it is the dog, and not the person, who draws the attention; the dog becomes the main topic of conversation.

This may not be an issue for other people, but because of my approach to life and disability, it was something that would annoy me intensely, and I wondered whether I would be able to tolerate it, or change it.

As an adult, I have always thought that the inconvenience of pets (the feeding, the mess, the smell, and what you do with them when you are away from home) was not worth the benefits of companionship and fun. This meant that the benefits I would gain from having a guide dog would have to outweigh the responsibilities I would acquire – feeding, grooming, walking and looking after an animal.

Finally, could I and my family put up with the doggy smell in the house? Clearly, a guide dog is an inside animal. Would its presence, including any smell, intrude on the life of my family and myself? I did not want to dismiss this issue lightly, because – unlike a strong cooking or other smell that can be removed by opening a window, using a deodoriser or by the passage of time – this dog was coming in for keeps. Also, as a person without the use of one sense, I worked hard to maximise the input from all of the others.

I was very conscious of bringing a dog into a home that was as much that of Maureen, Leon and Rachel as it was mine. While they assured me of their support, Rachel by chuckling and saying 'dog' repeatedly when I showed her pictures, I knew that there would be an impact for them.

*

I finally decided in the affirmative. The next steps were easy. I had an assessment, and soon after that the approval letter arrived. Jordana (aka Jordie – Jordana was just too pretentious a name for a dog, even a guide dog) came into our lives in September 1998.

Training with an instructor consisted of sessions around my local area, before we went into the city. We trained for several hours a day, which I fitted in around my work commitments. Working with a guide dog is very different to using a long cane. In the first few days, before you begin to develop a trust for the dog, you feel far more exposed. This is because you do not have control of something that is probing the space in front of you. However, my head told me that the dog was specifically trained to look out for my interests, and that I just had to deal with this hesitancy. It felt quite uncomfortable for a day or two, but I got used to it. I also began to enjoy the sensation of striding out freely, without the concentrated effort needed to use a cane effectively at the pace at which I walk – quite fast.

Learning the necessary basic commands is not difficult, and they are reinforced by repetition. The trickier process for me was working out the balance of control between myself and Jordie. I was not prepared to let her have total control, but I found that allowing her a reasonable degree of initiative and trusting her decisions made the process smoother and quicker. We didn't always get the 'teamwork' right, but it got better and better the longer we worked together and got to know each other's foibles. This, I have since discovered, is the standard handler and guide dog experience.

The teamwork starts in training, but continues for some time. On one occasion when I was uncertain as to whether I should curve left or go straight ahead, I let Jordie make the decision, and we became even more lost than we had been before. However, half an hour later I did the same thing and she took me exactly where I wanted to go. Just like humans, dogs are fallible, but a dog that can see, smell and has a good memory will often be closer to the mark than a totally blind person, even one with good orientation skills.

Travelling with Jordie meant a major decrease in the stress and tiredness caused by independent travel. This is particularly true on known routes. Between my home and the station, or the station and the building in which I do most of my work, I can – I imagine – use only about the same amount of concentration on my route as would a person with sight. This is a great relief and benefit for me. It also means that I can do much more walking for pleasure, something that I very much enjoy but that I did little of in the few years before Jordie arrived.

Jordie had a major impact on my independence. I moved around the city a great deal more during the day, completing tasks in my lunch hour that I would previously have delegated to someone else, done much more slowly by post or other means or just not done at all. I went for walks in the park while toileting Jordie. I'd seen the parks and thought they would be pleasant to visit but had never got around to it in the past.

Finding a place for the first time still had its difficulties. I did not have the same capacity to 'probe' with my cane for doorways or other landmarks. Also, because I was unsure of my environment, I was unable to give Jordie clear and decisive instructions. When your dog knows that you are uncertain she tends to become less confident, and therefore less effective. In such situations, whether using a guide dog or a cane, asking – although sometimes frustrating – is still the best method.

Walking with friends or colleagues is still not something that works well for me. During training I was encouraged to direct my dog to follow the other person. However, this is not the usual way that two people walk together – they would normally walk side by side. Because of the space that this takes up, and my dog's keenness to keep me in the centre of the footpath, this sometimes becomes clumsy. In some circumstances, I find it best to drop the handle and take the person's arm.

People talking to the dog is, as I predicted, one of the things that causes me most problems. I am insulted by the fact that most people talk to the dog before they talk to me. I try, at times unsuccessfully, not to respond rudely to this. However, for me it is one of the major disadvantages of having a guide dog.

A related problem is that the dog is distracted by people patting her and talking to her while she is working. If you assumed that common courtesy would be to ask permission before doing this, in many cases you would be wrong. I can tolerate this from children, who may not know any better, but from the adults who do it, it is thoughtless and puts my safety at risk.

My work requires me to travel, and sometimes I stay in hotels. This is generally not a problem except that – as for any new location – I have to find an appropriate toileting area. Apart from this she settles into the hotel room as if she were at home. Air travel is very easy. It is important that the airline is aware that I am travelling with a guide dog. However, I have included this information in my frequent flyer profile, so it pops up every time.

One problem with flying, internationally and on longer domestic flights, has been toileting facilities at airports – there are very few. On most occasions I have persuaded the airlines to let me walk down the stairs near the gate lounge and let the dog go on the ramp area. This is technically a security breach but, while staff are reluctant, they are often persuaded by me pointing out the alternative – the necessity of toileting on the aircraft. Of course this is unlikely to happen in reality, as I always encourage my dog to go at the last possible time before reaching the airport.

There are only two real challenges travelling internationally with a guide dog. The first is the number and diversity of forms that need to be filled in for quarantine checks. Also, the dog has to be vet-checked immediately before leaving many countries, or returning to Australia, so you have to allow time for this and for visiting relevant customs officials.

The second is the side of the road on which cars drive. Despite Jordie's regular visits to the United States, she could never get used to the idea of cars coming from the opposite direction, so I had to pay a little more attention when crossing roads there.

I have been refused access by only a few taxis and restaurants since I started to travel with a guide dog. For the taxis I was able to obtain their numbers from a bystander and lodge a complaint, and drivers have been fined. Of course there may have been others who have just not stopped, but I am not aware of them.

Several restaurants who refused were quite entertaining. In the first I showed my guide dog owner's card, which is signed by the NSW attorney-general and refers to the provisions of the relevant legislation. The manager accepted this, borrowed the card while we were eating, and showed it to all other staff – he clearly saw a good opportunity for a bit of impromptu staff training. In the second restaurant, the manager could not read the card. However, when I explained Jordie's purpose, he consulted the other patrons and took a straw vote as to whether we could stay. We were admitted with an overwhelming majority.

So, the proof is in the pudding, which has been eaten (metaphorically by me and literally by Jordie), and both of us are well satisfied.

18
Deputy commissioner

I had completed a meeting with some senior bank officials in Brisbane. Walking with my guide dog, I got into the elevator on the thirtieth floor of their building at the same time as another person. The lift buttons were not marked with raised letters or Braille, so I didn't know which one to press.

Turning to the other man in the lift I said: 'Could you press the button for ground, please?'

I got no response.

Thinking that he may have a hearing impairment – I was the deputy disability discrimination commissioner, after all – I looked directly at him so he could read my lips, and said a little more clearly: 'Could you press ground, please?'

Still no response.

Puzzled, I reached over and tapped him on the shoulder, and repeated my request.

'Oh,' he said, 'Are you talking to me? I thought you were asking the guide dog.'

My guide dog is good, but she hasn't learned to read lift buttons yet!

*

There are many similar stories of assumptions made about people with disabilities. In my experience, most of those assumptions are negative, and most of them are wrong – but they still keep being made.

I have known and experienced this for most of my life. But my good friend David Mason provided me with a greater opportunity to do something about it in 1999. David was the director of the Disability Rights Unit at the Australian Human Rights Commission, a role in which he had served since the commencement of the *Disability Discrimination Act* on 1 March 1993. I had worked with David in his former policy role at the commission when the legislation was being developed, and we remained in touch.

Elizabeth Hastings served as Australia's first disability discrimination commissioner from 1993 until 1998. As a person with a disability – Elizabeth used a wheelchair – and someone with previous experience at the commission, she made a good first commissioner. She was able, by words and example, to demonstrate the impact that discriminatory practices and attitudes have on the lives of the more than 20 per cent of Australians with disabilities. She sadly died not long after she finished in the role.

At the end of her term of office, the Howard government chose not to fill the position with a full-time commissioner, or with someone who had lived experience of disability. Instead, they asked Chris Sidoti, the then human rights commissioner, to take the role as a second job. Chris did so reluctantly, knowing that he would not have the time or experience to adequately fulfil the role, but also knowing that, if he did not do it, the job would simply not be done.

This situation continued for some time, but then Chris, having experienced the difficulty of carrying two commissioner roles and feeling that he could not do the job adequately, refused further appointment. Disability was passed, like the poor cousin of discrimination, to the then sex discrimination commissioner

Susan Halliday. Susan also felt reluctant about taking it on as a second role, but agreed to do so for the same reasons as Chris.

Chris and Susan both relied heavily for their knowledge and policy output on the commission's Disability Discrimination Unit. Led by David Mason, and including people with lengthy disability and policy expertise, this was one of the commission's most effective teams. They had run the initial awareness campaign for the *Disability Discrimination Act 1992* (DDA), and supported Elizabeth Hastings through her term as commissioner. They continued to provide excellent policy and advocacy work for Chris and Susan, but were hampered by the lack of a full-time disability commissioner.

Qualified as a lawyer and an economist, David has a sharp mind and a huge intellect, which he put to excellent use at the commission. Not only did he write numerous erudite and incisive speeches – many of which I delivered – but his capacity for delivery of policy papers and thinking was enormous. He loves music and comedy as well, and can recite long stretches of songs or Monty Python sketches as part of his conversation. Combining those two skills, he once had me begin a speech to the Deafness Forum with a verse he composed and set to the tune of 'American Pie'.

David's passion for human rights and the removal of discrimination, particularly but not only for people with disabilities, was almost unequalled. He gave much thought to the problem caused by the lack of a dedicated commissioner, and late in 1999 he approached me with a proposal. He had found a way to manage the unit's budget so that I could be appointed as a part-time deputy disability discrimination commissioner, to provide the expertise, experience and leadership on disability issues that the commission lacked. Given the way in which I was working on tribunals, this was an opportunity I jumped at and relished.

The role was officially to support the commissioner by providing some expertise and guidance in the disability area. But David and

I knew that it was much more. David wanted me to provide greater outside recognition of the disability role of the commission, to help re-energise the waning momentum of the DDA since Elizabeth's term had ended, and to work with his unit for greater policy progress towards the real change we knew the DDA could achieve. I couldn't have been happier.

*

Much groundwork in a range of discriminatory areas had already been done when I arrived at the commission, but I was able to work with the team to continue the momentum. Transport was perhaps the area where most progress had been achieved. In an early example in 1994, three people who use wheelchairs complained about inaccessible buses being purchased by the SA government. The commission made an interim order to prevent the purchase proceeding, and the complaint settled when the government announced that low-floor, fully accessible buses with ramps would come into use at the rate of one per week.

Similar complaints followed from around Australia. As a result, Accessible Transport Standards were developed, providing a timetable for some of the most major infrastructure change in Australia's history. The process was painstaking but necessary to get all stakeholders on board (pun intended!). The standards required that all vehicles newly entering public transport be accessible, and that percentages of accessible vehicles must increase over a 20-year period. Since their introduction in 2002, a number of states look like reaching 100 per cent accessible fleets well before the 20-year compliance target.

Transport systems began to accept that people with disabilities are part of the 'public' that they should serve. Standards for accessible public transport were approved in principle in 1996 (and formally by the parliament in 2002), and began to guide large-scale changes by many transport providers, including large investments in new vehicles and infrastructure.

The area of banking and finance also saw activity both before and after my arrival. The commission conducted an inquiry into electronic commerce for older Australians and Australians with disabilities. As a result of that inquiry, and in partnership with industry and people with disabilities, the Australian Bankers Association launched voluntary industry standards in 2002 with benchmarks for access. Some 14 years later they are overdue for review, but they form a solid platform on which to build.

Telecommunications is key in society today, and can be an area where people who are blind or deaf can be seriously disadvantaged. The decision in *Scott v Telstra* was an early landmark in the DDA's history, finding that, if Telstra provided telephones to people who could hear, it was also required to provide TTYs (teletypewriters) to people who were deaf. Since the mid-1990s a scheme has been in place to make these available.

The decision in *Maguire v SOCOG*, sadly not determined until after the Olympics, required the Sydney Organising Committee for the Olympic Games to pay Bruce Maguire $20,000 in damages when they failed to make their website accessible to people unable to read print. The ramifications of this decision have echoed loud and clear to the computer screens of web managers throughout Australia, and around the world. This was one of the issues on which I most frequently gave speeches in my early years as deputy commissioner.

The public inquiry we ran into the impact of digital mobile phones on people using hearing aids also had a positive result. This was one of the first DDA complaints dealt with as a public inquiry, because it raised issues of a broad systemic nature. It was conciliated, and all three mobile phone providers introduced schemes to replace or upgrade equipment for people using hearing aids when their digital mobiles caused interference to them.

Compliance with the DDA in the tertiary education sector was patchy at best. Some outstanding tertiary institutions accommodated students with disabilities in an exceptional manner. However, these institutions had to stretch their resources as more students with disabilities gravitated to them, because other tertiary institutions discouraged enrolment or continued participation by students with disabilities.

However, by early this century, more than half of Australia's universities had provided the commission with action plans under the DDA, varying from high-level frameworks for further planning to quite detailed action lists, with specific timelines. While an action plan is not a guarantee of the right actions, it is a public commitment to accountability for moving forward on access and equity.

Finally, and perhaps most importantly in my view, was the commission inquiry conducted on employment of people with disabilities, which concluded in 2005. Called WorkAbility, it clearly outlined the problems in this area, and set forward some excellent recommendations for solving them. Sadly, almost a decade later, the recommendations have largely not been implemented, and the issues remain the same.

In some respects, the power of the DDA as legislation is very strong. If the Federal Court upholds a complaint of discrimination, it can order essentially any action required to provide equitable access, or to compensate for discrimination – unless access would involve unjustifiable hardship. But at the same time, litigation and complaint processes are always going to be more limited in scope, and more expensive, than processes where potential respondents, and people with disabilities, work together to make systemic changes.

Standard-setting is particularly important in the disability discrimination area compared to areas like race and sex discrimination, because often equal access for people with disabilities is not simply a matter of removing discriminatory attitudes. With disability, there are more complicated issues of translating a desire to be accessible and inclusive into systems and facilities that people can actually use. Whether someone can enter a building, even if they cannot walk or pull open a door, depends on a host of practical details, not just on an organisation proclaiming a commitment to equality as a matter of principle. Therefore the negotiation of standards, or the running of public inquiries, where all parties sit around a table and negotiate on an equal basis, will usually achieve a more effective result.

The overarching question for me as deputy commissioner, as it had been in most of my work, was what sort of society do we want to be? For me, the answer is clear – we want to combine a commitment to excellence with a commitment to inclusiveness; we want all Australians to have a fair go; and we want to make the most of the abilities and potential of our diverse people, and that includes people with disabilities. As a team, the Disability Rights Unit did what we could to achieve this.

Sev Ozdowski was appointed human rights commissioner in late 2000, and the 'poor cousin' of disability was passed on to him as a second job. He held it for the next five years. Sev was the third commissioner who, while having the role, did not have an in-depth understanding of the lived experience of disability. However, he also did not seem to recognise that the team in the Disability Rights Unit had that understanding and strategic vision. His greatest contribution to the progress of change under the DDA came during the times when he let us get on with the job.

Unlike Chris and Susan, who recognised the benefit to the commission of my knowledge and skills, Sev appeared threatened by my presence. I was sad about this, because I accepted his role and had committed to work with him. However, his concerns were confirmed in his mind when I applied for the commissioner role at the end of his term, and he has not spoken to me since.

*

Sydney became a city of frantic construction activity for the two or three years before it hosted the Olympic Games – if construction had been recognised as an Olympic sport we would have been well on the way to gold. As a blind person who worked in the CBD every day, I found the process challenging as well as exciting. The noise and constant pavement replacement meant that my decision to get a guide dog was an even greater benefit to me. But it was impossible not to get caught up in the building excitement. And the fact that the Paralympics, a celebration of the sporting achievements of people with disabilities, was occurring just afterwards was an added bonus. Maureen and I managed to see the torch run past just a few blocks from our house early one morning, with three-year-old Rachel sitting on my shoulders.

The Olympic precinct was built with access in mind, although the access consultant must have been sick the day that the switchback queuing metal rails in front of the ticket boxes were constructed right over the top of the tactile ground-surface indicators intended to guide people who were blind directly to the ticket windows. The new railway lines built to the precinct, and the line to the airport, were both built accessibly. And bus fleets from around Australia were temporarily stripped of their accessible vehicles so that the games would be better served.

Maureen was a volunteer Olympic driver, ferrying officials here and there during the games. We did not attend many Olympic events, although I do recall a women's hockey game in which New Zealand were playing, where we loudly cheered: 'Come on, Bondi!' with many of the other Australians in the crowd. And I really enjoyed the weight-lifting event we saw, because the noises of the crowd, the weights rattling on the bar and the grunts of the contestants clearly told me whether the lift had been made successfully. I wasn't in the stadium when Cathy Freeman won gold, and did her iconic lap of honour carrying the Aboriginal flag, but I was riveted to Tim Lane's call of the race, and hearing repeats of it still gives me goose bumps.

As deputy commissioner, I was pleased to have the chance to be in the stadium for quite a few of the Paralympic events. As a person with a disability, it was incredibly exciting to hear my Paralympic Australian brothers and sisters cheered by the crowds as loudly and energetically as the Australian Olympians had been some weeks before.

The Olympics and Paralympics had a positive effect on the position in Australia of people with disabilities. Not only was there significant infrastructure improvement but, for a few weeks during the Paralympics, our Paralympians became Aussie heroes, and those of us who had not reached those heights basked in the reflected glory. Sadly, their achievements were not well remembered by many, and the legacy of more positive attitudes was not sustained.

*

I was still making a contribution in the broader blindness field, becoming president of the Royal Blind Society (RBS) in the late nineties. It had been recognised for some years that Australians who were blind or vision-impaired would be best served by one national blindness agency. This view was supported by Blind Citizens Australia, the national organisation of blind people, with which I was closely involved.

We had initially tried to draw in too many organisations, and the range of views and personal interests were too disparate to achieve a positive result. But the RBS board, which by then I chaired, was still keen to proceed. We adopted a strategy of trying to merge with one or two other large organisations, with the expectation that some or all of the smaller ones would follow. This proved to be correct.

We soon reached in-principle agreement for the merger of the RBS and Vision Australia Foundation. Word of these discussions got out in the blindness sector, as we had hoped it would and, two days later, the Royal Victorian Institute for the Blind asked to participate, and we readily agreed. I was appointed chair of the merger steering committee, which consisted of three nominees from each participating agency, and three nominees of Blind Citizens Australia.

I probably devoted one day a week to this work for the key 18 months of the merger and the start of Vision Australia, the new national organisation. I quickly recognised that not-for-profit mergers are far more complex than mergers or takeovers in the commercial world. In the latter, the bottom line is agreement on the dollars to be exchanged. But in the former, the process is achieved through garnering good will, finding common interests and approaches, and persuasion and negotiation. My skill set in all of these areas improved markedly.

It was a proud achievement for all involved when the merger was completed, and the first CEO – Gerard Menses – was appointed. Gerard came to us from the broader disability sector, and was not an employee of any of the existing organisations. This key appointment was the final of many tricky decisions to be negotiated through, and his protests at my debating technique described earlier did not limit my view of his strong capacity to carry out the role.

One of the first achievements of the newly merged organisation was running one of the television events of the year, *Carols by Candlelight* in the Myer Music Bowl in Melbourne. This had been a successful fundraiser by the Royal Victorian Institute for the Blind but, with changes at Channel Nine and with the merger taking place, the ball was almost dropped. It was well saved, though, by Carol Ireland, who came from the RBS to be Vision Australia's marketing and fundraising executive.

Carol and I worked together to ensure that the fundraiser not only continued but also placed people who were blind or vision-impaired in key roles during the carols performance. We knew that it was really important to use this television opportunity to show such people and what we could achieve. Carol suggested that I, as the new chair of the merged organisation, should make the one-minute pitch on behalf of Vision Australia to the hundreds of thousands of people in the Music Bowl, and the millions in the television audience. I jumped at the chance, but while only a short speech it had to be powerful, and this was the biggest audience I had faced by a long way.

It was tightly scripted, and we did test runs on a couple of occasions that afternoon, but the adrenalin was still pumping as I walked with Carol out onto the stage. I delivered the pitch – reading it in Braille, of course – and received warm applause as I left the stage. Once off-camera, we enjoyed a couple of champagnes, which made the early Christmas morning flight from Melbourne to Perth with Maureen and Rachel that little bit more testing.

*

In 2003, Maureen decided to offer herself for a contribution in local government. She threw herself into the task with her usual vigour and energy. The Ku-Ring-Gai Council electoral system, where she stood for the Roseville ward, was such that success is almost impossible to achieve without a running mate. Two people initially agreed to run with her, but for various reasons withdrew quite close to the nomination date.

Wanting to maximise her chances of success, and with minimal interest in local politics, I suggested that she add my name to the ticket. A wife-and-husband team may be seen by some as questionable but, since I had a public profile, I believed I could contribute to her voting tally. So our 'Rescue Roseville' campaign began, aimed at shifting the strong anti-development views on the council, and bringing some balance back to local decision-making. We didn't want to see that power swept away by a state government frustrated by the North Shore opposition to its share of the development Sydney needed to meet its significant growth.

As the campaign continued, and I began to conduct railway station clinics with the voters on my daily commute to work, I started to enjoy myself, and feel that I had a contribution to make to local government. Maureen's organisation was superb, and we ran a strong campaign.

However, no-one was more surprised than I was when Maureen called me several days after the election to tell me that, not only had she been elected, she had gained enough first preferences to have me elected as well.

I served on council for almost two years. I found it to be a small microcosm of state and federal politics where – as a result of the lesser remuneration and the larger numbers elected – some of the participants are significantly non-strategic, and driven by personal or sectional interests. However, I also worked with many who were committed to maintaining and improving their community, and it was just a question of finding the best compromise to achieve those goals.

I spent many nights and some days poring over council papers – in electronic versions, of course – and discussing the pros and cons of council direction and individual land use. I also spent time speaking with residents and developers, and my contemplative mornings spent on Roseville Station waiting for my train were often interrupted with people wanting to express one view or another on a particular matter before council. I learned how 'in your face' local grassroots politics could be. I only hope that my contribution to the process was worthwhile, given the amount of work I did and the insights I gained.

19
Parenting

In April 1998, eight months after Rachel's arrival, we moved from our house in Artarmon to a larger renovation project in Roseville. It rained the whole day of the move. When the removalists had left, we discovered that the back gutters on the roof of the house were blocked, and the rain was running down the inside of our back wall and pooling on the floor. So, donning my sailing wet-weather gear and getting the ladder from the garage, I climbed up to see if I could rectify the problem.

The sun made one of its rare cameo appearances for the day at about that time, and Maureen came out to advise and instruct on the gutter-cleaning from the ground, with Rachel in her arms. Rachel looked about her new surroundings, and spotted her dad, covered from head to toe in wet-weather gear, and standing on a ladder two to three metres above the ground, flinging down handfuls of wet dead leaves, dirt and bird droppings that had clearly been in situ for some time.

She puzzled about what she might do to remedy this situation, as Maureen could tell from the intensity of the frown on her little face. Then, haltingly but clearly she said: 'Bad Dad, off roof.'

Her first sentence took a minute or so to enunciate, but her meaning was crystal clear. She has been telling me what to do ever since.

*

As Rachel grew I was determined to continue my role in her parenting. A standard pram was never going to work for me. I couldn't see where the pram was going, and one of my hands was full with my guide dog harness. So we acquired a pram that could convert into a stroller, with a handle that flipped over the top so that it could be pulled as well as pushed. I held Jordie's harness in my left hand by my side or slightly in front of me, and reached back with my right to tow the pram. This caused a certain amount of body twisting, but I got the hang of it after a while.

I used to tug Rachel to a park nearer to our house on weekends and warm summer evenings. Jordie would mind the pram, and help me find it again if Rachel was being slightly uncooperative. Rachel would have me carry her, or just toddle, from one entertainment to the next – swings, merry-go-round, slippery dip. When I said it was time to go home, her toddling would become faster so that I could not catch her, but she always gave herself away with her happy giggling.

My constant fear of rolling the pram on the uneven Ku-Ring-Gai footpaths only became a reality on one occasion. I knew that I had really hurt Rachel because, rather than berating me for my poor driving, she cried. I took her home with a scratched face and sore arm, and was even more careful from then on.

*

After successfully establishing the Women in Business mentoring program, Maureen decided to go back to her first qualification of journalism. She took a job as a subeditor, first for a short time at

Fairfax and then for about ten years at News Limited. Once the stories are written for the paper, subs fact-check them, improve some of the grammar and set them out for inclusion in the newspaper. Most of their work does not start until later in the day, and they are the ones who 'put the paper to bed' or ensure it looks good before publication. For a few years Maureen worked that shift, starting at 6 pm and finishing at 2 am. This actually suited us, because I could get home from work and take over the night-time activities, ensuring that Leon had done homework and getting Rachel into bed – with a story, of course. I could then start things off in the morning, and hand over to Maureen before I went to work. We did not see as much of each other, but the kids got more of our time.

On one of those evenings when Rachel was about three, Maureen had gone to work and Rachel and I were playing out in the backyard before she went to bed.

'Dad, why don't you dare me to jump off this couch and onto the ground?' she challenged a number of times.

My repeated response was, 'Don't jump off that, Rachel, you will hurt yourself.'

Despite my entreaties she continued to jump. The last jump ended badly, as she fell and hit her shoulder on the edge of a low wooden coffee table. I was probably a little tired at the end of a long day, and annoyed with her because she had not done what she was told. My cursory response to her crying was that she should not have jumped, and that I would give her some Panadol and she could go to bed. I put her to bed as usual, but she was still whimpering a little as she went off to sleep. I thought no more of the jumping incident.

I got up early for work the next morning, and Rachel was not out of bed before I left. This was unusual, but not too much so. So I was shocked later that day when I called Maureen on a routine matter, to be told that Maureen had called an ambulance because Rachel was unable to sit up. She was carried out to the ambulance 'on Santa's sleigh' because they were concerned that it may be a neck injury. Thankfully, it was not.

When I came home that night, Rachel's little arm was in a sling, and to this day I am reminded of my heartless response when Rachel broke her collarbone.

*

Leon was 14 when Rachel arrived, so he too played a role in looking after her, and contributing to her learning and growing. Once he left school and went to graphic design college, he earned an income by looking after her one day a week. Leon has a great knowledge of nature and animals, learned both from his own dad and from his own interest. He shared this fascination with Rachel as she grew. He also loved to design and draw, and Rachel honed her creativity with his support.

Just before Rachel was born, we bought a house at Bar Point on the Hawkesbury River. It was an idyllic location, surrounded by bush and mountains and only approachable by water. We spent many happy weekends there as a family or with friends. We would drive up to Brooklyn on a Friday night, have fish and chips and a glass of wine at Lifeboat Seafood, and then take the five-kilometre boat trip up the river. You could feel the week's tiredness sloughing off like a worn-out skin as this process took place.

We had bought the house as part lifestyle and part investment. The lifestyle side worked really well for us. The investment was not so good. It was hard to obtain weekend or weekly tenants, repairs and breakages were expensive because tradies had to travel by boat, and – as both of our lives became busier – we just did not use the house enough to make it worthwhile. We sold it after a few years, but have missed it ever since.

*

There can be few scarier moments in the life of a parent than when your child becomes lost. Knowing where Rachel was when we were travelling by ourselves was a constant focus for me.

Imagine my reaction when, while at the Westfield shopping centre in Chatswood, I changed my mind about getting into a lift, and communicated that to Jordie but not to Rachel before the doors closed. She was in the lift going somewhere, and Jordie and I were not.

I tried to deal calmly with the situation, but failed. I just could not work out what to do next.

Should I catch another lift? At what floor would I get out? Should I report this immediately to Centre Management, and where would I do that? Should I call Maureen, and what could she do?

In the end, I was saved by the calmness of a mum, and the common sense of my daughter. The nearby mum walked up to me and put her hand on my arm.

'Hi,' she said, 'I just saw what happened. What is your daughter's name? You stay here and wait for her to come back, and I will go and report that she is lost.'

I told her the name, and agreed with her plan. But before she could leave the lift doors opened, and out popped an impatient four-year-old. I wasn't sure which of them I should hug first. Before I could decide, Rachel said: 'You and Jord were too slow, Dad, so I told the lady in the lift to push the three so I would come back. Come on, you promised to take me to Softplay.'

I thanked the mum and hurried off to enjoy a calming coffee while Rachel played among the little foam balls.

*

There is an important balance to achieve for a parent who is blind. The relationship is different to that of another parent, because the child has access to a lot of information that you do not have. I think it is okay to work with the child and use that information, but it is not okay to take away too much of that childhood freedom and lack of responsibility.

Maureen and I both worked to ensure that Rachel would be independent, and encouraged her to make her own decisions from an early age. Before she was two, Maureen would offer her clothing alternatives, and let her choose what she wanted to wear. If it was a cold day we would encourage her to wear something warmer, but not force the issue. We were not silly about this, but we wanted her to understand the consequences and learn from that experience.

I have tried to do the same thing in our relationship. We would talk about where we were going, and how we wanted to get there. I would often make decisions, but sometimes, even if I thought Rachel was wrong, we would follow through on her choice. Sometimes she was right, and other times we extended our travel as a result, but we both enjoyed the experience. The independent and mature young woman who now shares our house is proof of her capacity, and our parenting technique. Rachel has rarely been embarrassed or uncomfortable about being with me as a result of my disability, though she has certainly groaned sometimes at my behaviour as an embarrassing dad.

As she grew, Rachel and I travelled independently together. When she was smaller I would use my guide dog, but as she grew up we have walked together as Maureen and I do. We have both learned compromise as a result – me to be patient and wait when there are things that she wants to do or look at, she to have me walk with her and report back a little more frequently. As Maureen's and my trust in her has increased, the boundaries have moved further out. Inevitably we have not always got it right, and tensions have occurred, as they did with Leon and the stretchy wrist strap. But greater mutual trust has been a very worthwhile pay-off for this investment in effort.

20
Commissioner

It was a Sydney summer night you could taste in November 2005 as we drove to the Roseville shopping centre to buy fish and chips. This was a regular Thursday outing, and eight-year-old Rachel and I went into the shop to order while Maureen waited in the car.

My mobile phone rang, and I stepped outside to take the call. Several minutes later, after the call had ended, Rachel was amazed when – as she walked out of the shop carrying our order – I picked her up in my arms, fish and chips and all, and started jumping up and down in the air with excitement. Attorney-General Philip Ruddock had just called me to offer me the roles of human rights commissioner and disability discrimination commissioner.

Keeping the secret for the next two to three weeks was one of the hardest challenges I have faced. I had so many plans to discuss with my closest colleagues. But there's 'many a slip twixt cup and lip' when a decision such as that has not yet gone to Cabinet, so Maureen, Rachel and Leon were the only ones who knew until I had solid confirmation that Cabinet had approved my appointment.

I told David Mason and Michael Small at the commission before the announcement was made. They were very pleased, but not too surprised, as they knew I had applied. We immediately started plotting.

Next were my family. I told them the night before the announcement, as I was not quite sure that Dad in particular would be able to contain himself. Mum and Dad could not have been more proud, and Dad immediately started calling me 'commissioner' instead of 'magistrate', which he'd been using to acknowledge my tribunal work.

After that was the round of resignations to avoid conflicts of interest, perceived or real. I resigned from Ku-Ring-Gai Council the night before the announcement, causing a by-election. I reluctantly resigned as chair of Vision Australia. And I also resigned from all of my tribunal appointments.

By 2.30 pm on the day the attorney-general's media release announcing my appointment was due, David's frustration was building to a crescendo, and finally he screamed, 'Come on. Put out the bloody media release. There are only 1825 and a quarter days to go.' And that was the way we viewed my appointment. It was a limited time period, and we wanted to achieve as much as we possibly could. We lived like our hair was on fire.

As it happened, our window was widened, as I received further appointments extending my term until July 2014. But that sense of urgency always remained.

This was the job to which I had aspired for some time, because it gave me access to those levers I had dreamed about to improve society all of those years ago when I decided to study law. It remains the best job I have ever had.

*

The attorney-general agreed that I could devote equal time to my two roles as commissioner: human rights and disability discrimination.

I was determined that disability would not again be the poor cousin. Because of my deputy commissioner role, I had a better understanding of the organisation and its politics than probably anyone else appointed as commissioner, so I could hit the ground running.

I was determined to continually engage with Australians on human rights and disability, as I did not see how I could effectively advocate on an issue without an intimate understanding of how it affected people. So I networked constantly with relevant advocacy and support groups. Being 'as networked as a parrot' was the way David Mason would describe me if I was looking a little tired from long nights of such interaction.

I also engaged with ministers, shadow ministers and senior bureaucrats in the areas where I needed to work. It is easy for the commissioner to become just another advocate. There are already many advocacy groups in the community, and the commission needs to work with them, but not be part of them. There were times when I had to express views publicly, and sometimes those views differed from government views. At such times I tried to contact the minister or department before I made the statement, to give them the courtesy of having time to prepare their response. Often I received this courtesy in return.

I tried to build relationships each time I engaged with ministers and bureaucrats, and these relationships often paid me back. And sometimes, my disability could play to my advantage. I was sitting next to Brendan Nelson on a plane back from Canberra one evening when he was a junior minister. We greeted each other, and then got on with what we were doing. I heard him scribbling with his pen, which was clearly not working, as he tried to edit a speech. I turned and smiled in sympathy and, forgetting that my guide dog was on the floor next to me, he asked if he could borrow my pen.

Realising who he was asking, he squirmed a little in embarrassment. I assured him that he should not be embarrassed, and produced the pen I regularly kept in my pocket for signing documents.

'Keep that one, Minister,' I said, 'and you can tell your audience tonight that you wrote your speech with a blind man's pen.'

He never forgot the line, and we have worked well together ever since.

*

The commission has always had staff who are effective, committed to advancing human rights and passionate about their work. In fact, one of the problems we faced as commissioners was preventing staff from overworking.

I could not have asked for two better work colleagues than David Mason, managing the disability team, and Vanessa Lesnie, managing an equally powerful one in human rights. Vanessa is one of the best human rights and refugee lawyers with whom I have worked. She is smart, strategic, hardworking, and honest and direct. She is also an excellent manager, and the loyalty her team had for her was passed onto me. Knowing that internally things were in such good hands meant that I could focus externally more than I would have been able to if this had not been the case.

The commission had experienced significant budget cuts in the early days of the Howard government. This trend has continued until today, with some minor exceptions. I therefore knew that I would need to get maximum value from lessening resources.

One of my early initiatives was to change the role of my executive assistant. My computer skills, and the engagement strategy I was adopting, meant that I did not need a full-time level of administrative support, so I changed the role to an admin–policy mix. I then employed executive assistants who were young graduates looking for opportunities to learn and network as they advanced their careers. I knew that they would not stay in the job for long – around 18 months to two years – but the output I would get in that time, and the increased policy capacity, would pay me back for the inconvenience of a high turnover. This plan really worked for me, and there are now a number of young people progressing in their careers from whose energy and capacity our work benefited.

*

Perhaps because I was married to a journalist I knew that my roles would be more effective if I engaged heavily with the media. I was working with issues that did not play strongly across all strata of Australian society, and I needed to maximise impact. My first media adviser was outstanding – Janene MacDonald, who was already working at the commission, but had spent a significant time in the Canberra press gallery. The advice I received from her, and from Maureen, who was a journalist again working in the industry, was critical in showing me how to get my message across. Janene arranged some media training for me early on, but I learned much from her and Maureen's advice and experience.

One of the best pieces of their advice was to determine – at the beginning of work on any issue or any interview – what my message was, and ensure that I delivered that message. This seems obvious advice, but so many people do not take it. I learned that there was little harm in repeating my message over and over again, and I developed simple phrases to convey it. The three-word slogan has become a diminished form of this practice, particularly in recent politics, but the broader rule still applies.

I was always happy to background a journalist honestly, and give them contacts for other sources, sometimes of people who would not say the same things that I did. My objective was to get and keep the story running, not just push my side of it. I never refused to deal with a journalist because I did not like what they wrote or said. I sometimes told them that I did not like it, and civilly explained why, but then moved on and continued in the relationship.

I also never refused to engage with a particular media outlet, even when it was clear to me that they did not campaign for all of the issues for which I stood. *The Australian* and *The Daily Telegraph* are two examples, but I would put a number of shock jocks and radio hosts in the same category.

I found that pitching a story to one or two journalists was usually far more effective for me than putting out regular media releases. Most of the time these releases go straight to the trash – virtual or real – and are lost among the plethora of other similar missives. But once you have developed a relationship with a journalist, a phone call or text, followed up with something in writing, usually got me a better result.

*

The approaches of two men guided my time at the commission, and have guided me for much of my life. They are a man from South Africa and a man from Weemala, an institution for people with disabilities.

The man from South Africa is Zak Yacoob. He is a man of my age or older, of Indian descent (a 'coloured', in apartheid parlance), who is also blind. With those disadvantages, even post-apartheid his achievements are impressive. He was a lawyer, and a judge on the South African Constitutional Court. He gave the keynote address at the World Blind Union conference, which I attended in Cape Town in 2004.

The theme of his presentation was that, in order to be true to yourself in arguing for acceptance of your diversity, you have to accept the diversity of others. He told the story of a group of people with disabilities who sought to lobby against the inclusion of rights for gay and lesbian people in the new South African constitution. He had shown them how that contradicted their own demand for rights, and substantially weakened their own cause. This adoption of diversity, and acceptance of the rights of all, has been key to my work.

The man from Weemala is John Roarty. Weemala operated in Sydney for some time. Thankfully it, and many others like it, is now closed. It was a terrible place in which people such as John were confined for much of their lives, and his book *Captives of Care* is compelling reading.

Despite the disadvantage and isolation in which he lived much of his life, his commitment, determination and capacity to keep focus made him a role model for me. He had a great capacity to test proposals by whether they were going to improve the lives of people with disabilities. He focused on the impact on people, rather than the policy itself and what it would change. And he told stories of that change.

John would ask, and I did too: 'Will this improve our chances of employment? Has our accommodation improved? Has our access to public buildings and community facilities improved? Has our transport improved? Have our opportunities in education improved? Have welfare provisions for us improved? Are we more integrated into the community? Does the community have a better attitude towards us, as people with disabilities?'

The final chapters of my book show how I both applied the lessons I learned from Zak Yacoob and examined the questions John raised in my work at the commission.

21
Human rights

In November 2008 I gave a speech, crafted by Krista Lee-Jones, to the Henry Parkes Primary Schools Citizenship Convention. We used examples from Dr Seuss's books to illustrate human rights to these children. For example, *Horton Hears a Who!* illustrates the Universal Declaration of Human Rights. The arrogant turtle king in *Yertle the Turtle*, who forces other turtles to stand on each other's backs so that he has a higher throne, is toppled when a turtle at the bottom stands up for his rights with a burp. Diversity is applauded in *One Fish Two Fish Red Fish Blue Fish*, while *Oh, the Places You'll Go!* expresses the rights to freedom of expression and movement, and so on.

While these examples are fun, I worked seriously to communicate human rights in creative ways that would resonate with particular audiences. This must continue to be done if we are to convince the Australian community that human rights are for everyone, everywhere, every day.

*

The commission's decision to initiate a national inquiry on entitlements for same-sex couples was the first in which I took part as human rights commissioner. National inquiries such as this are resource intensive, and the challenge for the commission is deciding which of the many areas needing attention should gain this level of focus. But this discrimination was clear, patently unfair and relatively easy to address. The decision was a no-brainer.

The only difficult strategic decision was whether our inquiry should include the issue of same-sex marriage. Clearly, the barring of marriage based on sexual orientation is just as discriminatory as the economic discrimination on which we focused. We had to make a judgment call about whether including marriage would be a bridge too far and mean that we achieved nothing from the inquiry as a result.

In the end, I took the view that 70 per cent of something was better than 100 per cent of nothing, so we left out the issue of marriage. I was often criticised for this decision during the inquiry. But the current opposition expressed by conservative politicians – completely out of sync with the clearly stated public view in Australia, and some ten years after our inquiry – demonstrates that our judgment was probably correct.

Equal rights should be available for gay and lesbian couples to access the financial entitlements and work benefits that heterosexual couples take for granted. The right to non-discrimination and the right to equality before the law are two of the most fundamental principles of human rights law. Yet a raft of laws on Australia's books clearly denied certain rights to same-sex couples, in areas such as tax, superannuation, Medicare, aged care, social security and immigration. Our goal was to identify those discriminatory laws, explain the impact of those laws on real people, and recommend changes to those laws so that the discrimination disappeared.

During our hearings, we heard stories from many people against whom these laws discriminated.

In Sydney, Michael told us about the discrimination he faced after the death of his same-sex de facto spouse. At the time his partner died, Michael could not be noted on his partner's death certificate. He said: 'The exclusion from my partner's death certificate placed me in a very precarious situation when proving the existence of our relationship to a host of financial institutions and government bodies. I was excluded financially on more than one occasion from claiming monies that were in both our names, and some in his name only, until I could prove by other means that the relationship existed.'

In Melbourne we heard from some gay dads, Lee and Tony. They pointed out that there were many areas of government support to which they do not have access: 'We do not have access to the Medicare safety net as a family. We can not income split, share tax obligations or participate in superannuation incentives applicable to a heterosexual-headed family, especially where one spouse stays at home to look after the children (as has been the case with us).'

In Adelaide, we heard from Sue and Leanne, who had just become the parents of a five-week-old child. They had been together for eight and a half years. They contributed to the community through volunteer work, donations, and providing respite care to a foster child. They found it frustrating that they were allowed to care for foster children, yet they were not allowed to adopt children, or access assisted reproductive technology. Leanne said: 'We are an average suburban family. We are working hard and contributing to our community. We don't want special treatment – just what others can expect from their legal and social community. Our rights are denied simply because of who we love. We just want equality.'

Lynne, another lesbian parent, made a similar plea: 'I am not a second-class citizen, and resent my family and I being treated as such. All I ask is to be treated equally, no more and no less than any other Australian. Just equal.'

The purpose of conducting a national inquiry is to make sure that stories like this are heard loud and clear. The commission could easily produce a report, with recommendations about new laws, without leaving the offices in central Sydney. But there is little point in that. The commission needs to tell the government, and the community at large, that laws which discriminate have a real impact on real people. That is what we did.

Our report came out in June 2007, with an election due by the end of that year. Vanessa Lesnie and her human rights team had spent days and weeks researching more than 100 Commonwealth laws that discriminated against couples on the grounds of their sexual orientation. We developed proposals to amend those laws, which were all included in the report.

We worked hard, in conjunction with the GLBTIQ community, with Howard-government Cabinet ministers, many of whom were very supportive of our recommendations, to have them promise that they would enact the changes. That promise never came.

We and the community also worked hard with shadow ministers. When the Rudd government was elected, one of the first things Attorney-General Robert McClelland did was move to enact the proposals included in our report. They came into effect in mid-2008.

One of the problems with many commission inquiries is that the hard work of the inquiry is done, and the reports sit on the shelf and are not acted upon. Thankfully, that did not occur with this inquiry.

Some of those tears, which had been in my eyes at the hearings, returned as I proudly stood with my good friend Sharon Young in the back of the commission float in the Sydney Mardi Gras parade for two years in a row. We campaigned for the changes in 2007, and celebrated their enactment a year later. No longer were same-sex-attracted people economically discriminated against simply because of who they loved.

*

As human rights commissioner I led three inspections of Australia's immigration detention centres, and the human rights team prepared three reports on our inspections, which were provided to the Department of Immigration and the Howard and Rudd governments.

This process involved many interactions with people left in a form of purgatory, with little knowledge of when their situation might change. They were kept, in the main, in prison-like conditions, yet had committed no crime. They were referred to by the contractors who ran the centres as clients, when they were actually detainees. And as conditions became worse and more crowded, even the dignity of their names were taken away, and they were referred to by numbers.

As they told me, they reluctantly fled from the hell of their own countries to the purgatory of ours. This is not the Australia of which I am proud.

I find writing about this area of Australia's policy very hard. First, as an unashamedly proud Australian, I am profoundly ashamed of our record in this area. Vulnerable people, so vulnerable that they chose to flee their country of birth (which in most cases must be a decision made out of pure desperation), undertake a sometimes perilous journey, and arrive on our shores seeking asylum. Of course we need to do security and health checks, but we should welcome them in first. As individuals we would welcome our neighbours if they arrived at our house in such a state. But we lock them up – either in Australia or offshore – and give them little or no prospect of release.

Second, I met many of these people when I visited immigration detention centres. That was the toughest gig I had at the commission, and my memories of it are of overwhelming sadness.

Third, unlike most of the other areas of human rights in which I have worked, I see little potential to find a pathway towards change. Most politicians, in most areas of politics, show no propensity to change. Whether the reasons are principled, pragmatic and poll-driven, that is the case. We lack the vision of a Malcolm Fraser to take us in a different direction. I've spent my life finding a way, but this path is not clear to me.

So I have decided to turn to a creative approach. The rest of this chapter comes from the voices of asylum seekers and those who support their cause. Read these poems and then make your decision. I pray that in the future we will see the leadership and compassion that Australia so generously shares in lots of other areas, and that I and many others crave in this one.

Treasure Island, a sonnet
Within our happy harbourside retreat
we put on show of affluence and glee
and round the barbie with our friends we meet
or watch the footy final on TV.

Our leaders stop the boats, turn back the tide
of those who seek to storm our golden gates,
to let them know that God's not on their side
nor will we ever count them as our mates.

With every boat that sinks our grief's untold,
the smugglers just don't care they're overfull,
so join the queue, no need to bribe with gold
and get a proper visa in Kabul

or if we must, illegals to prevent
we'll just excise the whole damn continent.

by Brendan Doyle

Blind tiger
They repatriated this security risk.
You'll be safe back home,

they assured him, *the war's over.*

He knew about the war,
forced to fight when still a child.
And he knew about *over.*

Over was why he risked death
to escape to a place
that sounded so safe and festive:

Christmas Island. Only he was flown
to another island where men
hung from beams like strange fruit.

Now he sits on a footpath
begging for coins, his eyes
punched out by bicycle spokes.

You'll be safe there, they growled,
the war's over. He knows
what it means to be blind.

by Rob Wallis

Mother

Mother, again tonight I thought about you,
I imagined you in front of me sitting and listening to my
    sorrows my griefs my sadness,
When I groaned you took my head and patted it,
Guided me not to lose hope, not to give up,
To stand like steel and to spend happy times with my friends,
To learn from my time.
But what should I do

When I think about you I become sad,
You are not near me to hug me to kiss me to advise me,
Before I lose my life before I die,
I wish to worship my heaven which is your feet,
I wish to worship you before I die, before I pass away, before I
    leave this world.

by M, 15 years old, detained 13 months

One strong woman to another
Let us look forward.
We will get our chance one day.
And we will be called by our beautiful names.

We didn't come by illegal way.
We are not illegal.
We cry and cry.

No-one gives us a tissue.
We are refugees.
Flashbacks take us back

Where we cannot go.
Where can we go forward?
They will not let us settle.

Let us be strong.
Let us forget numbers
Let us call out
our beautiful names.

by Asmine (Darwin)

22

Race discrimination

When Tom Calma's term as Aboriginal and Torres Strait Islander (ATSI) social justice commissioner and race discrimination commissioner came to an end in early 2009, Attorney-General Robert McClelland approached me. He wanted to appoint the next ATSI commissioner, but wanted them to work full-time in just that role. Given the issues facing Aboriginal people, this was a very understandable view.

He asked me if I would resign as human rights commissioner and take on the role of race discrimination commissioner instead, as well as continuing my disability discrimination commissioner role. The human rights commissioner role could be carried out by the president of the commission, then Cathy Branson.

I thought carefully about this request. I was not sure how comfortable I was taking on this portfolio, given my experience as a white Anglo-Saxon Australian. But then I formed the view that I had worked hard to represent issues experienced by people who were same-sex attracted, and by asylum seekers, and that I could do the same in this portfolio.

I was also concerned that my term would end in about 18 months, and that this was not really long enough to do justice to a new portfolio. The attorney-general understood this concern, so extended my term, giving me another three years in both roles. I was ably supported by an excellent policy adviser in Amy Lamoin.

As federal disability discrimination commissioner, and a life-long disability advocate, I know the importance of using my own voice to tell my own story. The mantra of the disability sector is: 'Nothing about us without us.' There's no substitute for representative voices.

I did not have the same experience of discrimination that many in Australia had – discrimination, exclusion and unfair treatment based on race, ethnicity, colour or faith. I thought it was important to acknowledge this throughout my term.

I saw my role as race discrimination commissioner as being based on a partnership with my community stakeholders. I consulted heavily – which I know can be a burden on community groups, who already feel over-consulted, but not listened to, or not understood. I also sought to respectfully tell people's stories, illustrating and practically communicating important principles, gaps and risks through these stories.

Multiculturalism is Australia's norm. It has been for over two hundred years. With generations of migrants, and generations of people born to migrant parents, multiculturalism has been our past. It's our present – 50 per cent of Australians are born overseas or have an overseas-born parent. And it's also our certain future. Once we accept this, we'll realise that igniting and exploiting cultural or religious differences for the purpose of political expediency is the most dangerous legacy that governments, or politicians, can bestow, because it fractures our identity and constrains our development.

We need to delve into our collective wisdom, both ancient and modern – our stories – to find a shared solution for racism. We need a clear, considered and contemporary conversation about race, racism and race relations in Australia that properly recognises our individual and national connections to our region and the world. We need firm, bipartisan commitment to racial equality in Australia, and a durable plan to achieve it. It's often convenient to defer to our governments, but governments alone won't get us there. This is a serious conversation for us all.

*

When I think back over my time as race discrimination commissioner, the question I was most commonly asked was: 'Is Australia racist?' How do you answer that question without buying into the very headline, the divisive news grab, the quick political quip?

Figures often tell a clearer story than prose. The Challenging Racism Project research, released in March 2011, measured racist attitudes and experiences of racism in Australia. It was collected through telephone surveys, over a 12-year period. It found that around 85 per cent of respondents believed racism to be a problem in Australia. Around 20 per cent – roughly equivalent to the population of Sydney – had experienced forms of race-hate talk such as verbal abuse, name-calling, racial slurs, offensive gestures and so on. Around 17.5 per cent had experienced race-based exclusion from their workplaces and/or social activities; and around 17 per cent – roughly the population of Queensland – had experiences of racism in education.

While 12 per cent of respondents self-diagnosed, or admitted, their own racism, it's a much lower figure than the 33 per cent who admitted to being racist in Europe in a similar study. Meanwhile, 41 per cent of Australians had a narrow view of who belongs in Australia; and the same percentage of Australians had some anxiety about multiculturalism.

Aboriginal and Torres Strait Islander respondents returned much higher rates of experiences of racism. When it came to issues like contact with police and seeking housing, their experiences of racism were four times that of non-Aboriginal Australians. People born overseas also reported experiencing higher rates of racism than those born here. They were twice as likely to experience racism in the workplace, with some birthplace groups, such as those born in India and Sri Lanka, reporting even higher rates of racism.

In May 2009, over 4,000 students from Indian backgrounds staged a protest in Melbourne's Federation Square. They claimed that recent attacks on Indian students were motivated by racism, and that the government was not responding adequately. This followed an April 2008 protest outside Flinders Street Station staged by 500 taxi drivers from Indian backgrounds. It was in response to the death of a taxi driver of Indian descent, and called for improved safety measures. A month later, around 50 taxi drivers protested in response to another serious assault.

The Rudd government quickly dismissed the possibility that racism was the cause, or even a factor, in the attacks on international students. They referred to Australia's zero tolerance for racism. State governments followed suit.

This denial silenced people who had legitimate reasons to feel aggrieved, and showed that we dismissed, discounted and denied their stories. These negative public discussions about international students showed the rise of an outsider status for certain people in Australian society. Desperate people seeking asylum became queue-jumpers, while people who wore cultural dress became a threat. In places such as the WACA and the MCG – hallowed ground to many Australians – crowds vilified players for the colour of their skin. Such encouragement of an outsider status keeps the outsider vulnerable and disconnected. And it makes our societies fragmented and unequal, which means nobody wins.

*

One of the biggest experiences I had as race discrimination commissioner, and sadly one of the times where I felt least proud to be an Australian, was in Geneva in 2010, when Australia appeared before the United Nations Committee on the Elimination of Racial Discrimination.

Two Aboriginal elders also attended that session. They travelled for over 40 hours from their remote communities in the Northern Territory to deliver a pressing message to the committee about the survival of their Aboriginal brothers and sisters, and sons and daughters, who were living under the Northern Territory Intervention. They decided to participate in the session because 'we hoped it would ease our own and our communities' despair'. They said that they felt a need to step back from the Intervention to see 'what is left of us mob'. No community should ever have to ask this question – but particularly not a community whom we dispossessed 200 years ago.

These two elders obviously couldn't speak on behalf of all people who lived under the Intervention. However, they are both trusted community leaders, and some of the language that they used to describe their communities' experiences included 'loss and losing', 'grief', 'brokenness', 'numbness', 'fear', 'the death of feeling', 'the death of dreaming'.

In 2011, I visited some of the communities affected by the Intervention. As you enter them, you're greeted by tall blue signs that say: 'Warning: Prescribed Area, No Liquor – No Pornography.' These communities are people's homes. In sessions with the UN committee members, these two elders described the shame and humiliation they felt living between those tall blue signs. With their stories, the elders engaged the committee members in a way that I couldn't. They gave the process a level of legitimacy that I couldn't, because of their direct, lived experience under the Intervention.

The Northern Territory Emergency Response legislation – all five Bills and 480 pages of it – contained far-reaching measures, including suspension of the *Racial Discrimination Act 1975*. I don't dispute that the government has an obligation to promote and protect the right of Aboriginal people to be free from family violence and child abuse. However, I don't accept that to take the urgent action required, it was necessary to discriminate on the basis of race. Less restrictive and non-discriminatory action could have been taken to protect the rights of children and families. The entire legislative process – including a Senate inquiry – took ten days. This was a scandalously abbreviated parliamentary process, with no Aboriginal representative in parliament at the time.

The UN committee and special rapporteur branded the Intervention as racist, as did many of the people living under its terms. Throughout my term as race discrimination commissioner, I was concerned about the use, or misuse, of the provision of the *Racial Discrimination Act 1975* that allows the government to take 'special measures' for Aboriginal and Torres Strait Islander peoples. Delivering standard services to Aboriginal communities, that are available to all other Australian citizens, cannot be properly considered as special measures. It's wrong thinking that disregards the rights and diminishes the citizenship of all Aboriginal and Torres Strait Islander peoples.

*

There were some positive achievements during my time as race discrimination commissioner.

The first was the Rudd government's endorsement of the Declaration on the Rights of Indigenous Peoples on 3 April 2009. This declaration contains the minimum standards for the survival, wellbeing and dignity of Indigenous peoples. My colleague commissioner Mick Gooda identified achieving the aims of the declaration as a key priority for his term as social justice commissioner.

Second, in July 2011, the National Congress of Australia's First Peoples became operational. This gives Aboriginal and Torres Strait Islander peoples a say on the issues that are important to them. The commission was very proud to have assisted with the creation of the congress, through the work of the previous social justice commissioner, Tom Calma. Once again, there is a credible national platform for Aboriginal and Torres Strait Islander voices.

Third, in March 2011, the Gillard government launched its national multicultural policy, *The People of Australia*. This was the first effective national multicultural policy for more than a decade. It identified multiculturalism as a social norm, and a firm part of Australia's future; established the Australian Multicultural Council; and committed the government to examine the responsiveness of government services to clients from culturally and linguistically diverse backgrounds.

This was particularly important for new and emerging communities in Australia, such as African–Australian communities. In 2010, the commission produced the *In Our Own Words* report about the experiences of African–Australians. I attended some of the consultations, and was ashamed that when Australia welcomes new communities we don't follow what my mother always told me, and learn from our past mistakes.

The multicultural policy also committed to the development of a National Anti-Racism Strategy. There's a clear need for such a strategy, which must be sustained, and evidence-based. And the commission, with a full-time race discrimination commissioner, had a leadership role in its development.

*

Our future is online. More and more of us are connected more and more of the time. In most respects, these developments in technology are welcome. In fact, as a blind person, I couldn't do my job without them. They have connected the world's indigenous peoples, as well as ethnic minority groups, in a way that they've never been connected before – to share stories, coordinate their work and collectively organise.

However, this technology can also be used to cause serious harm. The proliferation of race-hate websites and online materials breed and incite real-world hatred. Complaints of cyber-racism more than doubled during my term as race discrimination commissioner. Cyber-racism can cause huge damage to victims, mental and physical. It's the same old racism in a new space, but with increased potential for anonymity, exponential capacity to go viral, and a complex inter-jurisdictional environment. Many organisations, here and overseas, are running effective anti-bullying programs and campaigns. The commission has had some success with discrimination complaints, and material and sites are being taken down.

Just like that broader conversation on racism, tackling cyber-racism will require partnerships between government, social networking sites and internet service providers, and the community. And it will require members of connected communities to stand up and say it's not okay.

This was a major message I pushed during my time as the race discrimination commissioner. We're all responsible for naming, and saying no to, racism. We must call it when we see it. We must call it when the talkback show host, the internet friend, or the person sitting next to us, starts their sentence with the seemingly innocent, but loaded phrase: 'I'm not racist, but ...'

Such a denial of racism is just a soft form of racism itself.

There's been a tendency to name race as a problem in this country. And in doing that, we've named some cultures as the problem.

But the real problem is not reaching full equality. We need to act together, without delay, to eradicate racism and racial inequality in all its forms – to find a solution. This is how a real zero-tolerance approach to racism would look.

23
The Disability Rights Convention

Much time in our community, and our legal system, is focused on punishing people who travel while intoxicated. The majority of them drive cars, although the Australian Road Rules do make it an offence to be drunk in charge of a wheelchair. People have been caught drunk in charge of a horse or camel. But I wonder if anyone has been charged with being drunk in charge of a dog, particularly a guide dog.

Come back with me to New York in August 2006. It was a warm Friday evening, and the United Nations Ad Hoc Working Group on a Comprehensive and Integral International Convention on the Protection and Promotion of the Rights and Dignity of Persons with Disabilities (you've gotta love the UN – why use three words when you could use 27?) had just agreed on the draft text of the Disability Rights Convention.

The excitement was palpable, and as my friend Kevin Cocks, who went on to become Queensland's anti-discrimination commissioner, put it: 'I was so full of emotion that some of it leaked out and ran down my cheek.' Cheering, applause, handshakes, kisses and hugs were in abundance throughout the room.

It will surprise no-one that festivities moved from the somewhat staid surroundings of the UN building to a range of hotels nearby. The Australian watering-hole of choice for the occasion was the Wheeltapper Inn, an Irish pub on 44th Street. So my guide dog Jordie and I joined the happy throng there.

Backs were slapped, rounds were bought and consumed, and the revelry continued. At one point I was called outside to do an ABC radio interview about the convention, and when asked whether I was pleased with the result I replied that I was elated, adding an expletive that rhymes with trucking. The considerate ABC journalist, to whom I have given a number of 'exclusives' since, suggested that I might wish to repeat my answer, and the first version hit whatever is the equivalent of the cutting-room floor in the digital world. I have since instituted my 'two drinks, no interviews' policy.

I was booked on an early flight home the next day, so at about 9 pm Jordie and I prudently returned to our hotel to pack. This task was completed before 10 pm, but the beer-fuelled adrenalin was still pumping through my veins, so I – perhaps less prudently – returned to the Wheeltapper to find the celebrations still in full swing. Thinking that I had a long plane flight during which I could sleep, and knowing we had successfully come to the end of five years of hard work, I enthusiastically rejoined the party.

My early days as a cricketer taught me that 'what goes on tour stays on tour', so I will not provide further details of the Australian delegation's Irish pub activities. It is rumoured that I enthusiastically delivered a post–witching hour version of the well-known Australian ballad 'The Man from Ironbark' to the whole bar – complete with translations of Australian idioms – but I'm sure this can't be true.

My watch must have malfunctioned during the celebrations, because the time it showed when I decided to return to my hotel had little connection with my reality. Still, I felt fine, and was confident of a few hours' sleep before my airport departure.

However, when I walked out of the Irish pub smog, and into the New York night air, things did not seem quite as clear. Somehow I had completely forgotten the location of the hotel where I had been staying for two weeks. So I did the only thing possible – leaned down, patted my guide dog on the head, and said: 'Take me home, Jordie.'

Three street blocks and two avenue blocks later, we walked confidently into the hotel foyer, where I promptly knelt and gave Jordie a big hug. She gave me a happy lick in response, appreciating praise for a job well done. My 'drunk in charge of a dog' experience had escaped the notice of the watchful New York constabulary.

*

A book like this is not the place to chronicle the tortuous process of crafting a multilateral treaty such as the Disability Rights Convention. Suffice to say that representatives from around 80 countries sat in a very large committee room in the UN for eight drafting sessions, each lasting for two to three weeks at a time, to get the job done. I was proud to be in that room, representing Australia, for all of those sessions.

The UN process is a gradual one. I joke that the formal sessions are 90 per cent boring and 10 per cent absolutely fascinating. You have to pay attention all the time so that you don't miss the important bits.

UN negotiations are about compromise. As Ambassador Don McKay from New Zealand, who was the most effective of our chairs, repeated often: 'The perfect is the enemy of the good.'

While he was not in the room in New York, David Mason figuratively sat on my shoulder throughout the process. I would draft notes of each day's activities, and email them back to him, sometimes from my hotel room that night, and in later years from the UN Committee Room itself. David would read these, and the reports of the day that were available on the internet, while I slept that night. In the morning, I would wake to his excellent emails providing analysis and guidance for the next day's discussions. It was almost like having him there.

*

Calls had been made since the early eighties, with little success, for the UN to adopt a convention recognising the rights of people with a disability. However, the pressure gradually built, and in December 2001, the UN General Assembly finally, and with overwhelming support, decided to adopt a resolution to develop a disability convention.

While five years of negotiation may seem a long time, it was one of the quickest UN treaties ever negotiated. The UN, for example, recently concluded a negotiation process over a declaration on the rights of indigenous peoples that took more than 20 years.

It was also, in UN terms, a revolutionary process, as it involved a high level of participation both by nation states and civil society. The development of the convention involved the highest level of participation by representatives of people with disabilities of any human rights convention, or indeed any other UN process, in history.

Australia did not initially support the development of a disability-specific convention. These were particularly difficult riding instructions for the Australian delegation to work with the first time we went to New York. However, following positive reports of the process by the delegation, on our return I met with Attorney-General Philip Ruddock to discuss the process.

Ruddock always carefully listened to what people had to say to him, and weighed it with the other information before him. I talked to him about how the convention could be a good-news story for Australia and the government. As a country with relatively forward-thinking disability discrimination legislation we could bring other countries with us, and improve the circumstances of many other people with disabilities throughout the world. I had done my homework, and shared with him my own experiences as a person with a disability, and referred to the experiences of his sister who also had a disability. The departmental representatives in the first Australian delegation gave him similar advice.

It is impossible in such situations to know exactly which argument changed his mind, but the government changed its position. We went to the second drafting session in support of a convention.

The development of the convention was particularly rewarding as the Australian delegation and non-government organisations took an active role in the negotiation process. We offered numerous constructive proposals on a wide variety of issues. Australian disability organisations punched well above their weight in their contribution to the process. I can confirm this because, as a member of the official Australian delegation, we worked together most of the time, and on some occasions they – quite appropriately – punched me.

*

The Convention on the Rights of Persons with Disabilities sets out the fundamental human rights of people with disabilities. It states general and specific obligations that aim to protect different types of rights: civil and political rights, economic, social and cultural rights, and rights to development. A state, in UN terms, is a country.

The convention contains traditional human rights concepts. It outlaws discrimination in all areas of life, including employment, education, health services, transportation and access to justice. It also deals with freedom. Freedom has two faces: there is 'freedom from', for example, discrimination, harassment, victimisation and so on. There is also 'freedom to', which includes freedom to participate fully in education, employment, the benefit of services and facilities, and artistic and cultural life.

The convention has added, modified and transformed traditional rights concepts to give them a more specific disability focus. Article 21, the right to 'Freedom of expression and opinion and access to information', extends the protection against state interference with personal opinion and expression into the positive state obligation to provide public information in accessible formats. The state is required to recognise sign languages, Braille, and augmentative and alternative communication.

It also translates the concept of liberty of movement into a requirement that public spaces and buildings be accessible to persons with disabilities. This right to 'accessibility' appears as a stand-alone article and as a principle underpinning the convention as a whole.

The convention also provides a right to 'personal mobility'. This article requires states to take effective measures to ensure that persons with disability enjoy the greatest possible personal mobility and independence. They are required to ensure that mobility aids, devices, assistive technologies and forms of live assistance and intermediaries necessary for personal mobility are of good quality, and are available at an affordable cost.

Although these articles spring from the principle of non-discrimination, and the right to liberty of the person respectively, their formulation transcends any previously existing human rights document.

The Convention on the Rights of People with Disability recognises the dignity and human rights of people with disabilities. Such international recognition is necessary and long overdue. It completes the human rights jigsaw for people with disabilities.

After those many weeks of negotiation, the convention was

adopted by the UN General Assembly on 13 December 2006. Kofi Annan, then the UN secretary-general, said: 'Today promises to be the dawn of a new era – an era in which disabled people will no longer have to endure the discriminatory practices and attitudes that have been permitted to prevail for all too long.'

The signing of the convention by the Australian government was an important symbolic step for disability rights in Australia. Its ratification was more than symbolic. It was a legal step. It made a commitment to our international colleagues, which reinforced the national laws we already had in place.

*

I still remember the day the convention was signed by Australia. We were not the first to sign, unlike Jamaica, which sprinted in true Usain Bolt style to ratify it on day one, while the rest of us were still marching into the stadium. It was 30 March 2007. At 1.40 am on a Saturday morning, Sydney time – Friday, New York time. I was having a few glasses of wine, watching online as Australia lined up with 80 other signing countries at the UN in New York. Yes, it's a bit of a tragic life I lead. But rest assured I wasn't the only one: David Mason admitted to me the following Monday morning that he had done just the same thing – although with a few gin and tonics instead. Clearly we all need to get out more.

Australia was among the first countries to sign the convention. Don McKay, the chair of the committee that negotiated the convention, summarised its basic purpose: 'What the Convention endeavours to do is to elaborate in detail the rights of persons with disabilities, and set out a code of implementation.'

My contribution to a major international instrument was completed. But once signed and ratified by Australia, the work had just begun.

The benefits that this convention should bring to Australians with disabilities are yet to be fully realised. There are some arguments for further legislative change. The main work must be done not by the law, but by policy. Federal and state governments need to fully recognise the rights and freedoms of Australians with disabilities as set out in the convention. As the late French human rights lawyer René Cassin said: 'It would be deceiving the peoples of the world to let them think that a legal provision was all that was required … when in fact an entire social structure had to be transformed.'

24
Transport

Jetstar treated a group of people with multiple sclerosis disgracefully in 2014 – refusing to let them fly because of its 'two wheelchairs' policy. This policy, applied by budget airlines such as Jetstar, Virgin and Tiger, is that – because fewer staff are available, and turnaround times are shorter – only two people using wheelchairs can be assisted onto the plane, and only two wheelchairs stored in the hold. So if you're the third wheelchair user to check in, you don't fly, even if you have a pre-existing booking.

Let's just imagine that it is the objective of airline executives to have fewer people on their planes.

Babies have equipment – prams and strollers – that needs to be stored in the hold, and they need assistance onto the aircraft. So let's only have two of them. Think of the benefits – much less distraction from babies crying, and no sooky baby talk from parents and other admirers in the seat next to you.

But why stop there? Footballers usually carry a lot of equipment. And while most of them can get onto planes under their own steam, some need assistance off the plane after enjoying the alcoholic benefits of business class. Now I know you'll say that limiting them to two per flight would mean an AFL team of 20 would have to fly to their games on ten separate planes. But this is really a small sacrifice to make in the cause of meeting the needs of airlines.

But wait, there's more. How about two parliamentarians? They usually carry a lot of political baggage, and probably expect assistance on and off the plane, whether they need it or not.

And finally, let's only have two airline executives. They would need large bags to carry the substantial salaries they earn, as they busily retrench Australian workers, and I'm sure they need some kind of assistance.

In fact, let's just rename it the Noah's policy; as in, 'no assistance', and have only two of everything on each plane. After all, given the way the airlines treat Australians with disabilities, we might as well be travelling in the time of Noah's Ark.

*

It's not just people who use wheelchairs who get a bad deal from airlines. As the *Flight Closed* report, prepared by the Public Interest Advocacy Centre, detailed, Australians with disabilities are not served well. Our governments have chosen a very hands-off approach, not regulating in this area.

I, and the rest of the disability sector, lobbied extensively for the whole time I was commissioner. Sadly, we were not successful. The Department of Transport's Aviation Access Working Group was the only government committee from which I publicly resigned during my term. That group's capacity to avoid, delay and otherwise dodge any effective action to improve the travel experience for people with disabilities was legendary in the disability sector.

Much of the problem is one of attitude – a limiting and negative attitude by many airline staff towards people with disabilities. It was typified when, on one of my visits to New York for work on the disability convention, I walked onto the aircraft and directed my guide dog onto the piece of floor next to my seat. A concerned flight attendant bustled up and said: 'Oh, you can't put your dog there. That seat is reserved for Commissioner Innes.'

'I don't think he'll mind,' I said, as I smiled and handed her my passport.

*

In many ways taxis provide the most flexible kind of public transport – they can come to where you want them and go to where you want them, at the time that you want them. The one unattractive feature that they have – no, it's not the drivers, the drivers' opinions, or what is playing on the radio – is the cost. So the decision about catching taxis is a balance of cost versus convenience.

This is also true for people with disabilities. The difference is that, for us, our choices – both for public transport in general and for taxis in particular – are much more limited. For us, there is less access to other public transport, and for many people with disabilities there is less access to taxis.

The *Disability Standards for Accessible Public Transport* (Accessible Transport Standards) – passed in 2002 under the *Disability Discrimination Act 1992* when I was deputy commissioner – apply to taxis in the same way as they apply to trains, buses, coaches, mini-buses, ferries and planes. They set out in detail what transport providers must do to comply with the law. The standards expect that the response time for an accessible taxi will be equivalent to that for a standard taxi. In hindsight, this measure was probably a mistake. It would have been better to just require a specific percentage of the taxi fleet to be accessible. Because obtaining an accessible taxi, if you have a disability, where you require one, continues to be a major problem.

Another problem can be carriage of guide dogs and assistance animals. Remember the beer ad, where a man wearing dark glasses walks into a bar, with a little dog on a string, and says: 'It's a guide dog, mate'? Well, some taxi drivers haven't seen that ad. A small number of taxi drivers around Australia refuse to carry passengers using guide dogs. Such conduct is against the law. It also restricts people's ability to use the public transport system, and to play a role in the community. I have been refused carriage by taxis in the past. I also know of cases where cabs have driven off from ranks where my dog and I have been standing. This has also happened to others, some of whom have complained.

Drivers must know that to refuse passengers with assistance animals is against the law. And this is an industry responsibility as well. I know that most drivers respect the rules. But being in a customer service industry, it only takes a few people to give the industry a bad reputation.

*

My legal action against RailCorp, now Sydney Trains, is the initiative for which I am most recognised in the street, particularly in Sydney. Because it was very personal to me, it is probably one of the hardest things I did during my time at the commission.

In 1983, when the NSW *Anti-Discrimination Act* was amended to include disability discrimination, it made less favourable treatment on the ground of a person's disability unlawful.

Now, if a transport provider tells people who can see – through signs, screens etc. – where they are on a train, and not a person who cannot see, isn't that less favourable treatment? Barry Chapman and others in Blind Citizens Australia thought so. So Barry lodged a discrimination complaint against the State Rail Authority about lack of stop announcements on trains. RailCorp did not resolve the problem. They said that they were working on it, and persuaded Barry – and the rest of us – to wait.

In 1993, when the federal *Disability Discrimination Act* (DDA) commenced, it introduced less favourable treatment, or discrimination, on the ground of disability. Again, some of us lodged federal discrimination complaints about the lack of stop announcements. RailCorp did not resolve the complaints. They said that they were working on it and persuaded us to wait.

In 2002, the government introduced the DDA *Disability Standards for Accessible Public Transport*. They set out a 20-year timetable for transport systems to become accessible for people with disabilities. They contained a requirement for information in alternative formats, meaning that what was on signs and screens had to be made available audibly. This was required to occur by 31 December 2007.

The issue of stop announcements on trains was one for constant discussion among people who are blind or vision-impaired. It was also frequently raised on accessible transport advisory committees. Blind Citizens Australia, Vision Australia and Guide Dogs NSW all lobbied for change.

RailCorp began to recognise their obligations. As newer trains rolled out, automated stop announcements became available. Unless equipment failed, automated announcements were made 99 times out of 100. But on older trains – around 70 per cent of the fleet – announcements were often not made.

I naively expected all stations to be announced by December 2007 – the five-year point of the transport standards. This did not occur.

Let's pause the story here. Let me talk for a minute about the impact of not knowing where I am. Of course I, and other people who are blind or vision-impaired, have other ways to work it out – we have used them for many years. We listen for the sounds of tunnels and bridges. Those of us with some vision watch for changes of light. We listen at the carriage door for announcements on the station, which can sometimes be heard. We use smartphone apps if we have such a phone, and if we have signal. We ask other passengers, and sometimes they give us the correct information. We can usually do it. Some of us do it every day. And sometimes we get it wrong.

Arriving at the wrong station is not just annoying and a waste of our time – it can be unsafe. I know of people who could not see on a dark unstaffed station at night, and of others who have been at risk of injury from falling off an unfamiliar platform, or from other passengers.

Making the extra effort required has a negative impact. I used to experience tension before the journey in my shoulders and neck, a feeling of nausea in my stomach, worry, and an uncomfortable and stressful journey. I had to be concentrating on where I was all the time, and could not read or work. After such journeys I was more tired, I got headaches, and I was more grumpy. My family felt the impact of this.

Other people shared my experience and symptoms. Many of them provided statements when I took the matter to court. Other blind and vision-impaired people told me that they avoided using trains, catching taxis instead. They talked of the extra cost. Some other people were concerned about their safety, particularly getting off at the wrong station. Most people tried to diminish the impact on them: 'Because you don't want to let that sort of thing get you down.' But it was there.

I had no capacity as a federal commissioner to initiate complaints. I raised my concerns with the CEO of RailCorp in September 2010 – almost three years after stop announcements should have been available on all trains. I also spoke with the new transport minister. On this occasion there was an action I could take – not as commissioner but as a private citizen.

I gave them six months. I advised them that after that period I would lodge a complaint every time a train on which I travelled did not have a stop announcement. I started lodging complaints in March 2011. I lodged my first 36 complaints under the DDA. These were the complaints that ultimately went to the Federal Court. I lodged the next ten complaints under the NSW *Anti-Discrimination Act 1977*. This was my insurance – providing me with a backup plan if RailCorp found a way to avoid my federal complaints. I then reverted to the DDA for the rest of my 78 complaints, for the 78 times I had travelled on a RailCorp train that did not tell me where I was.

I went to two conciliation conferences to deal with these complaints. I then went to two more when the matters were referred to the Federal Court and the State Administrative Decisions Tribunal. At every conference RailCorp did not resolve the matters. They assured me that they were working on the problem, and asked me to wait. This time I was not persuaded, and the first 36 complaints went to the Federal Court.

I'm not critical of anyone who hasn't lodged complaints. This stuff is hard. You have to be determined. You have to be persistent. You have to be prepared not to be ground down by the big bureaucracy – which says: 'Look, we're trying our best, we are doing fairly well, don't be mean to us, leave us alone and in time we will fix the problem.' RailCorp said that in 1983, 1992, 2002 and 2007. And it's only when I lodged complaints in large numbers, and used the media against them, that they really lifted their game.

Even when I had gone this far, and offered a settlement which involved them publicly committing to a target for percentage of announcements made, and a time to achieve it, they would not settle. So they spent $600,000 fighting me in the Federal Court – money that could have been far more effectively spent installing PA systems and training staff.

Why wouldn't they settle? Because they still hoped that – by delaying and delaying and delaying – I would go away. Well, I didn't. Taking this matter to the Federal Court was hard. Even with the support of the Public Interest Advocacy Centre, who represented me, and Kellie Vincent and Ben Fogarty, my senior and junior counsel, it was a difficult process. The morning that I was scheduled to give my evidence in the case was one of the most nervous times of my life. But my keenness to achieve a better community, for myself and many other Australians, drove me on.

As I sat in the court, hearing RailCorp staff give evidence against me, and their barrister continually outlining why what I alleged was not a breach of the law, I began to experience significant self-doubt. But again, my determination for change drove me on.

So when Magistrate Raphael read out his decision in my favour on that February morning in 2013, the waves of joy and relief washed over me like the soothing balm of salt water on a hot summer's day. Relief because the risk that I had caused to the lifestyle of my family and myself – by risking our house on legal fees – had not come to pass. Joy because I had achieved another step on that path towards societal improvement, which I had set myself around age 14 when I decided to become a lawyer. Once again I had found a way.

I learned a few lessons from this process about advocacy and campaigning. First, it's tough. The pressure of opposing a powerful organisation weighs you down – and if I find it intimidating as a tall, white, assertive human-rights lawyer who understands the process, what must it be like for many disempowered members of the community?

Second, it's much easier with support. I've really valued the support I have received during this time from a number of people – other people who are blind or vision-impaired, people in the street who regularly come up to me and shake my hand, but most of all from Maureen and my family.

Third, you are not a whinger if you use the DDA and lodge a complaint. Our rights don't just come to us – people had to lobby for them. It's the key role of organisations such as Blind Citizens Australia: campaigning together, working strategically, we can achieve systemic change – not just for me, but for all of us. The DDA is not the perfect tool, but it can be an effective tool. However, it won't have any impact if we leave it in the toolshed.

25
Equal access

Come with me to an intimate restaurant. The lights are low, the music soft. A well-dressed couple sit at a table, their heads close, looking intently into each other's eyes.

He draws a small box from his pocket. He speaks. As he does so, he raises his hand containing the box.

She slaps his hand away, stands up and leaves the restaurant.

If you could not hear the conversation, captions would tell you that he asked her to marry him. But if you did not have captions, he could have been telling her that he was having an affair with someone else, and been handing back his ring.

If you could not see the action, audio description would tell you what she did after he spoke. If not, you would sit there wondering why she hadn't answered his question.

This story demonstrates the need for captions for people who are deaf or hearing-impaired, and audio description for people who are blind or vision-impaired. We used an enhanced complaints process – turning complaints into broader public inquiries – while I was deputy commissioner and commissioner to achieve captions on television and in cinemas. They are not on every cinema screen, but on a significant number. Audio description is also there in cinemas, and the push is on to bring it to television.

*

The *Disability (Access to Premises – Buildings) Standards 2010* (Premises Standards) were a long time coming, and addressed a broad range of discrimination against people with disabilities. Many people put enormous effort into the development of the Premises Standards over more than a decade. It took too long, but was very worthwhile.

These standards are the most significant change to the way we design and construct buildings to improve accessibility. They improve the safety and usability of our built environment for all Australians.

The changes will, over time, have a profound effect on the ability of people with disabilities to engage as equal citizens in the economic, political, cultural and social life of our community. The reality of exclusion from our buildings, and the services that operate from them, is not just a matter of inconvenience. It effects every part of our lives.

It can limit our opportunities for work and play, and developing relationships and skills. It exerts control over our spontaneity. It can make a simple outing to a restaurant or cinema a major operation. It can, and often does, leave us with a feeling that only some people are valued, and only some people can make a contribution to our community.

Work on these standards commenced in 1995, and after more than ten years of development – including five years of negotiations, three national consultations, a number of Regulatory Impact Statements and parliamentary scrutiny – the Premises Standards finally came into force in 2011.

Among the improvements the standards brought were significant increases in the number of unisex accessible toilets required in buildings, the introduction of 'ambulant accessible' toilet cubicles within toilet blocks, improved circulation space in new accessible toilets, lifts and around doorways, introduction of passing and turning spaces on a range of passageways, improved information and signage about accessible facilities, and an increased number of hotel/motel accessible rooms and wheelchair-accessible spaces in theatres and cinemas.

On paper, this list does not look like much. But for those of us who could not get into buildings, or who could not traverse those buildings with safety and dignity, it is seismic change. And as Australia's building stock changes, which it does around every 50 years, more and more buildings will become accessible.

The other key point of these standards is to remove the need for complaints, because every time a building is approved for construction or major refurbishment that approval is tested against the Premises Standards. So instead of changing buildings complaint by complaint, systemic change takes place.

It is unusual to single out the work of one person in such a lengthy and comprehensive policy change process. But the contribution made to this process by commission senior policy officer Michael Small was extraordinarily important. Michael is a consummate public servant – he has served Australians with a disability, and the many others who benefit from these standards, in the true sense of the word serve. He committed a significant part of his working life to this success, and he has every reason to be proud of that commitment. It has taken a mix of attention to detail (detail after bloody detail), an ability to stay focused on the broad policy outcome, and persuasion skills to successfully build and maintain positive relationships to find compromise and ways forward. But most of all, Michael kept his eyes on the prize, and ensured it was achieved.

I am sure we imagine that quiet smile on Michael's face when he walks into an accessible building. He knows how much he contributed to equality for Australians with disabilities.

Michael chose the day that the Premises Standards were passed – 18 years and two days after he commenced with the commission – to celebrate his departure from the commission. It is absolutely in character that Michael would not leave before the job was done.

*

One of the many great things about being an Australian is our freedom to participate in the political process. But until relatively recently, there were around 300,000 Australians who did not get an independent secret ballot. Until 2007, I did not have an independent secret ballot. Someone else has filled in my ballot paper, hopefully in the way I directed.

Until five or ten years ago this was an inevitable – if unfortunate – consequence of my disability, and the fact that those who count the votes were too lazy to learn to read Braille. But now, technology is available to change this situation. And this human rights breach has been remedied.

I, in conjunction with the Australian Electoral Commission and disability sector representatives, worked with the responsible minister, Garry Nairn, to address this issue.

I'm sure it was done for all of the right reasons. But perhaps my comment to him, during our discussions, that the 2,000 blind and vision-impaired people per electorate was more than his current majority may have got us over the line. Doing the numbers and success in political parties have always been close bedfellows.

A trial was arranged at 29 polling places in different parts of Australia, and I voted in secret for the first time in my life. I remember walking out of the polling booth with ten-year-old Rachel, who couldn't understand why I was crying. 'It's only an election, Dad, you don't need to be upset,' she comforted me. I explained that I at last felt fully recognised as a citizen in my own country.

At the 2010 federal election, the opportunity for people who are blind or have low vision to vote was rolled out across the country. This has continued. True, it is not absolutely secret, as I need to tell someone in a call centre who I am voting for – but the registration makes me anonymous to them. It's a step along the path to a secret vote for all.

In New South Wales I can register by phone for a vote over which I have full control. I vote on or before election day via the telephone – I don't even have to attend a polling booth. My freedom to participate in the political process is almost complete.

The Australian Electoral Commission has also made it easier for people with various disabilities to participate in elections. More and more polling booths are accessible, and literature is provided in plain English to assist people with cognitive disabilities. Information videos are also captioned and prepared using Auslan (Australian Sign Language).

*

I have already referred to Bruce Maguire's successful discrimination case against the Sydney Organising Committee for the Olympic Games in 2000. Bruce's case was the catalyst for much improvement in this area. Digital access was the topic I was most asked to speak about as deputy commissioner for the next five years.

A 2003–5 US study by Forrester Research Inc. found that there is 'an increasing need for accessible technology to allow individuals to customize their computers to help overcome physical and cognitive difficulties and impairments'. The study found that up to 57 per cent of working-age adults in the United States were likely to benefit from the use of accessible technology. This means that digital access is not a niche market – it's the majority of the market. This percentage will only increase, both in the United States and Australia, as the working population ages.

More and more companies have realised that access is a strategic business activity. And because of the global nature of technology, what is occurring in the United States flows through to Australia. Apple has been one of the leading proponents of this move to greater accessibility. As the smartphone has grown in importance, along with the increase in wearables, it has led the charge to making products more usable for everyone. I don't move anywhere without my iPhone in my pocket and my Apple Watch on my wrist – giving me directions, playing me music, reading me books, passing on my texts and emails, and letting me surf the web. Apple has not been on its own. Other major providers have followed suit, as have operators of websites and digital delivery platforms, which increasingly play a key part in our lives.

Access is not just a smart business initiative. It is also the law. So, increasingly, supermarkets, banks, and others in the e-commerce environment are taking this lesson on board.

Of course, there are the recalcitrant organisations that either just ignore the problem or take a conscious business decision to do little about it. But they continue to be mopped up by the use of discrimination complaints, as well as business damage due to selling to a reduced market.

We need to do more than recognise basic access. We need to recognise the impact of disability on the individual, and have a system that has the capacity to address specific needs. Disability is, by its nature, diverse, and its impact is even more so.

Sadly, though, this diversity is not recognised. And universities, and other similar organisations, try to apply a one-size-fits-all approach to accessible technology. This, of course, is not how students and others without disabilities are treated. Not only is material available in print, but there is web access, overhead slides, audio and video. This breadth of material needs to be available to all in the form of captions, audio description and the like.

The smart operators – whether they're companies like Apple, education providers, employers or providers of services – will recognise these trends and move to meet them. Those who are not so smart will – like SOCOG – pay the penalties by successful complaints being lodged against them, and in missing out on engaging a huge segment of their market.

In the end we'll all pay the penalty, because a community that excludes by not making its facilities accessible is a community that – in diminishing individuals – diminishes itself as a whole.

26
Jobs

If you had been in a mid-city coffee shop some years ago, you may have seen four friends chatting around a table. There was Bert, who had dyslexia; Tony, who had epilepsy; Karen, who experienced anorexia; and Vivian, who had bipolar disorder. As an employer, you may have looked at these people and decided not to employ them because of their disabilities.

Big mistake! You would have been missing out on the genius of Albert Einstein, the athletic ability of Tony Greig, the singing and entertainment capacity of Karen Carpenter and the acting ability of Vivian Lee. Just think about how diminished your workplace would have been without these abilities.

*

I'm a lucky Australian with a disability, because I have a job. According to the OECD, 45 per cent of Australians with disabilities (about two million people) live in or near poverty – more than double the OECD average of 22 per cent. This is partly because the majority of us spend much of the small income we receive on services and supports we need. The National Disability Insurance Scheme will address this during the coming years.

Another reason is because we participate in the job market at a rate 30 per cent lower than that of the general population. When we are employed, we are significantly underemployed, with 800,000 of us living on the Disability Support Pension and not paying taxes. Any economist will tell you that this creates a problem, for people with disabilities and for Australia.

We want to work – I don't know anyone who is happy to live on the Disability Support Pension. I know plenty of people with disabilities who are actively looking for work. We can work – as those of us who are working demonstrate. Most of us don't cost any extra to employ, and the government pays the cost of workplace changes for most who do.

So why aren't we getting jobs?

As a country we've tried slick marketing campaigns. We've tried more training and education. We've tried spending money on government and private job-support services. The figures don't improve. In the Commonwealth public service, the employment of people with disabilities has dropped from 6.5 per cent to 2.9 per cent during the past decade, when we make up 15 per cent of the working-age population.

What could we do to change this? We could remove some of the structural disadvantage by not using recruiting mechanisms that exclude people with disabilities. We could recruit CEOs and other leaders to be role models on the employment of people with disabilities. We could set organisational targets for the percentage of people with disabilities to be employed, or to be recruited. We could set up schemes where people with disabilities are employed in highly visible places, such as the offices of our politicians. We could provide easily available support and advice to employers.

But most of all, what we should do is talk much more with

employers, through our representative organisations, and find out why they are not employing us. Employing people with a disability benefits the whole community. Jobs shift us from poverty, and mean we pay taxes. If one-third of people with a disability who are unemployed got jobs, our GDP would increase by billions.

*

The question most Australians ask when they meet someone at a barbecue or other function is: 'What do you do?' Jobs define us, economically and socially. So when we, as people with disabilities, are employed at a rate of 30 per cent less than the average in Australia, we are negatively defined.

I know this because, until Dave changed his attitude, I experienced it. I lived the crushing negative impact of not getting job interview after interview. Not because I could not do the job, but because I had a disability. I get this problem.

That is why, as a disability advocate, as a staff member and consultant in various organisations, and as a person with some influence over the implementation of disability policy in Australia, I have placed jobs for people with disabilities front and centre in my activities.

I have detailed my work in this area, in Blind Citizens Australia and Disabled Peoples' International; in the Disability Advisory Council lobbying for the DDA; in Qantas, Westpac and while working at the Australian Human Rights Commission. I have spoken about, advocated for, and banged on about jobs for people with disabilities most of my life. They are a game changer.

The only way people with disabilities will get jobs is if the attitudes of employers towards us change, and if employers commit to ensuring that their workforces represent the diversity of the Australian community. The only way employers will change their intent about employing us, so that it becomes a reality, is to set targets and then plan for how they will be achieved.

*

Here's just one scenario. Charlotte has a disability. She has had problems getting a replacement personal attendant carer to assist her in the mornings to get ready for work. Replacements have often not turned up or turned up late. She has also experienced travel delays, due to long waits for wheelchair-accessible taxis. Charlotte would like to catch the bus or train, but her local stops are not accessible.

Because of these issues, Charlotte is late for work, and her manager is not impressed. He says they will need to talk about her performance later in the week, and that he has been talking to Human Resources about her 'situation'. Every time Charlotte brings up the idea of flexible working hours, she is greeted with sympathetic nods of acceptance but no follow-up.

Charlotte feels really upset. As well as the hassle every morning, travel expenses are costing her a fortune, as her fortnightly Mobility Allowance meets only part of the total cost.

When Charlotte is finally at work, there is no accessible toilet on her floor, so she needs to go to ground floor every time. Not only is this time-consuming, it's very humiliating. 'Key for the toilet, Charlotte,' is the cheery greeting from the concierge across the foyer every time she comes out of the lift.

She thinks about moving jobs, but the workplace modifications to her workstation are not transferrable. Also, an employment service providor will not help her if she already has a job.

She would like to get better qualifications. She attended a special school, and the curriculum was not very challenging. Also, she found work experience difficult to get, so her resume is not very strong.

She would like to try for a promotion, but feels that she hasn't had the opportunity to demonstrate her full potential. She doesn't get training opportunities like everyone else. She's also not sure she can go to the team-building weekend in Dubbo, because she has heard some horror stories about smaller airlines making it hard for people with disabilities to travel.

These are the experiences of hundreds or thousands of Australians.

*

In 2005, while I was deputy commissioner, the Human Rights Commission conducted the WorkAbility national inquiry into employment and disability. The inquiry made it clear that people with disabilities face higher barriers to participation and employment than many other groups in Australian society. Employers do not employ people with disabilities because of the perceived barriers of cost, information and risk. However, these barriers are myths.

First, cost. Most employees with disabilities do not cost employers more money. For those of us who do, the costs are usually less than $500. They might involve adjusting the height of a desk, getting a telephone with a volume control, or buying a computer with speech or Braille output. And there is assistance available from the federal government, through the job access website, to reduce or remove these costs. Myth one busted.

Second, information. Many employers told the commission that they did not understand disability, and were uncertain what people with disabilities could do. Just like other employees, we tend not to apply for jobs we can't do – there's not a lot of point! And because we've lived with our disability for some time – most or all of our lives, in some cases – we've worked out ways to carry out day-to-day tasks, which often translate well as employment skills. In fact, studies suggest that we are better-than-average problem solvers, an excellent skill for an employee.

Because it takes us much longer to get a job, or a promotion, once we get it we make sure we keep it. Research available on the Australian Network on Disability website shows that people with disabilities stay in jobs for longer, take less sick leave, and are more committed employees. Myth two busted.

Third, risk. Employers told us that they would not employ people with disabilities because the risk of injury would increase, and workers compensation premiums would go up. Again, both these assumptions are wrong. A study conducted by the Work Health and Safety Authority confirms that employees with disabilities make fewer compensation claims and are safer than other employees. This, too, is not surprising – we've lived with our disabilities and worked out how to do things safely. Myth three busted!

The inquiry made 30 recommendations to address the barriers identified. They are available in the inquiry report. These recommendations need to be acted upon holistically. There is little point in asking people with disabilities to participate in the open workplace if there are no jobs to go to; the expenses of participation are higher than the wages earned; or there is inadequate access to the supports needed by employers and employees to ensure that the job can be done properly.

That is why the inquiry recommended that the Commonwealth government lead the development of a National Disability Employment Strategy for Australia. Commonwealth, state and territory governments would need to work together to create a level playing field for people with disabilities in the open workplace. Governments would provide the supports, services and incentives to ensure people with disabilities have true equality of opportunity.

However, the private sector would also need to play a role. Business peak bodies and individual corporations would need to help government identify what must be done to lower the barriers to employing people with disabilities. More employers are needed to pave the way, and demonstrate the business case for hiring people with disabilities.

Also, public and private recruitment services, public and private workplace support services, public and private vocational education and training institutions, community groups representing people with disabilities, and people with disabilities themselves have a role in bringing about the conditions that ensure equality of opportunity for people with disabilities.

Sadly, while some of these matters have been acted upon to a small extent in isolation, the strategic approach called for has never eventuated. The result is that we have the same or worse unemployment levels of people with disabilities now that we had in 2005, and the same or worse economic disadvantage is experienced. The Howard, Rudd, Gillard, Abbott and Turnbull governments share the responsibility for this situation.

I worked hard throughout my time as commissioner to have these recommendations acted upon in a holistic manner, but I was unsuccessful in convincing government to do this. On numerous occasions throughout my term and afterwards, experts in the disability employment sector agreed with me that all of the recommendations made in 2005 are still current. I've been assured that acting upon them as recommended would significantly address the employment challenges that exist for people with disabilities.

After I left the commission in 2014, Attorney-General George Brandis tried to convince the disability sector that active work was continuing in the disability space. He gave Susan Ryan, the age discrimination commissioner who he appointed to also act in the disability role, a reference to conduct a national inquiry into the employment situation for older employees, and employees with disabilities. He gave the commission the reference, but little budget with which to do it. As a result of this action, and the steady decrease in real terms of the commission budget since the beginning of the century, people at the commission doing other critical human rights work were made redundant.

In reality, the running of the inquiry in regard to people with disabilities was just 'busy work' – a way for the government to do nothing about the actual problem, but claim that they were actively seeking solutions. All government had to do was dust off the 2005 recommendations and implement them – the answers were there for government, they just did not want to hear them.

I don't seek to criticise the commission, Susan Ryan or the staff carrying out the inquiry. Many of them are my friends, and they are working hard and sincerely on the inquiry. But sadly, it is work for which the only point is to provide government with a reason to further delay addressing the problem. The people who suffer are the thousands of Australians with disabilities who desperately want to work but cannot get jobs.

*

I knew that jobs for people with disabilities were a game changer. I also knew that to get those jobs employers, and the leaders of those employers, would have to commit to the challenge. And I knew that we needed targets. I had delivered this strong message to hundreds of employers.

Then, in the midst of the campaign for the National Disability Insurance Scheme, also a game changer for people with disabilities, Bernie Brookes, then CEO of Myer, told an investment conference in April 2013 that the 0.5 per cent increase to the Medicare levy to achieve the scheme would be better for sales if it was going through his cash registers. I was outraged by his remarks, but did not publicly comment.

There was much social media activity following Brookes's comments. Most of those who reacted, including many people with disabilities and their families, found Brookes's comments offensive and hurtful. I shared that view.

The next day, Brookes apologised for his comments. It was a half-hearted apology. Most of those who continued to react on social media found his apology to be insincere. I shared those views as well.

I knew Bernie Brookes. While chair of Vision Australia I had had dinner with him in the Myer store in Melbourne. I knew that, while he was a tough retail executive, he was also a supporter of philanthropy. Myer had significantly supported Vision Australia through its *Carols by Candlelight*.

In an attempt to find that positive opportunity, I proposed a challenge to Myer. It was the same challenge I have proposed to hundreds of similar Australian employers during my life, and particularly during my time at the commission. I challenged Myer to set a target of 10 per cent of its workforce being people with disabilities, and to commit to achieving it within two years.

This was not an unreasonable target. The company probably already had significant numbers of employees with disabilities, and if Myer changed its workforce to one that welcomed people with disabilities, even more current employees would make their disability known. Had they agreed, it would benefit Myer, people with a disability and the broader Australian community.

I phoned Brookes's office to issue this challenge, and discuss the opportunity. I checked the commission website, to see if Myer had lodged a DDA Action Plan committing to positive actions in the disability space. They had not. I checked the Myer website to see if disability was referred to in their diversity policy. It was not. I further checked to see if there was a count made of the number of their employees who had disabilities. There was not.

Brookes did not return my call.

So, after a reasonable period of time, I issued the challenge in the form of a petition on the website change.org.

At the time Marks and Spencer in the United Kingdom had implemented an employment target of 10 per cent of its employees being people with disabilities. Companies in Australia such as Coles, Woolworths, Westpac, Commonwealth Bank, Telstra and IBM had policies regarding the employment of people with disabilities. Many of them also had targets – I knew this because I had discussed the targets with them. The Australian Network on Disability website is an excellent source for this information. I thought Myer, an iconic Australian retailer, could do better.

My action resonated with Australians. More than 36,000 people signed the petition. I heard from dozens of people who cut up their Myer cards in protest at Brookes's comments and half-hearted apology. Some people chose to perform this action in my presence. Others did it outside and inside Myer stores in Melbourne and Sydney.

I continued, throughout the events that followed, attempting to contact Brookes. I phoned his office, and I emailed him. I know that the messages and emails were received, as I spoke several times to the media manager for the store. I believe that, had we been able to sit down face-to-face, we would have found a positive solution for Myer, and for people with disabilities. Brookes is a reasonable man. I had negotiated similar resolutions many times in the past with other employers.

Brookes's comments, and the subsequent social media activity, were inevitably reported on by the broader media. *The Australian* ran numerous stories, setting out the Myer side of the situation. Although my mobile number is known by many journalists at *The Australian*, they waited until after 5 pm, rang and left a message on the Commission Public Affairs landline asking me to call back, and then published the one line that 'Commissioner Innes was not available for comment at the time of publication'. Given the way that *The Australian* had dealt with the commission in the past and would deal with it in the future, this was no surprise.

My actions in lodging the petition were not viewed positively by some within the commission. The president, Gillian Triggs, was probably the most concerned, and we had much internal discussion to determine a concerted approach. Against my better judgment, I agreed not to make further public comment on the story.

I knew that refusing to comment would make me and the commission look defensive and not confident in its approach. Had I commented, I strongly believe the outcome would have been far more positive, both for the commission and myself.

Gillian tried to negotiate a resolution of the Myer matter with its board chairman Paul McClintock, after he wrote to her in regard to my actions. Following that meeting, a draft joint statement was prepared by Myer and sent to the commission for our endorsement. I would not sign the draft because I regarded it as significantly compromising both the commission and myself. I prepared an amended version, but Gillian thought Myer would not agree to it so no joint statement was ever made.

The media on the issue died down, and most at the commission thought the matter had gone away. I didn't. Then, on 1 July 2013, the launch date of the NDIS, Paul McClintock was again published in an op-ed piece in *The Australian*, criticising my actions and the commission as a whole. He asserted that it was not my role, nor that of the commission, to dictate actions to private organisations. He said that my challenge was outside my ambit as a Commonwealth statutory officer.

He conveniently ignored two important facts. First, my challenge to Myer had been a response to the negative comments made by Bernie Brookes, and provided them with a way to rectify the damage that Brookes had done. Second, that I, and every other commissioner with whom I worked during nine years, had issued similar challenges to numerous private organisations in letters and speeches and media releases. I had chosen another vehicle with which to issue my challenge.

The timing of McClintock's opinion piece was as significant as its content. To have the piece published on the day of the NDIS launch indicated that he was either uninformed and insensitive, or that he intended specific offence both to me and the broader disability sector.

Pleasingly, his response was lost to many busy with the celebrations of the day marking such important disability policy reform. Again, at Gillian's request and against my better judgment, I made no response. In my nine years at the commission this was the only major issue on which I stayed quiet. In early 2014, once the election was over, I spoke to a Fairfax journalist so that another side of the situation was on record.

27
Arts and culture

Conjure images of these people in your mind: Ludwig van Beethoven, Ray Charles, Rock Hudson, Andrew Lloyd Webber, Whoopi Goldberg. What's the link between them? This is a little like a trivia-night question, but it's far from trivial. They have all made a contribution to the world's art and culture. But that's not the link I'm looking for. The link I'm thinking of could be described as the 20 per cent link. Because the link between them all is disability.

Just like 20 per cent of the Australian population, they all had or have one.

*

Some 20 per cent of Australians have disabilities. They are part of the creative industries – as artists, as performers and as those who attend and enjoy arts and culture events. It's one in five of us; so, if you're not in the group yourself, the person sitting next to you or a family member or friend probably is. Lots of disabilities aren't visible – such as HIV/AIDs, psycho-social disability, or hearing impairment – so just because you can't see them, don't think they're not there.

Let's think first about those who participate in artistic and cultural events as performers. It would be most unusual (although not unheard of) for a man to play a woman's role. It would be disappointing if the role of a person of Aboriginal or Torres Strait Islander descent, or of a person of Afro-Caribbean descent, was played by a person with white skin. Or for the role of a person of Asian ethnic origin to be played by someone of Anglo-Celtic origin. While acting or performing involves the ability to represent and play the role of someone else, those sorts of differences are not lightly dismissed.

Yet routinely, people with disabilities are played by people who do not have disabilities. I'm sure you can think of a number of movies over the last decade or two involving a person who is blind in the key role. But name one where the actor was actually blind. In *My Left Foot*, a movie based around a person's disability, the actor playing the role did not have that disability. This continues through a broad range of performances and cultural events.

What is this saying about the way people with a disability are viewed in the community?

Your first possible assertion may be that such actors or performers are not available. Even if this were correct (which it isn't, as Accessible Arts Australia will show you), their lack of availability would demonstrate the diminished view of people with disabilities in this sector. It would mean that they are not receiving the same opportunity for training as other actors, artists and performers.

Vision Australia benefits each year from Channel 9's *Carols by Candlelight*. However, even though this is Vision Australia's event, it has been rare to have a performer who is blind or vision-impaired. This began to change while I was chair, and it has continued to do so. But there is still a great need for Accessible Arts Australia's 'Don't play us, pay us' campaign.

*

In the staging of arts and cultural events, all of society is not included. If I proposed that an arts or cultural event should be held in a large venue such as the Opera House without a public address system, you would be appalled. However, arts and cultural events regularly take place without the use of a hearing loop, thus removing sound to people with hearing impairment.

If I suggested that, as a cost-cutting measure, chairs were not going to be provided for a seminar, many would not be happy. Some would have brought their own chairs – particularly those who wheel in them – but most would be standing for the time of the seminar.

If you were asked to pay the same price for a seat behind a pillar, so that you could only hear but not see the performance, you would rightly complain. But I regularly go to arts and cultural events that are not audio-described, so that I – as a person who can't see – only get part of the performance.

If I said that no-one with grey hair (more and more of us) could attend a well-known and regularly held film festival in Sydney, I would be laughed at. Yet that same festival is held in venues that are not accessible to people who use wheelchairs, or have mobility disabilities, so they are not allowed to attend. This is viewed by many as quite acceptable.

'Oh, it's a heritage building,' we're told. Or: 'We are from the cash-starved arts sector; we can't afford a venue that has access' – and that's supposed to be okay.

While commissioner, I was advised by letter that it was acceptable for a modern Melbourne office building not to put in audible announcements of the floors their lifts had reached because: 'Most other Melbourne office buildings don't have such announcements, and the vast majority of our tenants don't want them.' I told them that was not acceptable either.

*

So, the arts and cultural community do not perform very well in regard to people with disabilities.

Yet many venues are accessible and provide such things as hearing loops and audio description. And many organisations are inclusive of actors, performers and artists with disabilities. I congratulate those people and organisations who have been inclusive; in the same way, I have criticised those who are not.

Any report card on the world of arts and culture reflects the situation across our community. In New South Wales we've had disability discrimination law for more than 30 years, and 20 at a federal level. Sadly, it's honoured in the breach as much as in the compliance.

The law, at state and federal level, makes it unlawful to discriminate against people on the grounds of their disabilities in all areas of public life. This includes participation in arts and cultural events – whether as a participant or audience member. If a venue does not provide physical access, doesn't have a hearing loop or doesn't have audio description, then the people putting on that performance, and/or the owners of the venue, are open to having a complaint lodged against them. The legislation is complaints-based, so it's not being regularly policed by discrimination officers in blue uniforms writing out discrimination tickets.

Most arts organisations are probably in breach of discrimination law in some way. It's a question of risk minimisation. Do you take actions necessary to make your venue or performance accessible? Or do you wait for someone to lodge a discrimination complaint, with all the risks of bad publicity, and go through the complaints process, and then have to fix the problem, and pay damages to the complainant. I'd be fixing the problem, rather than waiting for it to 'fix' me.

Sustainability is an important consideration here. There is a strong correlation between age and disability – almost 50 per cent of people over the age of 50 have some hearing loss, and 70 per cent of people over the age of 65 have some vision loss. The numbers of people with disabilities will also increase as more babies with disability survive, more people injured in accidents and wars survive. We cannot afford to exclude people with disabilities – a community that excludes is not sustainable.

The arts and cultural communities have – in many instances – been the vanguard of change in our society. One of the functions of this sector has always been to challenge established or accepted thinking, and lead the way to a different approach. The challenge is to continue to progress this change in the area of disability.

I have a vision of an arts and cultural sector where difference is celebrated: where people with disabilities perform and participate on an equal basis; and where venues, performances and exhibitions use technology to minimise the impact of disability in the form of hearing loops, captions, audio-description and clearer signage. Where physical barriers such as steps, steep slopes and lack of spaces for people using wheelchairs are not put in front of audience members wishing to attend artistic and cultural events. I have a vision of a community in which people with disabilities (one in five of us) are treated in the same way as all other members of the artistic and cultural community. We don't want to be treated as heroes, nor as victims, but as agents of our own destiny.

28
Powerful stories

Powerful stories drive successful advocacy. Here are a few stories that I heard during my time as disability discrimination commissioner.

The parents of a seven-year-old boy – let's call him Duncan – are worried. Duncan's about to be suspended from school. Duncan and his family live just outside a regional town in Victoria, Australia. He catches the bus to school each day – the first stop on the route is right outside his house, so he gets the seat right behind the driver. He returns on the bus at the end of the school day. He's doing all right at school, and getting on with friends. But the school says he has been violent towards other children on the bus in the afternoons.

Duncan has autism. The school principal is supportive of Duncan's attendance, but the school has a strong anti-violence policy with which she must comply. She can only conclude that the school day is too tiring for Duncan. Mum and Dad both work, so can't pick him up. Grandma – who minds him in the afternoons – doesn't drive. Parents and teachers have talked to Duncan about the problem, but the reports of hitting and pinching keep coming. Suspension seems the only option.

Duncan's mum has read about the Convention on the Rights of People with Disability, the Victorian Charter of Human Rights, and state and federal disability discrimination legislation. She knows how much Duncan loves school. She wants to do everything she can to help him stay there. As a last resort, she talks to a Disability Rights Advocate.

The advocate contacts the principal, and details Duncan's rights to education, and the need for the school to provide reasonable adjustment for Duncan. The principal agrees that the advocate can observe Duncan for a day at school before she imposes the suspension.

The advocate sees that Duncan is happy on the way to school, and during school. The problem only occurs on the way home, when all of the kids rush onto the bus, and Duncan can't sit in the front seat. With a small change to routine to let Duncan get on the bus first, and sit in the front seat, his education continues.

*

It was a Friday morning in September 1990 when 12-year-old Bella's parents announced suddenly, 'You're having your appendix out today!' Though horrified at the thought of being operated on: 'I was as quiet as a mouse about it because my mum and dad said I could have a special doll if I was a very good girl,' recalls Bella, now 34. 'So I was as good as I could be.'

The day after her operation, Bella was promptly given a blonde-haired, blue-eyed doll she christened 'Polly'. She hugged it tight, wrapped it in a little blanket and pretended to feed it. For years she played with that doll, imagining she'd one day cradle a real baby of her own.

Nine years later, Bella had all but forgotten about the operation when, during a routine pelvic exam and pap smear, she was told it was her uterus, not her appendix, that had been removed. 'I was so shocked I felt all choky here,' says Bella, lifting a hand to her throat. 'My parents lied to me,' adds Bella, with a quavering voice, 'but when I yelled at them that night my mum cried a lot, too. I never talked about it again. She said I wasn't clever enough and might have dropped my baby or forgotten to feed it. That really hurt.'

Bella, who works as a kitchen hand, experiences a mild intellectual disability, caused by repeated epileptic seizures as a baby. Without her knowledge or consent, she became the victim of forced sterilisation – surgery on girls with intellectual or physical disability to prevent them from menstruating or becoming pregnant.

This invasion of bodily integrity doesn't happen that often in Australia. As far as I am concerned, once is too often.

Australian women and girls with disabilities are twice as likely as women and girls without disabilities to experience violence throughout their lives. Women with disabilities are 20 per cent of the female population, and over one-third experience some form of intimate partner violence.

Despite this evidence, women and girls with disabilities are often not included in consultation on this issue, or on structural changes in service systems to stop this violence.

My friend Elizabeth Broderick AO, then the sex discrimination commissioner, and I worked on this issue during our time at the commission. We supported the Stop the Violence Project, and hosted numerous activities, including a national symposium.

Many stories were told about this issue. Three particularly remain with me.

Women with disability who live in institutions, boarding houses or group homes, are often victims of violence and sexual abuse. This is particularly true of women with psycho-social disability or mental illness. Often cigarettes are used as currency, and 'a smoke for a poke' is reported as a regular occurrence.

The comment that revolted and saddened me most was that of a woman who responded to the researcher: 'Are you talking about rape? I've been raped heaps of times. You just have to get used to it.'

Imagine being a woman using a wheelchair and being in prison. We heard of one such woman in a Queensland prison whose case was to be heard in a court, which required a drive of several hours over a windy mountain road. The transport provided for her was a ute, and her wheelchair – with her in it, unrestrained – was tied into the back. As a result of the ride she was flung about, fell out of her wheelchair and vomited. The response from police on arrival was: 'Why did you do that? Clean it up!'

The third story is a positive one. During the commission's access to justice consultations, we visited the Women's Crisis Centre in Katherine in the Northern Territory. The manager told us how she had worked to change the centre – and the culture of the staff – to welcome women with disability, particularly women with cognitive and psycho-social disability. She told us how, in many places, there is a clear policy to bar women for bad behaviour.

She challenges this, saying that the circumstances that may have prompted that behaviour have to be looked at. She leads by example, calmly talking with women who acted differently during their stays, or on arrival, at the centre. Her approach is that the centre is a safe place for everyone, not just those who fit a particular model that some of us might prefer.

This is a great example of inclusion. It didn't require more resources – just a change of attitude.

The Stop the Violence Project is creating the momentum to do more in this area. These and other stories made me much more focused on an issue to which I was already strongly committed. Women with disability must not be forgotten as we Stop the Violence.

29
National Disability Insurance Scheme

The campaign for the National Disability Insurance Scheme (NDIS), in which I played a part, caused the greatest change in Australia's social welfare system since the introduction of Medicare. We have not yet seen the full significance of that change, but it will be a new dawn for people with disabilities around the country.

For a long time Australia's disability service system has been broken and broke. People with disabilities, and our families, are the disadvantaged ones as a result. The individual stories about people with disabilities have been graphic. Stories of people who only get two showers a week, adults who spend their lives in nappies, and others who only leave their houses two or three times a year are common.

We have also been prevented from contributing. Limiting and negative attitudes block us from moving from welfare to work. Australia is wasting the capacity, and ability, of people with disabilities. It is doing the same for carers, who spend much of their lives trying to make up for the support that we do not have, when they could be contributing in other ways.

I said at a Melbourne rally in 2013: 'I'm a proud Australian. We live in a great democracy, with one of the strongest economies in the world. I'm not proud of how we treat Australians with disabilities – some of our most disadvantaged citizens. We are all ashamed that, in such a strong nation, that treatment continues.

'That's the message we want to send out today – to politicians, to bureaucrats, and to all Australians. This shame can no longer continue. So let's fix the system. Let's have an NDIS so that not some but every Australian counts.'

*

On many disability rights issues, we're used to a glacial pace of change. It's over 60 years since the Universal Declaration of Human Rights declared human rights for everyone, without discrimination – but somehow managed to miss mentioning disability. It's 30 years since the International Year of Disabled Persons. It's over 20 years since the enactment of Australia's *Disability Discrimination Act 1992*.

We've spent decades trying to build a society that's fit for all of us to live in. Chipping away at the barriers that exclude men, women and children with disabilities from full and equal participation in, and contribution to, our society. Certainly, we've seen progress. But on issues like access to public transport, and buildings, and information and communications, it's painfully slow, patchy and incomplete.

In some areas we've much to do. Many people with disabilities continue to have no choice but to live in institutional environments, including the disproportionate numbers in our prison populations. Disability employment rates are way below average. And this in a period where technological developments ought to have been reducing, or eliminating, many barriers.

Years – in fact, decades – go by in the areas I work, and in the lives of people with disabilities around Australia, with barriers still shutting people out and shutting people in. But sometimes a moment comes when change happens quickly. The development of the NDIS was one of those times.

Some form of compensation scheme for people with disabilities was seriously discussed during the reforming years of the Whitlam government back in the early seventies. Proposals got to Cabinet, but were blocked – many have suggested – by the self-interest of compensation lawyers. As Paul Keating once said, you should put your money on self-interest in every race – it's the only horse that's really trying.

The proposal was revived in the early part of this century. The groundbreaking recommendation for an NDIS was initiated by Bruce Bonyhady at the 2020 Summit. And from that the government sought the report of the Disability Investment Group. It recommended an NDIS, and an early investment in a major disability research and policy body.

Much lobbying occurred, from Bruce and others – including myself – in the disability field. The government resolved to look further into this issue, and Kevin Rudd tasked the Productivity Commission to investigate. It delivered its final report on 31 July 2011, recommending an NDIS, involving close to doubling of current funding for disability services and supports and major shifts towards consumer choice.

By this stage, the internal and external lobbying campaigns were well under way. Just eight days after the report, the prime minister, the assistant treasurer, the relevant minister and the parliamentary secretary for disability were out in public releasing the report, committing in principle to implementing it, and allocating $10 million for initial processes to work towards implementation. Almost immediately, support for the recommendations came from the Opposition (both by its leader and its disability spokesperson) and by most state and territory governments. And just ten days after that, the Council of

Australian Governments signed on – not to every detail – but to working in quite a short period to having an NDIS in place.

Leading up to the release of the report, and in the federal parliament since then, members from both sides, and the cross-benches, supported the implementation. I can't remember any other major public-policy initiative in the last 30 years with support like that.

How did this happen?

We should acknowledge the work of the Productivity Commission, and the decision by government to ask them to conduct this inquiry. This was a report with great weight – and I don't just mean the two-volume paper version. The Productivity Commission did people with disabilities in Australia, and the country as a whole, a great service. It highlighted and analysed exclusion, and loss of opportunities for people with disabilities, as major economic issues worth significant investments.

The tide of support continued. Surveys indicated that more than 70 per cent of Australians were in favour of a 0.5 per cent increase in the Medicare levy to partially fund the scheme – the most positive support for a tax increase in our history.

The Productivity Commission report provided strong analysis, supporting the argument, which many of us had been putting over the years, that an NDIS would have overall economic benefits likely to substantially exceed scheme costs. This would be achieved by facilitating greater economic and social participation by people with disabilities, and families and carers.

The report also emphasised that limitation of people's social participation, and life choices, is itself an economic issue, even when it can't be measured directly in dollars. This was consistent with the approach of Treasury, and the Australian Bureau of Statistics, which both emphasised human wellbeing, rather than solely GDP, as the appropriate measure of economic progress.

I and many others in the disability sector have been making these points since the eighties, but having them made by recognised economic and statistical authorities pushed the issue significantly up the credibility scale.

The Productivity Commission report showed that thwarted potential and limited life chances for people with disabilities don't need to be invisible to policy-makers, and to the wider Australian community. And that social and economic arrangements that exclude, or restrict, participation by people with disabilities is felt in people's lives.

For too long, people with disabilities in Australia, and their families, have been paying for disability with social and economic exclusion, and lack of choices. As a whole, Australia has been paying as well – both economically and socially – by missing out on making the most of the contribution that the millions of people with disabilities in this country have to offer. Bill Shorten, then parliamentary secretary for disability reform, said that this is as unjust, and unacceptable, as putting a wall around one of our capital cities, and condemning everyone inside to inferior life chances and outcomes.

The Productivity Commission produced evidence that better equality in economic participation for people with disabilities could bring billions of dollars of economic benefits. It said that a society that effectively includes all its members will be a more prosperous, as well as a fairer, place. Where were they back in those days when I hefted cases of wine from my garage, and told stories about scaring bikie gangs in Gundagai?

The report did not neglect the human dimension. There are passages that describe starkly the injustice faced by people with disabilities in Australia, and present an irresistible case for change. Here's one:

Mike has an annual income of $150,000, which he spends on basics of life, but also holidays, a nice house and a car. In contrast, Mary, who has a severe disability, has an annual income – after government transfers – of $25,000, and she gets around half of her reasonable personal care needs met. Beyond the basics, she can't buy the things that Mike can. She is so poor that she can't afford to top up her support needs to an adequate level. She would need another $15,000 to do so. She can't get out much, she needs a nappy because she can't get enough personal care, and she endures discomfort and indignity.

There are many people like Mike in Australia, and relatively few people like Mary. Under the NDIS, 15 'Mikes' give up $1,000 each ... Mary now has an income equivalent to around $40,000, and the 15 'Mikes' have $149,000 each, only a very little lower than before. The loss in wellbeing experienced by each Mike is low. The gain for Mary is high.

Being able to present this sort of story, and analysis, depended on listening to, and taking seriously, the experience of people with disabilities and our families and organisations. These stories need to be relayed to the public, and to decision-makers. Also critical was the extensive input from a wide range of organisations. To mention just one, the Business Council of Australia was clear in its support for an NDIS.

Another key factor was how clear and consistent the message was from people with disabilities, and our families and organisations. The work of the Every Australian Counts campaign and the voices of more than 100,000 Australians with disabilities and our families and carers was critical.

It was recognised that support for an insurance approach, rather than expanded welfare, would be a key factor in moving disability issues from a welfare-charity model to one based on rights and entitlements, ensuring a scheme promoted access and participation in all areas of life, rather than only providing an improved funding model for segregated services and segregated lives.

Despite how many of us there actually are as people with disabilities in Australia, disability has too often been strangely invisible in public discussion. I know that nothing cuts through like real human stories. We saw that in the media response to the Productivity Commission report, and the campaign. It was overwhelmingly supportive.

The enthusiasm of some state leaders to move forward with large-scale initiatives as early as possible was also immensely important. In New South Wales, Barry O'Farrell and Mike Baird, supported by ministers such as Andrew Constance and John Ajaka, realised that the state could not afford not to have an NDIS. In Victoria, Denis Napthine and Daniel Andrews came to the same view. Other states provided support, and some were more recalcitrant. But once over half the country was on board the momentum became overwhelming.

That iconic photo of Sophie Deane with Julia Gillard, celebrating the achievement for which we all worked so hard, is an image inscribed on my memory and my heart. Gillard's tears as she launched the scheme are demonstrative of the passion and commitment she made to this reform. She and her colleagues will be thanked by Australians with disabilities and our families across the country for many years to come.

Jenny Macklin, the responsible minister, also deserves much credit for making the scheme happen. I remember her steely determination to succeed prior to the September 2013 election, which I suspected she knew in her heart Labor would lose. My comments, emails and texts of advice and support to her, and her adviser Corri McKenzie, were, I am sure, also given by other individuals from across the sector.

*

The scheme is not fully in place as I write these words. But the success of the launch sites is overwhelming. Some media coverage has been carping, saying that the scheme costs will blow out, and that the aims of the scheme cannot be achieved. But the scheme reports to date demonstrate clearly that this is not the case.

As always, though, rather than the media and political commentators, I turn to the voices of people with disabilities. Those in the launch sites who have been surveyed are overwhelmingly supportive – positive survey results show over 95 per cent.

I was proud to be involved in the campaign for the scheme, and to have given input into its architecture. It will positively change the lives of Australians with disabilities, and our families and carers. The sector put together the most unified voice it has ever had on an issue. We moved disability far more to the centre of the conversation in Australia, and you can't put that genie back in the bottle.

30
Twenty years of the DDA

In 1993, Australia was a markedly different place. The High Court had just recognised native title; Australia had just been chosen to host the 2000 Olympics, and the John Fahey Olympic leap was top of mind. Internet use was beginning to gain momentum in industry and homes.

In the world of popular culture, Scottish band The Proclaimers announced a few years before that they would walk '500 Miles'; while a doleful Bill Murray rehearsed the same day over and over on the big screen in *Groundhog Day*.

This was the time in which the *Disability Discrimination Act 1992* sprang to life, commencing on 1 March 1993. Its twentieth anniversary provided a chance to assess our progress. It was a chance to ask whether we'd traversed the miles that, like the catchy song, we declared we would. As advocates for the DDA's objectives, we wondered whether we were repeating ourselves: covering the same ground, getting a little ahead, and then confronting the same examples of injustice in our own respective groundhog days.

At the DDA's introduction, Deputy Prime Minister Brian Howe described its vision as: 'a fairer Australia where people with disabilities ... can participate in the life of the community in which they live, to the degree that they wish; where people with disabilities can gain and hold meaningful employment that provides wages and career opportunities that reflect performance; where control by people with disabilities over their own bodies, lives and future is assumed and ensured ...'

So, as any child on a car journey will ask – are we there yet? Addressing injustice can mean embarking on a lengthy expedition; yet, frustratingly, we often find ourselves waking to familiar territory – distance we may have travelled evaporating overnight. Just when we think we cannot explain, argue or advocate one more time, our efforts pay off. The stars align, the sun comes up and, modest though it may seem, a new day has dawned.

To what extent has this occurred under the DDA? Those involved in its development knew that we had a long way to go. We knew that legislation was the start, rather than the end, of the journey. I remember sitting in parliament, listening to the DDA debate, and thinking that – even hearing the words of support – we had a long way to go.

For the first time, Australians had national, stand-alone legislation that sought the elimination of disability discrimination as its overall objective. A dedicated commissioner had been charged with pursuing disability rights. The full participation of Australians with disability was now on the national agenda.

As the first disability discrimination commissioner, Elizabeth Hastings, described it: 'In this sense, having a specifically named *Disability Discrimination Act* may serve in a way analogous to the access symbol on [a] door ...' This access symbol was quickly identified, and the door swiftly opened to confront longstanding discrimination.

People travelling with guide or assistance animals received compensation when they were barred from restaurants and accommodation. University degree ceremonies were moved from venues with inaccessible platforms. Employers paid compensation when reasonable adjustments were not made so that people with disabilities could do their jobs.

These are areas in which – after much rehearsal – we are achieving real, if halting, improvement. There are others, however, in which we continue to greet a day that looks disturbingly familiar.

Despite repeated investigations over many years, women and girls with disability are still forcibly sterilised; abuse of people with disabilities continues in residential institutions; and too many people with intellectual, psychiatric and cognitive disability remain trapped in prison systems. Sixty per cent of adults in the prison system experience an active mental illness. In NSW prisons, people with intellectual disabilities, who make up 1–3 per cent of the general population, represent 9–13 per cent of the NSW prison population.

A WA Aboriginal man, Marlon Noble, is a distressing example. After being accused of sexually assaulting two girls in 2001, Noble – who has a cognitive disability – was found unfit to stand trial in 2003. He was therefore never convicted. However, he spent ten years in prison before his recent release. The conditions attached to his release treat him like a convicted criminal. The WA legal system failed Marlon Noble. The commission was aware of similar cases – a stark reflection of an entrenched lack of access to justice for people with intellectual disability, which the commission and I addressed as a priority.

The DDA was originally proposed as employment discrimination legislation. Advocates insisted on a more general anti-discrimination law. It is ironic that there are less measurable outcomes in eliminating employment discrimination than in almost any other area. Overall employment rates for people with disabilities have been stagnant since the DDA's passage. Despite employment complaints at 42 per cent representing the largest number brought and conciliated under the DDA, there are few examples that have had a discernible impact in achieving the elimination of discrimination, rather than providing an individual remedy.

Since the commencement of the DDA, the commission has received more than 11,000 complaints. In the last decade it received an average of 716 DDA complaints each year. Since commencement, the commission has successfully resolved more than 4,200 DDA complaints, about 41 per cent. In the past ten years the commission has, on average, successfully resolved 45 per cent of all finalised DDA complaints. Yet, when my term ended in July 2014, Attorney-General George Brandis felt that it was appropriate to ask Susan Ryan, the age discrimination commissioner, to carry out the role as her second job. Susan has done the best she can, but has no lived experience of disability.

Undoubtedly, individual complaints are a force for systemic improvement. The Premises Standards are just one example. As well as complaints, the provision of standards represents a recognition that we do not have to wait for the right set of circumstances to arrive at our door. Despite initial concerns that to define rights may limit them, time spent waiting for the perfect complaint is time during which inaccessibility is further entrenched.

Similarly, although it seems counter-intuitive to use exemptions as a positive way to achieve compliance, they have certainly proved effective in managing the transition to non-discrimination. Captions are the best example of this. They may not be perfect, but there are far more captions on TV and in movies than there would have been without use of the DDA exemption power.

Meanwhile, public inquiries have also been useful – enabling wide participation, and the spread of information; and clarifying issues. An inquiry arising from a complaint regarding access to local government elections in Newcastle produced broader outcomes than all previous DDA electoral complaints put together, precisely because of its public nature.

It's important to remember that, despite preliminary fears, the transfer of the commission's hearing function to the Federal Court has not meant its decline. Concerns that the process would be too lengthy and costly have not been borne out. The court is no more ready to take a narrow view of discrimination, nor more keen to award substantial costs against complainants, and it has the added advantage of being able to make legally binding orders.

So what do these lessons mean for the DDA two decades on? Are we experiencing our own series of groundhog days, or have we made genuine headway?

At the 20-year point we were not where we hoped to be. People with disability continue to live without alternatives to institutional environments, including in disproportionate numbers in our prisons; while digital controls on many consumer appliances are reducing, rather than increasing, accessibility in homes.

Australia is ranked last out of 27 OECD countries when it comes to relative poverty risk for people with disabilities. Year 12 attainment is around 25 per cent for people with disabilities, compared to just over 50 per cent for the general population.

The Australia we, and Brian Howe, sought has not yet come to pass. We are not there yet, but we are closer than we were; there are some areas in which we have gained real ground. We need to celebrate those as we plan for the future.

One such success is the NDIS which, through restructure of service provision and decision-making, will position people with disabilities as agents of our own destiny, rather than as passive recipients. The DDA played a role in this, changing what we consider possible, redirecting the journey onto better terrain, setting us on a path to challenge what Bill Shorten, at the time, described disability as – 'the last frontier of practical civil rights'.

Naming discrimination can be powerful. DDA complainant Bruce Maguire recalls that, following his complaint against

SOCOG for failing to provide the official Olympics ticket book in Braille, he explained on radio that, if the Olympics were indeed 'for all Australians', a blind person had as much right to study the complex information as anyone else. A blind caller queried, 'Doesn't he realise that we just have to accept things, and not rock the boat?'

Maguire remembers: 'It was only when I realised that I was advocating not just for myself but also for a view of disability that rejected the beliefs put forward in that radio program, that I was able to see the complaint through.'

He continues: 'The impact of the DDA, then, is in the many subtle and immeasurable ways in which it is helping to shape attitudes, and replace the paradigm of benevolence with one of equality. Without this emancipatory vision, promoted by the DDA, I would almost certainly not have challenged SOCOG.'

As advocates for the DDA and its objectives, each of us has travelled many miles, experiencing many challenges along the way. Each time we do so, however, may just be the last iteration needed to move us to the next phase. We do wake regularly to a different outlook; as the sun rises on each new day, the horizon of equality gets closer. So, let's celebrate the successes, learn from the challenges, and walk that next 500 miles, or next 20 years, towards our equal, included and rightful place as part of a fairer Australian society.

*

Many anniversaries are recognised by launches and speeches that are soon forgotten, and by reports that gather dust on shelves. As commissioner at the time of the DDA's twentieth anniversary, I wanted to find a form of recognition that would further advance Australia on that pathway to equality. It is ironic that I, as a person who is blind, chose film as the medium.

I did so because I knew that film would bring the stories of what had been achieved using the DDA to life. And, knowing what I do about social media, I realised that short films could be shared on little screens – in computers and smartphones – as well as on big screens, on TVs and in cinemas.

In early 2012, I went to then commission president Cathy Branson with this proposal. I had put in much time planning how it could be achieved, and was excited about it. Cathy, as she always does, listened carefully to what I had to say, and read the document I had prepared.

'It's a fantastic idea, Graeme,' she said, 'And a very powerful way to utilise the twentieth anniversary celebrations. The only problem is, the commission does not have the $100,000 necessary to make the films.'

Cathy, in her insightful way, had with her negative response achieved exactly the positive result she had hoped for. She had given me a challenge, and I set about finding a way to achieve it. All of my negotiation and advocacy skills were put to the test. Through seeking funds from government, corporate and philanthropic sectors, the target was achieved.

We contracted with Attitude Pictures to make ten of the films, and sponsored community organisations to make the other ten. These films remain as an outstanding record of how people with disabilities used the DDA to achieve change – not just for themselves but for hundreds of thousands of other Australians with disabilities. You can see them all on the commission's website (humanrights.gov. au/twentystories/videos.html). They are recommended viewing.

*

Staff at the commission, and at Attitude Pictures, worked feverishly to achieve the deadline of 1 March 2013, the date set for the anniversary celebration and the launch of the *Twenty Years: Twenty Stories* films. I asked Governor-General Quentin Bryce, a former sex discrimination commissioner, to launch the films. I felt that the occasion merited recognition at this level, but I also wanted to set an absolutely solid launch date so that the project could not slip. Quentin graciously offered the use of Admiralty House, which served my purposes on both counts.

Plans were made for the evening, and 100 guests invited. We had a marquee on the croquet lawn overlooking the harbour so that a selection of the films could be shown. All of those who had appeared in the stories, and made the change possible, were invited to attend. Many did.

It was fortunate that we arranged for the marquee, because, despite beautiful weather for the week before, it was windy and raining all that Friday, and into the evening. The weather caused the function to be slightly delayed – which created havoc with all of my pre-programmed tweets about what was taking place. That aside, it was an excellent night.

The night was made even better for David Mason and me when – at Michael Small's suggestion – the governor-general acceded to my request to present David's Public Service Medal to him just before the event started, and announce the presentation before the whole audience. This was a fitting recognition of the key role David had played in both the development of the DDA and the first 20 years of its operation.

It was a night of pride and celebration for many leaders in the disability field in Australia, who had made huge individual sacrifices to achieve change for themselves and many other Australians. Just like me they had found a way. It was also a night of pride and celebration for the many people in the background – family members, commission staff and other supporters – who had travelled on that journey with them.

The speeches and films may have been interrupted by strong gusts of wind shaking the marquee, and the loud blares of ships' horns as they left the harbour, but nothing could dampen the flame of achievement and excitement that glowed on all of our faces that night.

The one slightly comical part of the evening for me was my interaction with the governor-general. I was sitting down after the formalities, enjoying a glass of champagne and sloughing off some of my evening's stress, when she came over to chat. Many people were crammed into the marquee, so it was cramped and noisy. I had not realised quite how close she was as I stood to talk with her, and – leaning slightly forward as I got up – I executed a beautiful if somewhat gentle headbutt to her excellency. To this day I claim the title of the first Australian to have headbutted our head of state. She took it all in good grace.

31
Reflections

During the Gillard–Rudd government much work was undertaken to consolidate the commission's operating legislation. This was led by David Mason. Many positive changes to the way the law would be administered, and the way complaints would be dealt with, were proposed. Definitions were improved, and the law was made less complex. It was an excellent piece of work, with improvements to legislation that had not seen major changes for many years.

The amendments included the abolition of the position of human rights commissioner. Since I had moved to the race discrimination commissioner role, this position had been held jointly by the president: first Cathy Branson and then Gillian Triggs. Given the increase in the number and responsibilities of commissioners, with Age and Children gaining their own commissioner and Race being separated from Aboriginal and Torres Strait Islanders, the position of human rights commissioner was unnecessary and confusing. Both sides of politics agreed to its abolition.

The one controversial part of the consolidation laws was the improvement of section 18C of the *Racial Discrimination Act 1975*. This is the section that deals with racial vilification. It was proposed to be extended to the other grounds of discrimination. There was so much adverse reaction to that provision of the law that Attorney-General Mark Dreyfus decided to withdraw the law from consideration altogether. This was a disappointing decision, as he could have removed the vilification sections and proceeded with the rest of the Bill. It would, in all probability, have passed the parliament once that section was removed. He did not take that course. In so doing, he provided an opening for George Brandis in the next government.

I do not intend to comment in any detail on the Bill that Attorney Dreyfus withdrew, although I did support all of it, including the vilification changes. People who have not experienced vilification and its impact do not understand the damage it can cause. This is the case, whether it is on the basis of race, disability or any other ground.

Following the election of the Abbott government, it was made clear to me by a Brandis staffer that the McClintock view of my Myer actions were shared by the new attorney-general. I explained my position, but to little effect. I continued with my work, but this cloud hung over my head.

Then, in January 2014, the attorney-general announced a new human rights commissioner. Tim Wilson had been the policy director at the Institute for Public Affairs, a conservative think-tank, when it had put forward the proposal that the Human Rights Commission should be abolished. This commissioner role, unlike all of those before it during my time as commissioner, was not advertised, nor was the commission involved in any selection process.

Had Attorney-General Dreyfus proceeded with the remainder of the Consolidation Bill, and had it been passed by the parliament, the human rights commissioner position would not have been available to be filled. How it could be filled in this way by Brandis, and how

Tim Wilson could accept it given the position he had advocated while at the IPA, I find incomprehensible.

The consequence of all of these decisions meant that, when the government delivered its 2014 budget, it could either allocate extra money to the commission for Tim Wilson's position or not fill mine when my term ended in July. The second course was the one that Brandis took. I found out not through a phone call from the attorney-general's office, as had always been the course in similar important changes in the past, but by reading the budget papers.

I was not upset about my own term coming to an end. I had been a commissioner for nine years, and it was time I did something else. I was very upset, and remain so, about the downgrading of the disability discrimination commissioner position.

*

In my speech to the National Press Club at the end of my term as commissioner, I assessed policy change at the commission throughout my time there using the stories of Australians with disabilities – Elliot, Judy and Amy.

Elliot is a 30-something tax accountant. He has worked for the same firm for eight years. He uses a wheelchair. Let's look at two days in Elliot's life – in 2005 as he starts this job, and in 2014.

In 2005, Elliot lived with his parents in a wheelchair-friendly home in the suburbs. He wanted to live independently, but it was impossible to find a suitably accessible apartment, let alone one in his price range, near transport. He doesn't drive, and buses in his area were among the more than 75 per cent not yet accessible.

Each morning, Elliot travelled in his wheelchair to the station. Stairs made the ticket office inaccessible, but he bought an annual pass, and entered the platform via an accessible gate. That worked going in but not coming home, where steps barred him from being on the right side of the tracks. Lack of kerb cuts frequently prevented him from accessing a footpath or shop, and extended his journey to the office from 300 to 500 metres. He had to settle for bad coffee, as the good stuff, though close enough to smell, was up a step.

His employer made minor office adjustments, widening a corridor and installing a height-adjustable desk. A small ramp was needed for Elliot to wheel into the building, but the owner said it would look out of character. There were no mandatory requirements to provide access to buildings, unless a complaint was lodged under the *Disability Discrimination Act 1992*. Elliot lodged his complaint, and a successful conciliation by the Human Rights Commission ensured access through the front door.

On this day in 2005, Elliot left the office early to fly to Melbourne to attend an evening seminar. Usually Elliot booked flights early, since most airlines only allow two wheelchair users per flight. But dates were changed the week before, so Elliot caught an earlier flight. This meant hanging around Melbourne for two hours before the seminar. Or maybe not, depending on whether his pre-booked accessible taxi turned up. Like most places in Australia, demand for accessible taxis far outstripped supply.

The picture is clear. In 2005 Elliot, a well-educated, successful accountant, struggled to overcome basic accommodation and access barriers.

How about employment? Initially, he found it hard. Eventually, he accepted a job with a firm run by a friend of his father's, although his pay was 17 per cent less than the other five accountants, due to his inexperience, or so he was told ...

Five years later, he landed his current position.

Let's fast-forward to the present. The debate over the NDIS has moved disability more into mainstream conversation. Elliot now lives independently, in livable design housing, thanks to the Livable Housing Australia initiative. There isn't much of it yet, but more than there was. Greater government and industry support needs to occur fast, if the aims of the NDIS are to be achieved. A voluntary model was agreed as a Rudd-government initiative, but most of industry and government are still on their way to the party.

Community support is starting to become available through the NDIS. It is providing people with disabilities with choice and control, and the capacity to move from being 'leaners' to 'lifters'. It must continue to roll out, if community participation is to become a reality. There have been some glitches, but the surveys of people with disabilities now on the scheme overwhelmingly indicate high satisfaction.

Building and footpath access have certainly improved. The Premises Standards commenced in 2011, revised to meet the objectives of the DDA. Any new building, or existing building undergoing significant renovation, must comply. Elliot now gets that great skinny latte, and has a shorter journey to work.

When he visits his parents, both sides of the railway station are now accessible. The Accessible Transport Standards, passed in 2002, are arguably the largest infrastructure change, and the biggest spend, in Australia's history. Accessible buses are well ahead of the timetables in the Accessible Transport Standards; although expensive rail and tram infrastructure is not keeping up across the country.

But the transport and jobs pictures are not all rosy, as I have detailed in previous chapters.

Let's go back to 2005 with Judy – a 50-something woman of no fixed address. She spends some nights with her partner, but when the abuse and violence get too much she sleeps rough, or couch surfs. Judy has an intellectual disability. Like many people with intellectual disabilities, she also experiences depression.

Violence against women like Judy was hard to quantify in 2005. The ABS doesn't disaggregate statistics on violence, women and disability. We know that 90 per cent of women with intellectual disability experience sexual assault at some time during their lives. We know that, if Judy reports the violence, the justice system will deal with it inadequately. And we know that a higher than average proportion of the population with intellectual or psycho-social disability have prison as their accommodation option.

Judy loves pretty greeting cards, and helps herself to her favourite ones from local shops. She is frequently in trouble with the police, and charged with summary offences. The magistrate is told of her intellectual disability, yet it is rarely given consideration. She has never been offered a support person in court.

Judy doesn't comprehend the court process, and acquiesces just to get it over with. She is encouraged to plead guilty when she is unfit to do so. Her lack of access to appropriate court support programs are a barrier to justice. They are a social cost to her, and an economic cost to the community.

How is Judy faring now? Sadly, no better. We have a long way to go to address levels of violence, particularly against women with disabilities, and to ensure all people with disabilities are treated equally before the law. This applies particularly to Aboriginal people, and people who are culturally or linguistically diverse. That's why the commission's report, which I launched in 2014, called upon every jurisdiction to implement a disability justice strategy.

Amy is a diligent Year 11 student in 2014, just like my daughter Rachel. She loves English and history, and stands up for what she believes in. As a member of the Deaf community, Amy uses Auslan.

Amy takes Auslan for granted, and finds it odd that another young student, Jacob Clarke, had to take his ACT school to court in 2004 to be provided with an Auslan interpreter. Amy appreciates that many before her have fought for their, and her, rights.

One of them was Sekou Kanneh. A year or two younger than Amy, in 2012 he took his complaint to the commission for conciliation to level his playing field – or running track, in his case. He's a champion sprinter, who broke the Queensland record for his age group. He, too, is deaf, and just wanted a flashing light when the others got the starting gun. His actions won him, and others like Amy, an equal chance.

Amy enjoys movies with her friends. Thanks to the discrimination complaint of John Byrne, and negotiations with industry that I led, the latest movies are captioned on 230 cinema screens around Australia, so Amy sees the dialogue her friends hear.

This is also true for captions on television, which have increased significantly in the last eight years due to positive use of the commission's exemption process. Although I, as a blind person, get audio description in the same cinemas, I am still waiting for it to be more than a short trial on ABC.

Amy, of course, is a digital native. Her smartphone, like mine, is never far away. Apps remove significant barriers for Amy and me. In 2012 Media Access Australia, a not-for-profit social enterprise, launched Access iQ, advocating for media that is accessible for people with disabilities. The site helps those launching video content to include captioning, or to make the content accessible to blind users. SOCOG may have prevented Bruce Maguire from enjoying the full Olympic experience in 2000, but the 2012 London games were accessible for all.

*

Let's consider the broader picture of significant reforms to the disability rights framework.

Accessible Transport Standards passed in 2002, while I was deputy commissioner. The Premises Standards finally passed in 2009, after significant delays in the Howard era. Australia ratified the Disability Convention in 2008, which COAG then used as a foundation for a National Disability Strategy in 2011. For a time, our own Professor Ron McCallum AO – Senior Australian of the Year 2011 and a definite disability lifter – chaired the convention expert committee. Sadly, we did not put forward another nomination when his term ended. In 2014, Australia signed the Marrakesh copyright treaty, which will help to end the worldwide book famine experienced by people with print disabilities. The NDIS commenced in mid-2013. It will represent a seismic shift in choice and control for 500,000 Australians with disabilities.

Thanks to those changes, and a number of DDA cases brought by disability legends, it's a different landscape. So what might the future look like for Elliot, Judy, Amy, Graeme and many others like us?

Disability is a normal part of the diversity of the human experience, and the life of our community. But it's still not viewed that way. We see retail chains who think it's okay to sell t-shirts with 'retard' across the front, when 'nigger' or 'slut' would not pass muster. Such language diminishes us, and we are viewed as either victims or heroes, when we should be viewed as agents of our own destiny.

Another indirect consequence of the NDIS, as well as providing us with much more choice and control, is the uniting and strengthening of the disability sector. Once divided and somewhat ineffective, the NDIS campaign has shown the benefits of a united stand, and now 'the force is strong in that one'. It will need to be, to combat the challenges ahead – to contest the 'lifters and leaners' paradigm, to continue to challenge the negative and limiting view of disability, to ensure that the NDIS delivers real change, to continue to use the DDA to challenge systemic discrimination, and to lobby for a jobs plan for people with disabilities. The sector can do this, but it will need to ensure that more young leaders are nurtured, that technology, the internet and social media are harnessed, and that the faster political and media cycle are used to our advantage.

Sector participation will also be critical because the role played by the Human Rights Commission has diminished. This is not because I left, but because the resourcing for the commission has been on a downward slide, in real terms, since the mid-nineties. The capacity to produce continued positive results through the passion and commitment of commissioners and staff is not sustainable. The commission will do its best with the hand it is dealt, but that is becoming a weaker and weaker hand. When I began as deputy commissioner in 1999, there were four policy staff dedicated to disability issues, and a significant program budget. The passion and commitment in that team, and what we achieved together, was outstanding.

As I left my role, I urged government, the community and the disability sector to commit to more jobs, more equal justice, and a community attitude that celebrates and enhances the contribution of people with disabilities.

Quality of life for Australians with disabilities will continue to improve, and one day we will have another full-time disability discrimination commissioner with lived experience of disability. In the meantime, I'll follow the dictum often attributed to that great human rights advocate Dr Seuss: 'Don't cry because it's over, smile because it happened.'

*

I have three major regrets about my time at the commission, and my lack of success in the implementation of proposals that would have achieved significant and positive change. These were not my ideas – they were David's. I was an active and continual proponent, because I saw the wisdom and merit of them all.

The first relates to the complaints system. The complaints system was run as a well-oiled machine, and is still effective at maximising conciliated results for individuals in a reasonably short and efficient manner. Not all complaints are going to be conciliated, but the rate the commission achieves is admirable.

However, we never got in the helicopter and looked at the system more strategically. There is nothing in the legislation that would have prevented us from pulling together a group of complaints against the same employer or service provider or educator, or on the same topic or about the same industry, sitting down with those respondents and working with them to obtain a systemic solution.

This is what we (largely David and I) did with complaints lodged by deaf and hearing-impaired people against cinema operators. When John Byrne lodged his complaint against a Perth cinema, because the movies he went to see there with his family every Saturday were not captioned, it was clear that this complaint on its own was not going to achieve change. David and I persuaded others at the commission to let us morph that and other complaints into a roundtable discussion with the three major cinema chains in the country, and the people who imported and distributed the movies. This work resulted in a conciliated agreement for captioned versions of movies to be brought into Australia and shown in 12 cinemas around the country three times a week. It was a small start. As the cinema industry went digital, the concept was rolled out to 130 cinema screens across the country, and audio description was added for people who are blind or have a vision impairment.

This approach could equally be applied to systemic workforce issues for women, a code for the few operators who still distinguish service delivery on the basis of race, or numerous other examples in the disability space. The people who administered the complaints system did not grasp the possible benefits of the tools at our disposal, and opposed me at every step.

My second regret was not being able to convince the commission of the benefits of co-regulation. As is demonstrated elsewhere in these pages, and graphically on streets and rail lines and in buildings throughout Australia, huge infrastructure changes have occurred as the result of Accessible Transport and Access to Premises standards. In the first case, the transport industry were around the table with governments and people with disabilities negotiating the content. This was also true of the building industry in the second case, but these changes are even more effective because the standard sits in the Building Code of Australia, which effectively means that access becomes part of the building approval process.

The problem with the development of such standards is that they take a very long time, are resource intensive to develop, and can be drawn down to the lowest common denominator. The huge advantage they have is that we don't have to make our transport and buildings accessible one train or building complaint at a time.

The same result has been achieved to a limited extent at a far lower cost by positive use of the exemption process under the DDA. Some industry bodies have agreed to have an exemption from the lodging of individual complaints on condition that they gradually increase access across the board. Captions on television is a classic example of this process working very effectively.

Many industries are loath to apply for such an exemption, as they are concerned that they could be seen to be avoiding their legal responsibilities. Also, apart from the Disability Rights Unit and the DDA, the commission has not actively encouraged the use of the exemption power in this way.

This reluctance could have been addressed by giving the commission a co-regulatory power. Using this power, the commission could have encouraged industry and the relevant representatives of the people discriminated against to sit around a table and negotiate an industry code. With the appropriate legislative authority the commission could have then approved that code. This is regularly done by other regulatory bodies in Australia, and by discrimination bodies in the United States.

The systemic benefits of such an approach could have been huge. Industry codes could have been developed on sexual harassment, employment of Aboriginal and Torres Strait Islander people and people with disabilities. The benefits to such affected groups are obvious, and the benefits to employers are that everyone would have known the rules with which they had to comply. Complaints would then only have to be lodged when someone went outside those rules. Employers and others are far less likely to do that when they understand exactly and in detail what the rules are.

Sadly, once again I could not persuade the commission or the attorney-general's department of the benefits of such an approach. I hope in years to come that others will have more success than I did. They will receive my energetic support.

My final regret relates to the development of the NDIS. I absolutely support the introduction of this scheme, for all of the reasons so eloquently set out by the Every Australian Counts campaign and many others. But the NDIS legislation, with a small tweak, could have been far more effective than it is currently being at removing the many barriers in the general community that people with disabilities face. That small tweak is subrogation.

The well-known insurance principle of subrogation occurs very commonly throughout our society. If we have a car accident, we do not immediately commence legal proceedings against the other driver. That responsibility is subrogated to our and their insurers. Insurers have, very sensibly, systematised this process so that most claims are quickly and efficiently resolved, and the court system is not hopelessly clogged with hundreds of claims. David and I proposed the same approach for the NDIS and the DDA.

We proposed that clients of the scheme could choose to subrogate their DDA rights to the National Disability Insurance Agency.

This would mean that a representative of the agency, being made aware of the fact that a particular local council did not provide accessible services, or the operator of a shopping centre was effectively excluding people with disabilities, could sit down at a table and discuss that issue with the council or shopping centre. The chances of finding a reasonable resolution to the barrier being faced would be significantly increased because, when the agency representative sat down at that table, they would bring with them the right to lodge a significant number of DDA complaints on behalf of the scheme clients affected by the barrier. In reality, in the vast majority of cases those complaints would never be lodged, or the court actions would never be taken. The knowledge that the agency had that option would be enough incentive to resolve the problem.

I came very close to persuading Jenny Macklin, the then minister, of the merits of this approach. But in the rush to get the scheme legislation passed, which I very much supported, I could not obtain quite enough traction for the idea. The rush was absolutely necessary, as a conservative government would have been far less likely (in my view) to take the scheme forward, or support it in the form we now have it, but my proposal was a casualty. Again, my energetic support will be behind anyone who revives the idea.

*

One of the saddest parts of the commissioner's job for me was that the time and energy it took meant that I missed time with my family. The quality of the time I spent with them was often reduced, because I was tired and grumpy, and not so easy to get on with. Sometimes, the build-up of stress and tension placed way more strain on my relationships with my family than was appropriate. Sadly, you don't get that time back.

I also spent less time with friends, and with my passions of sailing and cricket. I regularly missed twilight races on Wednesday summer nights, and found the week tougher to get through as a result. Maureen would often gently chide me for being tired by saying that it was well past time I went for a sail.

Leon was 22 by the time of my appointment, so was off enjoying adult life. I regret missing much of Rachel's growing up. We differ on the number of Father's Day school breakfasts that I attended, but whichever of our figures is right it is still too small a number. I was often in New York working on the Disability Convention in September, and no amount of New York presents can make up for the lack of an at-home presence. I am saddened by the number of times I was not there to get the goodnight hug, or to enjoy the family breakfast banter with Rachel and Maureen.

However, Rachel was often in my mind, and regularly appeared in my speeches. She used to become a little annoyed at my stories, particularly when other people told her I had mentioned her, but now it has simply become part of the dad territory.

Rachel has been completing her Higher School Certificate as I have been completing this book. I have been around much more for the 'code yellow' food emergencies, been a willing resident in the passenger's seat for the de-stressing late-night drives, and an active participant in using social media as a work avoidance technique. Rachel rues the day that Maureen introduced me to Twitter and BuzzFeed.

I am enjoying this time while I can, because I know that university, friends, partners and life will move her away from me. We have been grasping the chance to ensure that we reinforce a solid relationship that will serve us well into the future.

Rachel and I have many of the same traits, and there could not have been a prouder dad than I when she started the Social Justice Club at her school. We are noisy, argumentative and – to use

Rachel's word – 'complainative' together, and many are the times, I am sure, when Maureen has wished that 'the Inneses' would give her just a bit more personal space.

I am sure that my relationship with Maureen would have been smoother if I had put the quality time into it that it deserved. We managed to get through with a few close shaves. I am working hard to repay that debt since my term at the commission ended. Since God has come back into our lives in a much bigger way in the last three or four years, I'm sure that he is smoothing our path.

It's tough for two motivated people to achieve to the maximum in both their career and family life, and I often think that I got the better of the deal. I moved Maureen twice – across the world once and across the continent the second time – to follow my career, and that may well have set hers back. I am keen now to play more of a support role as she seeks success in business.

The last nine years have also meant that I had less time for my mum and dad. I am sure that Mum would have enjoyed more frequent visits. Dad, who fell and had to have a hip replacement in April 2006, died as a result of his heart not being able to cope with the related post-operative stress during a time when I was interstate. I had spoken about the importance of events and conferences being accessible to all Australians at a tourism conference on the Gold Coast, and took Rachel with me for a day off at Dreamworld. We had a wonderful day running from ride to ride. After nagging her all day, I eventually convinced her to try 'The Giant Drop' with me. She loved it so much that we raced back around and got on a second time just before closing.

We were waiting for our flight in Brisbane airport when Maureen rang me with the news. The tears streamed down my face as I told Rachel I had lost the man who supported me and barracked for me so much throughout his life, and the man I most loved in the world. She had lost a doting granddad. Her evocative saxophone playing at his funeral was probably the toughest part of the service to get through – even harder than the eulogy I gave. That hand on my shoulder, described in the introduction to this book, is one of the memories that lift me up when the going is particularly tough.

*

Early on in our relationship Maureen and I had to travel to Tasmania. We had finished our work there and were having dinner in a restaurant four or five blocks from our hotel. Because I was travelling with Maureen, I had taken her arm during our walk to the restaurant, and left my white cane in the hotel.

As sometimes happens in any relationship, we had a significant disagreement. We argued strenuously at the time, although now I don't even remember what it was about. I'm pretty sure, though, that I had done the wrong thing. We were both very annoyed with each other, and in different circumstances would probably have walked back to the hotel on our own.

Maureen did not talk to me at all on the walk back, and I could feel the tension running through her arm. But, despite how she was feeling, her guiding of me on her way back was as protective and assiduous as ever. She didn't let her feelings about what I had said or done impact her concern for my welfare. That's Maureen.

Bill Withers's sentiments in the song 'Ain't No Sunshine', which I apply wholeheartedly to my feelings about Maureen, are reinforced as my ringtone whenever Maureen calls on my iPhone.

As this book details, Maureen has shared with me almost half my life journey, and made a huge contribution to what I have achieved. Now that Rachel is an adult, and has her Higher School Certificate, Maureen and I are both looking forward to the journey ahead of us together.

My life has been thrice blessed. I began it with a supportive family, who worked hard to minimise the impact of my disability, and set me a high bar. I have been provided with many opportunities to contribute to the improvement of my communities, work for which I studied and on which I thrive. I have participated in and enjoyed a wonderful life partnership that has provided me with the foundation to grasp those opportunities. The journey of finding a way couldn't have been much better, and I am excited about what is still to come.

Acknowledgements

Thank you to all those who endured the process of writing this book with me – I have always practised the principle that a burden shared is a burden halved. Thanks to my wife, Maureen, who planted the seed of this book many years ago, although I did not believe her at the time. Thanks to the publisher representatives, and other friends, who convinced me that – as is usually the case – Maureen was right. Thanks again to Maureen for encouraging me to write during the times I got 'stuck', and for smoothing off some of the rough edges.

Thanks to my family, friends and colleagues, who provided the basis for much of the content. Thanks to my agent Brian Cook, and my publishers University of Queensland Press, who turned my words into what you now have in your hand.

Chapter 22, 'Race discrimination', is adapted from a National Press Club speech prepared substantially by Amy Lamoin, with assistance from Brinsley Marlay and myself, which I delivered at the end of my term as race discrimination commissioner.

The airlines story that begins Chapter 23, 'The Disability Rights Convention', was originally published on *The Hoopla*.

Bella's story (in Chapter 28, 'Powerful stories') was originally published in *Marie Claire* as part of the commission's advocacy work on the rights of people with disabilities.